Comments on ou̯ ̩es from readers & reviewers

"Tightly written volun̯ ̩d with lots of wit and humour about famous and infamous Canadians."
Eric Shackleton, *The Globe and Mail*

"The heightened sense of drama and intrigue, combined with a good dose of human interest is what sets Amazing Stories *apart."*
Pamela Klaffke, *Calgary Herald*

"This is popular history as it should be... For this price, buy two and give one to a friend."
Terry Cook, a reader from Ottawa, on **Rebel Women**

"Glasner creates the moment of the explosion itself in graphic detail...she builds detail upon gruesome detail to create a convincingly authentic picture."
Peggy McKinnon, *The Sunday Herald,* on **The Halifax Explosion**

"It was wonderful...I found I could not put it down. I was sorry when it was completed."
Dorothy F. from Manitoba on **Marie-Anne Lagimodière**

"Stories are rich in description, and bristle with a clever, stylish realness."
Mark Weber, *Central Alberta Advisor,* on **Ghost Town Stories II**

"A compelling read. Bertin...has selected only the most intriguing tales, which she narrates with a wealth of detail."
Joyce Glasner, *New Brunswick Reader,* on **Strange Events**

"The resulting book is one readers will want to share with all the women in their lives."
Lynn Martel, *Rocky Mountain Outlook,* on **Women Explorers**

THE BLACK DONNELLYS

AMAZING STORIES

THE BLACK DONNELLYS

The Outrageous Tale of Canada's Deadliest Feud

CRIME/BIOGRAPHY

by Nate Hendley

PUBLISHED BY ALTITUDE PUBLISHING CANADA LTD.
1500 Railway Avenue, Canmore, Alberta T1W 1P6
www.altitudepublishing.com
1-800-957-6888

Extreme care has been taken to ensure that all information presented in
this book is accurate and up to date. Neither the author nor the
publisher can be held responsible for any errors.

Publisher	Stephen Hutchings
Associate Publisher	Kara Turner
Series Editor	Jill Foran
Editor	Geoff McKenzie
Digital Photo Colouring	Scott Manktelow

We acknowledge the financial support of the Government
of Canada through the Book Publishing Industry Development
Program (BPIDP) for our publishing activities.

Altitude GreenTree Program 🌲
Altitude Publishing will plant twice as many trees as were used
in the manufacturing of this product.

National Library of Canada Cataloguing in Publication Data

CIP data for this title is available on request from the Publisher.
Fax (403) 678-6951 for the attention of the Publishing Records Department.

ISBN 1-55153-943-8

An application for the trademark for Amazing Stories™
has been made and the registered trademark is pending.

Printed and bound in Canada by Friesens
2 4 6 8 9 7 5 3 1
_____

Cover: Clockwise from left, Jennie Donnelly, James Donnelly, and William Donnelly.
(The photo of William Donnelly by permission Ray Fazakas, author, *The Donnelly Album*)

To Ken Quantz,
who got the whole thing rolling.

Contents

Prologue

Eleven-year-old Johnny O'Connor trembled as he lay beneath the bed. From his hiding spot, he watched as the vigilantes milled about the kitchen. There were 20 men inside the farmhouse, armed with clubs, spades, and rifles — weapons that had just been used to kill four Donnellys.

The boy's heart tightened as one of the vigilantes entered the ground floor bedroom where he was hiding. This man dumped the contents of a metal canister on the bed and furniture. It was coal oil, a highly inflammable liquid. Another man tossed a torch into the room. The bed above Johnny's head began to burn as the members of the posse made their way outside.

Terrified, Johnny waited until he was sure the vigilantes were gone. Then, in a blind panic, he slid out from under the bed and rushed through the burning home. Flames were everywhere, engulfing the walls and furniture. Desperate to escape the Donnelly death house, he raced past the battered bodies of his neighbours and made his way towards to front door.

Chapter 1
A New Land

James Donnelly stood in the middle of the partly cleared field, surveying the scene like a king surveying his lands. It was early spring, 1847. James grinned as he moved his boots in the verdant muck of Biddulph Township, southwestern Ontario.

The soil beneath his heels was rich and fertile. James was certain he could wrench a living from its surface.

While most of the property around James had been cleared of trees, much of it was still wooded. The areas that had been cleared were full of rocks and stumps. An enormous amount of work would be required to create a farm from these fields. The prospect of such a challenge delighted him.

James Donnelly was short and stocky, with work-hardened muscles and thick, curly black hair. He had a handsome face and ruddy skin. James, who was also known as Jim, was born in Ireland in 1816. He grew up in Tipperary, a particularly violent part of the Emerald Isle. James's knuckles bore testimony to years of fist fighting and hard living.

Sitting on the ground near James, skirt billowing out around her, was his wife Johannah. A solidly built woman, Johannah was better known for her brawn than her beauty. She had big hands, blue eyes, and dark brown hair. Born in 1823, Johannah had also grown up in Tipperary.

Near Johannah were two little boys — James Jr., who was five, and William, who was two. William slept in his mother's arms while James Jr. played in the dirt.

Hands swinging by his sides, James strode towards his wife. He stopped before her and pointed to an empty spot in the field. There, he declared, was where he would build a house. Then, as though he could conjure a homestead out of thin air, he cast his big forearm about the lot: the privy would go there, the barn over there, and the fields yonder.

One small detail might have daunted a less ambitious man: the land belonged to somebody else. But James Donnelly wasn't one to be put off by a technicality. He would claim these fields through hard work, resourcefulness, and brute force. And who would argue with that?

Certainly not Johannah. She knew from the day she'd laid eyes on Jim that the man knew how to settle a disagreement. That day was in 1840, at the Clonmel County Fair in

Ireland. There was a fight at this fair, involving rival gangs of youths. At the first sign of trouble, James waded into battle and began lashing out with his fists and boots. He never turned down a chance to brawl.

A young Johannah Magee was standing nearby when the donnybrook started. According to family legend, Johannah was so impressed by James's fighting spirit that she handed him a shillelagh — an Irish wooden club — to finish off his enemies. As Johannah watched in admiration, James used the club to break the skulls and bones of his opponents.

Kindred spirits, Jim and Johannah fell deeply in love. On November 8, 1840, just a few months after they met, the couple was married. A year later, they had their first son, James Jr.

But Ireland offered few prospects for a young family. The country was poverty-stricken and wracked with sectarian strife. Irish Catholics fought English and Scottish Protestants in a brutal internal war.

As fond of brawling as they were, James and Johannah took no part in these conflicts. They treated Protestants with civility — a habit that did little to endear the couple to their fellow Catholics.

In fact, a secret society of Irish Catholics, called the "Whiteboys," made it their business to persecute Protestants and their sympathizers alike. They called fellow Catholics who got too chummy with Protestants "Blackfeet," and they did their best to make their lives miserable.

Of course, a bit of name-calling wasn't going to hurt the

Donnellys, and James knew a thing or two about sticks and stones. But while James's Whiteboy opponents could be pummelled into submission, he faced another foe that was not so easily thwarted.

In the mid 1840s, Ireland faced a massive famine. Most of the potato crop — the staple food of the Emerald Isle — was destroyed by blight. Two million Irish citizens starved to death, and another two million emigrated. The country's population was cut in half within a few years as citizens fled or died.

Despite these hard times, in January 1845, the Donnellys had a second son, William. Little William had a clubfoot — considered a bad omen at the time — but James and Johannah loved him all the same.

With the birth of his second son, James Donnelly took stock. Ireland was a sea of poverty and strife, and it took all his and Johannah's efforts simply to survive. Around that time he heard rumours and reports from relatives who claimed to have found the good life in the Territory of Canada. At the time, Canada was still a part of the British Empire. The colony possessed huge tracts of land that had yet to be settled. It was an excellent place for a young, poor family looking to fight their way up in the world.

In early 1846, Jim packed up his family to embark on the long, dangerous ocean voyage to Canada. The ship the Donnellys boarded was a floating slum, barely fit to navigate the storm-tossed North Atlantic Ocean. The family spent their voyage huddled below decks, careful to guard their few possessions against the hoards of equally desperate emigrants packed in the hold of the leaky ship. Disease ran rampant through the cramped quarters, and Jim and Johannah struggled to keep their young boys clean and healthy.

After enduring the terrible voyage, their ship docked at Grosse Isle, an island north of Montreal. The Donnellys gingerly made their way down a gangplank and onto a dock. Johannah carried William in her arms, while James Jr. trotted alongside his father, hand-in-hand.

A clutch of grim-faced officials awaited the family at the bottom of the gangplank. By way of welcome, these officials herded the Donnelly clan into a huge, filthy shed containing dozens of other families. The shed was an enormous, windowless building that provided scant relief from the elements. Government officials built it, and others just like it, in order to control the movement of newcomers to Canada. Typhus and cholera raged inside these sheds, taking countless lives.

The Donnellys were quarantined in their dismal shed for several weeks. Armed soldiers kept the sheds under guard to prevent any premature departures. At last, the authorities issued the family a clean bill of health, allowing them to leave Grosse Isle.

James Donnelly had a destination in mind. Other immigrants had told him about a far-off place called southern Ontario. Ontario possessed some of the best farmland in

Canada at that time (the prairies had not been settled yet). Southern Ontario was flat and not heavily populated.

Dreams of a bountiful farm helped the Donnellys endure another long, slow journey, this time from Grosse Isle to southern Ontario. To make this trek, they travelled by river barge from Montreal to Kingston, lake-boat from Kingston to Toronto, and finally, wagon and oxcart from Toronto to Forest City (now known as London, Ontario).

The Donnellys settled quickly into their new home in Forest City. James gained employment as a tradesman, and established a reputation as a hard worker. The family managed to accumulate some money, which they used to buy a horse, a cart, and various tools.

But the Donnellys didn't stay long in Forest City. Johannah disliked the "big town" atmosphere and longed for a country house. At the time, Forest City boasted a population of 5000 people, making it one of the larger municipalities in the region.

In the spring of 1847, James moved his family once again, this time on a horse cart. He was too poor to buy a farm of his own, so he simply picked a plot he liked in Biddulph Township and set up house.

Biddulph Township still had a raw, frontier atmosphere. Some of the first pioneers in the area were African Americans fleeing slavery in the United States. They arrived in the 1820s, but didn't stay for long. By the mid 1840s, most of the former slaves who had settled in Biddulph Township were gone. In their absence, the area filled up with Irish families.

The 100 acres that James Donnelly claimed as his own was part of a tract called "Government Lot #18." His farm was located in the southeastern quarter. An absentee landlord named John Grace owned the lot, but paid so little attention to his property that it was years before he realized someone else was living on his land.

The Donnelly "squat" was located near Roman Line Road, which acquired its name because of all the Irish Roman Catholics in the area. Roman Line Road led to Lucan, the largest settlement in the Township. Lucan had a population of about 500 people, most of them Irish like the Donnellys. The distance from the Donnelly homestead to Lucan was about six and a half kilometres.

Because of the extensive Celtic settlement in the area, Biddulph Township featured some of the same religious rivalries that divided Ireland. Certain pubs in town were known as either Catholic or Protestant haunts.

As in their homeland, the Donnellys had little time for petty religious quarrels. Jim was willing to wheel and deal with anyone, Catholic or Protestant. He was more concerned with building a home and a farm than engaging in religious turf fights.

With only a handful of tools, Jim set up a rudimentary log house on his stolen property. He dug a well and lined it with stone, built a privy, and went about getting his farm in order.

James hired himself out as a labourer to various Lucan locals, and slowly built up enough capital to purchase seeds, ploughs, and other farming implements. He worked furiously, both at odd jobs in Lucan and on his farm. Not that he had much choice; Jim had heard stories about the vicious Canadian winters and knew he had to provide proper shelter and sustenance for his family if they were to survive.

James and Johannah moved rocks off the property and dug up stumps with the help of their one horse. In this manner, they managed to clear several acres. When she wasn't helping her husband, Johannah was busy raising the children. In a few short years, she produced a line of healthy, strapping boys. She took primary responsibility for raising her sons, feeding them and dressing them in homespun clothing.

The family's third son, John, made his appearance on September 16, 1847, a few months after his parents moved to Biddulph Township. He was their first child born outside of Ireland. Patrick Donnelly arrived two years later, on April 15, 1849. Michael was next in September 1850, followed by Robert, on November 9, 1853. The seventh and final Donnelly son was born on August 30, 1854. His parents named him Thomas.

The boys grew up strong and fit in the rustic environment of Biddulph Township. Even William, with his clubfoot, had no problem keeping up with his brothers. But while Jim and Johannah didn't treat William differently from his brothers, the same couldn't be said for some of the townsfolk.

According to Irish folklore, crippled or clubfooted children were conceived by the Devil. Jim and Johannah weren't worried about such superstitions, but many of their neighbours still believed in the myths from the old country. To them it was clear that the Donnellys were different, and William in particular drew many a sidelong glance around town.

The Donnellys, however, didn't really care what the townsfolk thought. If the Donnelly name didn't inspire feelings of trust in the residents along the Roman Line, so be it. Feelings of fear were just as good.

Chapter 2
The Fuse Is Lit

The Donnellys lived in relative bliss during their first few years in Lucan. The boys eagerly obeyed their mother and father, and worked hard to make the farm prosper. Neighbours kept their distance, however, viewing the family as a pack of thieves usurping another man's land.

While they might have disapproved, none of the Donnellys' neighbours ever confronted the family about the ownership of their farm. It took an outsider named Patrick Farrell to bring the issue of property rights to a boil.

A bearded Irishman, Farrell had broad shoulders and a short temper. He was heavy-set and very muscular, a natural state for a former blacksmith. Farrell wanted to become a farmer and leave the forge behind. To this end, he rented 100 acres of land near Lucan, with the intention of farming the rich soil. Unfortunately for Farrell, the land he leased was part of none other than Government Lot 18 — the very lot the Donnellys called home.

One day in 1856, Farrell travelled out to Lucan to inspect his new farm. To his astonishment, he discovered a rudimentary farmhouse sitting on what should have been an empty field. Snorting in anger, he stormed over to the house. As he approached, a short, dark-haired Irishman and a brood of kids stepped out of the dwelling to greet him. A masculine looking woman in a long dress followed. The entire Donnelly family stared at Farrell with tough, uninviting eyes.

Farrell demanded to speak with the owner of the farmhouse. After sizing up the stranger, Jim said that he was the one who had built the structure. In a mock-innocent tone, he then asked if something was amiss. Farrell spat on the ground and emitted a series of colourful Celtic curses. His short fuse was burning fast. He called Jim a squatter and a thief. Then he told the Donnellys to get lost, threatening to move the family himself if they didn't leave immediately.

The former blacksmith was taller and heavier than Jim, but the head of the Donnelly clan wasn't the slightest bit concerned. In fact, he welcomed a fight with the foul-mouthed stranger; he was happy to defend his family's honour and his land. Jim calmly took off his coat and handed it to one of his sons. He winked at his boys and told them to watch carefully.

As the Donnelly boys cheered, their father walked up to Farrell and drew his hands up into fists. For an instant, Farrell didn't react. Men usually cowered before the burly blacksmith. Recovering from his surprise, Farrell snarled and vowed to make short work of the damned squatter who dared to challenge him.

Farrell and James began throwing heavy punches and kicking each other. Within seconds, the pair was wrestling and grappling in the dirt. To Farrell's shock, his opponent quickly got the upper hand. Jim pinned Farrell to the ground and battered his face with his fists.

Finally deciding that Farrell had had enough, Jim calmly got to his feet and wiped the dirt off his clothes. He was sweating and heavily bruised, but in far better condition than Farrell, who lay groaning on the ground. The former blacksmith's head was swimming. Through half-shut eyes, he could see James Donnelly and his whelping brats standing triumphantly over him.

Bloodied and humiliated, Farrell slowly got up. He shook his head until his eyes went back into focus. Once he could see properly, he cast a wary gaze at Jim, to see if he was planning on punching him any more. But Jim was content to smirk at his vanquished opponent and pat his boys on their shoulders. His sons danced about, delighted at their father's easy win.

James smiled and told Farrell never to return. Aching from countless blows and burning from an unfamiliar sense of humiliation, Farrell nodded his head. He cursed Donnelly in a low voice and vowed revenge.

At first, Farrell tried to get the local constabulary to take up his cause and kick the Donnellys off his land. The local police seemed greatly disinclined to do so. Some accounts suggest that James Donnelly had friends on the force. Others state that the police were intimidated by the head of the Donnelly clan and didn't want to risk a beating by serving him an arrest warrant. In either case, the authorities dawdled and the Donnellys stayed put on their stolen land.

Seeing as he was getting nowhere with the constabu-lary, Farrell decided to sue Jim in court. The case dragged on through 1856 and 1857. The legal system in southern Ontario was fairly primitive at the time, and courts moved sluggishly.

When a judge finally got around to hearing Farrell out, the justice did his best to be impartial. While it was true that Jim's family was squatting illegally, they had proven to be excellent stewards of the land. Not only had they turned Government Lot # 18 into a thriving farm, James had also built two houses on the land, one after the other. The Donnellys' second homestead was much grander than their first. It was a two-storey shingle-sided frame house with three bedrooms upstairs and one bedroom downstairs. The new structure had a parlour, a big kitchen, and enough space for the boys to run wild. Candles and oil lamps illuminated the inside.

In the end, the judge hearing Farrell's case tried to

balance property rights with justice. He declared that the land would be split in half. Each man would get 50 acres. James Donnelly could keep the northern 50 acres of his farm, while Farrell got the southern half.

Farrell took over the land the judge had awarded him and worked it with a vengeance. Some days, the former blacksmith could see his hated neighbour toiling in the northern fields. Donnelly and Farrell ploughed their respective plots, each man glaring at the other and dreaming of having all the land for himself.

The war of wills between Farrell and Donnelly soon escalated into bloody combat. On one occasion, Farrell discovered that three of his cows had been poisoned. The cattle subsequently died. Another night, his barn burnt down.

Farrell couldn't prove who was behind these outrages, but there was no doubt in his mind. Fearful of taking another pounding, however, Farrell did little to strike back at his enemy. Still, his hatred of Donnelly increased with every new atrocity.

The animosity between the neighbours reached its climax at a barn-raising bee held for Bill Maloney on June 27, 1857. It was common at the time for farmers to hold "bees" when they needed help with a big project. Like bees labouring together to build a hive, members of the community would gather to share the work at hand. Whoever called the bee would typically serve liquor to his guest workers to keep their spirits up. Booze gave the event a party flavour and made the bee more enjoyable. As the men worked and drank, their wives and daughters prepared enormous meals.

Jim arrived at Maloney's bee with a hammer, a saw, and his 12 year-old son William. On the verge of manhood, William was eager to help in any way he could. His clubfoot didn't impede his movement or make him self-conscious. In fact, William had a cool disposition and was slow to anger.

Patrick Farrell also showed up to the bee to lend a hand. He spent most of his time glaring at Jim and William, who ignored him.

Both James and Farrell drank heavily all day. While the alcohol seemed to relax James, it loosened Farrell's tongue and put him in a foul mood. He denounced Jim Donnelly as a common thief and his family as a bunch of criminals. The other men at the bee observed warily as Farrell taunted and goaded his opponent. Some of the men told Farrell to watch his mouth. Farrell, however, was enjoying the rare opportunity of being able to insult James in a public setting. The former blacksmith continued to issue blustery broadsides as the day went on.

Jim took Farrell's insults in stride. Far from getting angry at his old foe, Jim pretended he didn't exist. This calm attitude drove Farrell to greater heights of intoxicated fury. Soon the blacksmith was talking openly about teaching "the squatter" and his "devil clubfoot son" a lesson with his fists. Farrell staggered about the work site, gulping liquor and screaming at Jim. All the rage that Farrell had bottled up against the

Donnellys came surging out as the day progressed and the supply of hard alcohol dwindled.

Finally, William decided he'd had enough. He ceased hammering and told Farrell to stop insulting his father. In a calm voice, William said that his family had struggled to build their farm and deserved to stay on the land. William also suggested that Farrell was only mouthing off because he was drunk. Were he sober, Farrell wouldn't be so cocky.

The men building the barn froze when they heard these words. They stared at the former blacksmith to see what his reaction would be. As everyone at the work site watched, Farrell stepped forward and slapped William hard across the face. The boy reeled backwards from the force of the blow. Farrell grinned. At last, he had struck a blow against one of the hated Donnellys, if only a young boy.

Jim Donnelly had been sitting down, taking a break, when the altercation broke out. After William was hit, Jim got up slowly, and coolly told Farrell to go home. With calm dignity, he told his foe he was drunk and needed to sober up. Other men began chiming in, urging Farrell to apologize. But instead of apologizing, Farrell screamed, then charged headfirst at Jim, knocking him off his feet and onto the ground.

Once more, Jim and Farrell rolled in the dirt, smacking each other with work-hardened fists. The men at the work site quickly formed a circle around the grappling opponents and gawked at the spectacle. The women present stood at a distance and watched with horrified eyes.

The two enraged fighters got up off the ground and exchanged blows at close range. Their punches lacked precision, but not power. At one point, it looked like Farrell was winning. He was extremely angry and badly wanted to avenge the beating Jim had given him the year before.

Some witnesses would say that Farrell grabbed an axe and waved it above his head, ready to slam it down on Jim's skull. Other accounts have it that Farrell was determined to subdue Jim with his fists alone. In any case, Jim grabbed a handspike (a device used for climbing trees) and brandished it as a weapon. He slammed the handspike into Farrell's head and then staggered away.

Farrell collapsed and writhed on the ground, bleeding profusely. As drunk as he was, Jim knew it was doubtful that Farrell would recover from such a blow. The farmers gaped at Jim with shocked eyes. "If Farrell dies, that makes you a murderer," one of them said. The possibility was terrifying even to a man as fearless as James Donnelly. The strictest penalty for murder was death by hanging.

Jim raced back to his farm, running far too fast for his clubfooted son to keep up. Once Jim made it home, he blurted out a quick account of the fight to his wife. Johannah listened with mounting horror. She wasn't concerned by the fact that Jim had been in a brawl, but rather by the thought that he might be wanted for murder. Johannah came to a quick decision: Jim would have to flee. The alternative was the jail cell or the hangman's noose.

Johannah hurriedly gathered up some provisions and handed them to her husband, along with warm clothes and blankets. After a brief farewell, James and Johannah parted, while their sons looked on, dazed and scared. "Obey your mother," Jim ordered his boys as he tore out of the farmhouse. Two days later, Farrell died. James Donnelly was now a murderer.

In the days following the fight, constables searched hard for James. They dropped by the Donnelly homestead and interrogated his grim-faced wife. Johannah wouldn't tell them anything, nor would her sons. Even Thomas, the youngest Donnelly boy, remained tight-lipped when officers asked if he knew where his father was.

The constables searched the Donnelly farmhouse and property, but came up empty-handed. They also poked around the homes of the Donnellys' neighbours. But they couldn't find Jim. As far as the officers could surmise, the Donnelly patriarch had high-tailed it to the United States.

Actually, James hadn't travelled far at all. For the most part, he hid out on his own property. His farm still contained thick stands of trees, and it was there that he made his refuge. Jim started a new routine: he stayed outside all day, only daring to venture back home under the cover of night.

Throughout the summer of 1857, Jim remained on the lam. On certain days that summer, a heavy-set woman with a long dress and bonnet could be seen working the fields of the Donnelly farm. This field hand had a bulky build and looked none too feminine. The Donnellys' neighbours suspected the hired help was actually Jim, wearing one of his wife's outfits. They were right, although none of them were foolish enough to confront Johannah or inform authorities. Farrell's death had made Lucanites even more leery of the Donnelly clan. The police didn't catch wind of Jim's masquerade and he remained a free man.

Adding further evidence of her husband's presence, Johannah grew noticeably pregnant during the winter of 1857–58. Local gossips were amused: the dour Johannah, with her pack of unruly boys, was hardly a temptation for the men about town. Since few men were daring or desperate enough to take Johannah to bed, they reasoned, James had to be the father.

While happy to have sired a new child, Jim's future looked grim at best. He could spend another winter out of doors, and risk freezing to death, or he could surrender himself to the tender mercies of the law. Jim knew he faced a long jail term or even death if his case went to court. So, despite all the discomforts involved, he decided to remain an outlaw. He sheltered himself as best he could against the howling Ontario winter, relying on Johannah to provide food and boost his morale.

In the spring of 1858, Johannah had her baby. The child was a girl, which came as a delightful surprise to both parents. Johannah named the girl Jennie, and raised her while taking care of all the household work and her seven strapping sons.

Jim probably could have hidden out indefinitely. But in the end, he decided to turn himself in. He did so partly on the urging of James Hodgins, one of the only people in all of Biddulph Township to remain on friendly terms with Jim and Johannah after Farrell's murder. Hodgins was a justice of the peace, so the Donnellys trusted his judgment in matters of the law.

Hodgins assured Johannah that her husband stood a good chance at getting a light sentence. After all, Farrell was as much to blame for the fight as Jim; it had been Farrell, not Jim, who had struck the first blow. Johannah repeated these words to Jim, who was swayed by Hodgins's logic. He also dreaded the thought of spending another winter out of doors. So, in May 1858, the proud head of the Donnelly clan emerged from hiding and gave himself up to authorities. He was hustled off to jail in preparation for trial.

The trial opened in late spring, at a courthouse in Goderich, Ontario. Several townspeople made there way there from Lucan to witness the trial, as it promised to be great entertainment.

Inside the packed courtroom, the Donnelly clan, along with various enemies and acquaintances of the family, watched the proceedings intently. A parade of witnesses described the animosity between Jim and Farrell, and the tense atmosphere at the barn raising. They offered details about the fight between the two men, including the climactic moment when Jim struck Farrell with the handspike. Jim didn't deny hitting Farrell, but claimed he acted in self-defence. Even witnesses for the prosecution more or less confirmed his story.

Nonetheless, no one was surprised when the court found James Donnelly guilty of murder. Johannah had been prepared for just such a verdict. She clasped her hands together tightly and hoped her husband's punishment would be light.

The judge glared at the defendant, then pronounced his sentence. He ordered James to be hanged by the neck until he was dead. The sentence would be carried out in September 1858. Jim's face turned ashen as his wife screamed. Even the Donnellys' enemies gasped in horror at the severity of the court's decision.

Johannah and her sons looked on in shock as Jim was taken from the courthouse and placed back in his cell. Having just spent a year in which they had seen their patriarch only sparingly, his family feared they were about to lose him for good.

Chapter 3
Hit First, Talk Later

Johannah Donnelly sat stiffly on a pew inside St. Patrick's Catholic Church in Lucan. She held baby Jennie in one hand and a white piece of paper in the other. Next to Johannah were her seven boys, looking unusually well scrubbed and neatly dressed.

The Donnellys acted like model citizens during the service. They sang hymns along with the rest of the congregation, took mass at the altar, and listened attentively to the sermon. Once the service was over, they rose and, on Johannah's signal, moved outside the church at a fast clip. Marching through the open doors of St. Patrick's, they arranged themselves in a line outside. Johannah positioned herself near the church door, while her boys stood next to her. As the farmers and small-town merchants who made up the congregation stepped outside, Johannah made sure she caught their attention. She held out the paper in her hand and asked parishioners to read it. It was a petition, calling for clemency in the case of one Jim Donnelly, sentenced to hang for killing a man.

Johannah had put the petition together with the help of Jim Hodgins. Hodgins felt it was the least he could do, having convinced Johannah's husband to surrender to what now seemed like certain death.

The petition didn't ask for Jim's release. Even Johannah knew her man would have to be punished for murdering Patrick Farrell. Instead, it simply asked that Jim's death sentence be put aside, for the sake of justice. It stated that James Donnelly was of good character and deserved a better fate than the hangman's noose.

Petition in hand, Johannah bustled about Lucan, trying to collect as many signatures as possible. She planted herself at strategic locales where crowds were likely to gather, and offered up her petition for inspection. Her boys often accompanied Johannah on these missions.

Lucanites were impressed by Johannah's quiet dignity. She didn't weep or beg people to sign her petition. She let them read it, and then quietly asked for their support. As a result, a surprisingly large number of people signed Johannah's petition. As disliked as Jim Donnelly was, few people were ready to see him die. It seemed pitiless to hang the father of such a large family. And the general consensus was that Jim had acted in self-defence when he'd clobbered Farrell.

Over the course of the summer of 1858, Johannah managed to get over 125 people to sign her petition. A few days before her husband was to be hanged, she handed the petition over to Justice Hodgins. Hodgins, in turn, passed it along to the proper authorities.

The petition did the trick: Jim's death sentence was commuted. He was given a term of seven years in jail instead. His sentence would be carried out in a federal penitentiary in Kingston, Ontario.

The Donnelly family was delighted by this turn of events, but they didn't let their joy overwhelm them. Even with good behaviour, Jim would have to serve the full length of his sentence. In his absence, Johannah was faced with raising a huge family on her own.

After the court dismissed Jim's death sentence, Johannah held a family meeting at the farmhouse. As Jennie played on the floor, Johannah looked at each of her boys in turn. She reminded her sons that she was the head of the family now that Jim was in jail. If the Donnellys were to survive, the boys would have to obey her every command and work as hard as full-grown men. Johannah outlined the various tasks she had in mind for her boys. She divided up the farm chores, from feeding the animals to cutting hay and bringing produce to market. After explaining their responsibilities, Johannah asked her sons if they were up to the challenge of living without a father for the next seven years. With Tipperary pride in their eyes, the Donnelly boys, from youngest to oldest, accepted their mother's challenge. They told her they would do what it took to get by.

Johannah smiled. With her family solidly behind her, she continued her lecture. She said it was time for her leather-hard boys to become even tougher. No one would push the Donnellys around while Jim was in jail. Johannah wanted to transform her sons into brutally efficient fighting machines. To achieve this goal, she encouraged them to brawl amongst themselves. The oldest boys scrapped with each other, the youngest with the youngest.

Fight etiquette was not part of the boys' curriculum. Johannah trained her sons to fight dirty. A knee to the groin, a thumb to an eye, all was fair as long as a Donnelly prevailed. "Hit first, talk later," she told her boys. It was an adage she repeated endlessly while Jim was in jail. In Johannah's mind, it was better to be feared than to be loved.

Under their mother's rough tutelage, the Donnelly boys gained reputations as vicious brawlers. They were quick to anger and liked to settle grievances with their fists. And while they didn't win all their fights, they never gave up and never turned down a challenge, real or imagined. Even adults became wary of the Donnelly boys.

Soon the family was known around the township as the

"Black Donnellys" — as in black-tempered, black-Irish, and Blackfoot. To the Whiteboy factions in Lucan, the Donnellys were particularly egregious because they didn't discriminate against Protestants. Like their father, the Donnelly sons brooked no prejudices when it came to religion. They were happy to pummel Catholics and Protestants alike.

As part of her toughening program, Johannah allowed her two oldest sons, James Jr. and William, to consume alcohol and smoke tobacco. Her permissiveness came at a price, however. James and William could drink all they wanted, but they were not allowed to sleep off their hangovers. Johannah insisted they get up at dawn, as usual, and put in a hard day's work, regardless of what they'd been up to the night before.

In addition to becoming feared pugilists, the Donnelly boys began to steal. It's unclear whether Johannah encouraged such thievery or just turned a blind eye. Whatever the case, Biddulph Township experienced something of a crime wave while Jim was in jail. Harnesses, milk cans, ploughs, and yolks began disappearing from neighbouring farms. Stores were broken into and supplies went missing. The Donnellys, it was whispered, were responsible for most of the thefts.

As time passed, Johannah's boys graduated from petty theft to more serious offences. In February 1860, the Donnellys were accused of setting fire to a barn belonging to a farmer named Thompson. A few weeks later, a horse belonging to Tom Kennedy had to be destroyed after its tendons were cut. And then in March, another barn — this one belonging to a farmer named Breen — was set ablaze. A group of farmers having a party in a nearby house managed to save the barn before it was completely destroyed.

While the Donnellys were the leading suspects in these crimes, Lucanites learned the hard way that it was unwise to turn to the authorities for help. In the early 1860s, a neighbour named Bob McLean, angry at the loss of his tools, pressed charges against the Donnelly boys. Shortly thereafter, his barn burned down, his house was set on fire, his cattle were poisoned, and his horses had their throats slit.

Arson became commonplace in Biddulph Township. Between August 1864 and August 1865, there were seven major fires in the area. The Donnellys weren't responsible for all of these offences. It is difficult, however, to sort out the crimes they did commit from ones they were merely suspected of.

Nevertheless, there's no doubt that while Jim was incarcerated, his sons established a reputation for violence, vandalism, and theft. Lucanites shuddered when they contemplated what life would be like when Jim returned to the family fold.

* * *

One clear fall morning in 1865, seven rowdy young men and one shy little girl stood by the Roman Line, eagerly awaiting the arrival of a stagecoach. In the midst of this boisterous gathering stood Johannah Donnelly, a look of hope and

A photograph believed to be of James Donnelly Jr.
(Used with the permission of J. Robert Salts, author of *You Are Never Alone)*

expectation on her weather-beaten face.

Even decked out in their best clothing, the Donnelly boys were a ferocious sight. The oldest sons — James Jr., William, and John — had grown into strong, powerful young men. Their arms and shoulders rippled with muscles formed by relentless farm work. James Jr., who was in his mid 20s, was regarded as the wildest of the Donnelly boys. He was

William Donnelly, the self-styled leader of the Donnelly boys
(By permission Ray Fazakas, author, *The Donnelly Album*)

six feet tall and husky, with dark curly hair worn in a middle-part.

While James was the wildest, it was the second-oldest son, William, who was the natural leader of the Donnelly boys. Unlike his brothers, who had broad faces and coarse features, William had a narrow face with a thin nose and lips. The brains of the family, he had a cool nature and always maintained an eerie serenity, even during violent punch-ups. While his brothers kept their hair short, William kept his dark locks long. His hair flowed over his ears and almost to his shoulders.

The third son, John, was a strong teenaged boy with a wide grin. The fourth son, Patrick, was thoughtful, hardworking, and sober-minded. His younger brother Michael was the opposite: quick-tempered but quite lazy when it came to physical labour. The youngest boys, Robert and Thomas, who hadn't grown into full manhood, stood with their family by the road, twitching and squirming.

One member of the Donnelly clan stood out from the rest. Little Jennie, a beautiful young child with twinkling blue eyes hid shyly behind her mother. She peeked out from behind Johannah's s skirts, peering down the road.

After an interminable wait, the Donnellys picked up the distant sound of hooves on the ground. Each member of the family strained their eyes to catch sight of the approaching horse. Would it be the stagecoach or just a farmer pulling a wagon?

A stagecoach came into view, and the family braced themselves for the arrival of their patriarch. The coach rode right up to where the Donnellys stood, then halted. Out of the passenger compartment stepped a short, powerfully built middle-aged man. His hair was much greyer than it used to be, and his face was lined with stress and age, but Jim Donnelly carried a bounce in his step as he set foot on the Roman Line for the first time in seven years.

In an instant, his whooping family had swallowed him up. Johannah and her sons took turns hugging and patting James on the back as they shrieked in collective joy. Little Jennie hung back. Frightened by the noise, she shied away from this stranger.

After accepting the tumultuous greetings of his wife and boys, Jim knelt down to bring himself face-to-face with the daughter he had never seen. "This must be Jennie," he said. "A little Irish princess is she."

Jim picked up his daughter in his big hands and placed her on his shoulders. His arms pinched a bit as he lifted her. During his years in prison, he had begun to suffer the effects of arthritis. He was nowhere near as quick as he used to be.

The entire Donnelly clan strode down the streets of Lucan, making as much noise as possible. Their cheers attracted the attention of local merchants and farmers. Storeowners stepped to their windows to see what the commotion was about. Farmers nervously whispered to each other as they watched the proud parade sweep by.

Jim Donnelly was back. His family was united once more.

* * *

A few hours after Jim arrived home, a small knot of hooded men left the Donnelly homestead on horseback. The riders carried blazing torches, giving them a demonic appearance in the dark night.

The torchbearers made their way to the barn owned by Liam Haskett. Haskett was one of several men who had testified against Jim in court. Now that Jim was out of jail, the time had come to settle old scores.

The men rode up to Haskett's barn, then dropped their torches on the ground by the walls. Within seconds, the barn was engulfed in flames. Choking smoke filled the air as the Donnellys kicked their heels and raced their horses away from the crime scene.

Haskett rushed out of his farmhouse and tore into his now blazing barn. He managed to free his horses and save them from a fiery immolation, but the fire raged on. Haskett stood a safe distance away, watching glumly as his barn collapsed in a mass of flame and embers.

* * *

The years following Jim's release were filled with momentous events for the Donnelly family. In the late 1860s, Patrick, the only Donnelly son who didn't enjoy fighting and feuding, left Lucan to live in St. Thomas. There, he trained to become a blacksmith, and later entered into marriage with a girl named Mary.

In January 1867, Jim Hodgins died. Jim Donnelly was quite upset; the justice of the peace had been kind to him, even after he left jail. Hodgins was one of the very few people in Biddulph Township that Jim could honestly call a friend.

As self-contained as the Donnellys were, Jim had appreciated having at least one ally in the community.

On February 11, 1871, John Donnelly married his sweetheart, Fanny. John took to farming on a plot of land near his parents' homestead.

In January 1872, Lucan officially became a town. It now had 1100 people and had become a major cattle-trading area. Nearby London was experiencing its own economic boom, with a population that had reached 15,000 people.

Lucan was prosperous enough to support two different stagecoach lines. In the pre-automobile era, coaches were one of the main forms of transportation between communities not serviced by rail lines.

The two coach lines consisted of the McFee stagecoach company, owned by Hugh McFee, and the Hackshaw Company, owned by Bob Hackshaw. In the early 1870s, William and James Jr. took jobs working as stagecoach drivers for the McFee line. To the great surprise of Lucan residents, William and James Jr. proved to be excellent workers — fast, efficient, and courteous to their passengers. They treated their clients with grace and kept the notorious Donnelly temper in check.

It appeared that the Donnellys had abandoned their criminal ways. The boys were settling down, starting families, and channelling their energies into legitimate business activities instead of brawls.

Chapter 4
Stage Coaches and Wedding Belles

May 24, Queen Victoria's birthday, was a holiday in the Dominion of Canada. And while the Donnelly clan had little regard for British royalty, Victoria Day 1873 was an occasion to celebrate all the same. The day marked the launch of the family's new business.

Earlier in the year, William and James Jr. had bought out their boss, Hugh McFee, and taken over his stagecoach company. The brothers were now entrepreneurs. On May 24, decked out in their finest clothes, the Donnellys watched proudly as William positioned himself on the wooden driver's seat at the front of the stagecoach. William had grown a moustache to complement his long hair, and it gave him the roguish air of a stage actor. He held onto the reins of the horse in front of the coach and tipped his hat at his parents. Jim and Johannah beamed with pride. Their dream of a better life in Canada seemed to be paying off.

The Donnelly clan gazed admiringly at William's stagecoach. It was spotless: all gleaming surfaces and polished wood. The coach weighed roughly 2000 pounds and offered compartments for passengers and their baggage. The passenger compartment was cramped, containing a handful of leather-covered seats. The coach could hold about nine passengers inside, and maybe a dozen more on the roof.

A clutch of passengers stepped into the coach. William greeted them warmly and waited for them to settle inside. Then, he cracked the reins and sent the horse galloping ahead. The Donnelly clan let out a series of wild cheers. The family stagecoach was off on its inaugural run.

William and James Jr. operated their line with help from brothers Michael, John, and Thomas. The Donnelly coach journeyed from Lucan to London and Exeter. Through hard work, the Donnellys hoped to drive their main competitor, Bob Hackshaw, out of business. On this score, they succeeded all too well.

Feeling the heat from the Donnellys, Hackshaw gave up. In the fall of 1873, he sold his company to a Lucan resident named Patrick Flanagan. A powerfully built Irishman, Flanagan was extremely stubborn and had no intention of letting the Donnellys dominate the stagecoach trade.

Soon, William and James Jr. found themselves locked in a bitter rivalry with a tough opponent. Flanagan wasn't afraid of the Donnellys, and openly announced his intention to bankrupt their stagecoach company. After that, it was all-out war between the two competitors. Both companies tried to outdo the other with price cuts, faster service, and longer hours.

Despite the excellent service the Donnelly boys provided, customers were hard to come by. Many Lucanites were too scared of the Donnellys to patronize their stagecoach. Most residents preferred to give their business to Flanagan, whose company thrived as a result.

At the same time that William was locked in a losing economic battle with Flanagan, he found himself falling in love. The object of his affection was an attractive young lady named Maggie Thompson. Maggie was pale and petite, with blue eyes and black hair.

William and Maggie had known each other for years. However, the second-oldest Donnelly boy didn't take much notice of the pretty young woman until he attended a St. Patrick's dance at a local schoolhouse. William was an excellent dancer and, with his long hair and devilish charm, many Lucan women found him attractive.

As a fiddler played traditional Celtic reels and jigs, William boldly invited a series of young ladies to join him on the dance floor. In a corner of the schoolhouse, Maggie Thompson watched William's every move. She was sitting next to her father, John, a dour man who despised the Donnellys. John Thompson was not at all happy to see William at the dance.

In time, Maggie caught William's eye with her intense gaze. With typical boldness, he walked over to the fragile-looking young lady and asked her to dance. Before her father could interfere, Maggie leapt to her feet to accept.

As her father scowled, Maggie danced several jigs and reels with the dashing Donnelly boy. During some of the dances, William held Maggie close to him. Her body seemed bird-like and fragile in his rugged hands. The more they danced, the more William was attracted to Maggie. By her soft gaze, it was clear that Maggie felt the same.

John Thompson finally broke up their two-step. He stood next to his daughter and suggested that the Donnelly boy might want to find another partner. William wasn't in the mood for a fight, especially not in front of such a charming young woman. He reluctantly surrendered Maggie to the loving graces of her father. Thompson quickly ushered the charming colleen back into a corner of the room.

William was about to leave when another woman stepped up and announced she would be happy to take Maggie's place. William's new dance partner was physically the opposite of Maggie. She was tall and thin, with red hair, freckles, and a boisterous manner. Her name was Hanora Kennedy, but she called herself Nora. She too had set her sights on the dashing Donnelly boy. Though he danced a few times with Nora, William's heart wasn't in it. To Nora's disappointment, he excused himself and left.

William was deeply smitten by the lovely Maggie. And Maggie, for her part, had fallen in love with the most dangerous of the Donnelly boys. The two might have married in short order, but John Thompson had other ideas. The thought of his beloved daughter marrying a Donnelly and bearing his children was enough to make him black with rage.

At first, William tried to work his charm on Maggie's father. Just as he could be courteous to his stagecoach customers, William was capable of acting respectful when need be. He launched a good-will campaign to win over John Thompson. He never lost an opportunity to tell Thompson how lucky he was to have such a fine daughter. In addition, he regularly regaled the man with tales of his new life as an entrepreneur. William tried to convince Thompson that he was a sober-minded business owner, not a wild, violence-prone youth.

But Thompson proved immune to William's wiles. He told William that he would rather kill the damned devil clubfoot than let him near his precious daughter.

This threat, of course, didn't stop William from going after what he wanted. While he schemed to win Maggie away from her father, other members of the Donnelly clan were pursuing romantic relationships of their own. Two days before Christmas, 1873, Robert Donnelly married Annie Currie, whose family lived in St. Thomas, Ontario. Not being

The charming Jennie Donnelly
(Used with the permission of J. Robert Salts, author of *You Are Never Alone*)

part of the Lucan community, the Currie family wasn't swayed by popular prejudice against the Donnellys. In fact, Annie's brother, James, had taken quite a shine to Jennie Donnelly.

Jennie had grown into a lovely young woman, with laughing blue eyes and a charming, pixie-like manner. She was the only member of the Donnelly clan liked and admired by everyone in Lucan. In addition to being beautiful, Jennie didn't harbour any of her family's less than appealing traits; she was good-natured and even-tempered.

While his brother Robert busied himself as a newlywed husband, and his sister Jennie enjoyed the attention of her handsome suitor, William kept busy hatching a wild plan to secure the love of his life.

Shortly after New Year's Day, 1874, William gathered some friends and family members together and outlined his plan. Seeing that John Thompson wasn't willing to give Maggie up, William decided to kidnap her. He was certain Maggie wouldn't mind.

On the night of January 9, William put his plan into action. With brothers Tom and Michael by his side, he rode his horse onto the Roman Line. A group of family pals tagged along with the Donnellys, including Jim and Dan Keeffe, Pat Quigley, Bob Corcoran, and Bill Atkinson. All of them were pleased to be on such a grand caper.

These hard-riding men cut through the bitter cold, bodies protected by thick coats, faces covered in scarves. They quickly made their way through the snow to John Thompson's farmhouse. They stopped outside the house, tied their horses up, and then banged on the door until Thompson himself opened it.

The men barged past Maggie's father, stomping their snow-covered boots on the farmhouse floor and swaggering into the warm kitchen. They slapped their cold hands together and did their best to look threatening. Once they were all inside, Thompson slammed the door shut and crossed his arms. He glared at the intruders and said nothing. The posse milled about, unsure of what to say or do. Thompson, meanwhile, remained as silent as a statue.

Biding his time, William spoke up. In a casual voice, he explained that he had gathered his friends together to help him search for Maggie. The gang of snow-covered ruffians were ready to fight, if need be, to rescue Maggie from the grasp of her overprotective father.

Far from cowed, Thompson laughed uproariously. He uttered a few salty curses then told the assembled throng that Maggie wasn't home. A few days earlier, Thompson had spirited Maggie away; she was staying at another farmhouse and her father wasn't about to offer directions on how to get there. The invaders looked at each other sheepishly. They hadn't counted on this hiccup.

William cleared his throat and said his posse would check to see if Thompson was lying. The posse stomped around the farmhouse conducting a quick search for Maggie. With sinking hearts, the young men had to concede that she was nowhere to be found.

Muttering vague threats, William led his defeated company out of the house. "This isn't over," he warned Thompson. "I'm going to track down Maggie even if we have to search a thousand farmhouses." Thompson howled with glee and escorted him to the door.

William went back to work on the stagecoach, feeling

more determined than ever. He was deeply in love, and John Thompson's machinations only spurred his desire to win the man's daughter.

A few days after his failed raid, William heard about a new opportunity. He discovered that Thompson's son — who was also named William — was getting married. Surely Maggie would attend the celebrations.

So, on an evening in late January 1874, William Donnelly, plus assorted friends and family, mounted their horses and set out once more. Their new target was the farmhouse of William Thompson, the groom. The men wore thick scarves to protect their faces from the cold and to hide their identities.

Inside Thompson's home, the wedding celebration was in full swing. William Donnelly gazed at the farmhouse, so brightly lit against the black sky and white snow. He could hear music and the sounds of men and women making merry. Certain that Maggie was inside, he patted the long-barrelled revolver he had brought along with him and smiled. The Donnellys didn't care much for guns — viewing them as weapons of cowards — but in this case, William made an exception.

With a signal from William, the posse began to ride in wild circles around the farmhouse, whooping and screaming. Some of the men were armed, like their leader. They pulled out their pistols and fired into the air or at the smoking chimney of the farmhouse.

The party music inside the house came to a stop. Nervous faces pressed up against the cold glass windows as guests tried to figure out who was attacking them. Was it some kind of Native ambush?

William's plan was to create a huge ruckus that would distract all the wedding guests, particularly Maggie's father. The guests would think the posse was conducting a shivaree — a wild rural celebration that often accompanied a marriage. Amidst all the chaos, Maggie could slip outside and join William on his horse. Then the kidnappers would ride off, and William would be united with his love. Whether Maggie knew about this fanciful plan is anybody's guess.

The ruffians continued to race their horses around the farmhouse, bellowing and firing rounds. After several minutes, it occurred to William and his posse that they had been outsmarted again. There was no sign of Maggie, either at the window or on William's saddle.

The dispirited young men decided to leave with a literal bang. They stopped their horses and peppered Thompson's farmhouse with gunfire. The wedding guests dived away from the windows, fearing they might present tempting targets. William's co-conspirators reloaded again and again, blazing away until all the windows in the farmhouse were shattered. They fired so many rounds into the chimney that it nearly toppled over.

Sticking their smoking pistols back in their belts, the young warriors issued a few final war whoops then rode off.

No amount of gunplay, however, could hide the fact that William had failed once more in his mission of love.

While William despaired, John Thompson delighted. He looked out of a bullet-shattered window and smiled as the posse disappeared. Thompson was shrewder than William had anticipated. He had kept his daughter away from the wedding celebration, just in case the devil clubfoot tried to snatch her. The marauders might have ruined the party, but Maggie was still safe.

* * *

Two weeks after the one-sided gun battle at the Thompson farmhouse, Jennie Donnelly married James Currie in Grace Anglican Church in Bothwell, Ontario. The couple settled into a farmhouse near St. Thomas, where they would raise a family.

Michael Donnelly got married soon after. On May 25, 1874, he wed a young lady named Ellen (Nellie) Hynes. In some ways, Michael was quite unlike his brothers. While the other Donnelly boys were tough but hardworking, Michael was tough and lazy. He never learned to read, and he avoided straining himself at any task he undertook.

To his family's astonishment, Michael took a job as a brakeman for the Canada Southern Railway in the 1870s. He had always liked trains, and proved to be a diligent employee. His bosses were satisfied with his work and didn't seem to care that he was illiterate.

William, meanwhile, continued to brood over Maggie. Not only did Maggie remain hidden away from him, her father insisted on pressing charges against William and his posse. In due time, William, Michael, and Thomas Donnelly, plus their friends, were arrested for various offences stemming from their mock shivaree.

A few days after Michael's wedding, the Donnelly boys and their friends appeared in court. In the end, they were found not guilty due to a lack of evidence on the prosecutor's part. The riders had kept their faces concealed and no one in the farmhouse could properly identify them.

William Donnelly walked sullenly out of the courthouse, rehashing a list of grievances against John Thompson in his mind. But as he was about to discover, Thompson had one last card to play.

Shortly after William went on trial for shooting up the Thompson farmhouse, Maggie was forced to marry a man she didn't love. The wedding was a disaster, with the bride sobbing throughout the ceremony. Though it was a sombre occasion for his daughter, John Thompson couldn't hide his satisfaction; he had outwitted the wiliest of the Donnelly boys.

William was horrified when he heard about Maggie's betrothal, but he knew there was nothing he could do; he had been roundly beaten. Angry and dispirited, he tried to concentrate on his stagecoach business and forget about his ladylove.

And Maggie? In time, no doubt, she would forget about her rough-hewn hero.

* * *

William may have been defeated, but he was still a Donnelly, and not one to wallow for long. He set his sights on a new prize: the spirited Nora Kennedy. Nora was every bit as inclined towards William as Maggie had been, and her family was every bit as dead-set against him. They did their best to scuttle the relationship, but Nora proved to be made of tougher stuff than Maggie. She refused to be bossed around by the male members of her family when it came to matters of the heart. On January 28, 1875, she and William were married at St. Patrick's church.

But Nora would pay a steep price for her independent attitude. When she and William kissed at the altar of St. Patrick's, virtually no one from her family was there to watch. The only spectators were the Donnelly clan and a few assorted friends. Their boisterous spirits more than made up for the empty pews, however.

After the wedding, the Donnellys held one of their typically rowdy, alcohol-sodden celebrations. They made merry, in inimitable Donnelly style, and welcomed Nora into the family. Nora danced with her husband, and looked forward to life with one of the wild Donnelly boys. She was to live in a farmhouse with William, a few kilometres away from Jim and Johannah's homestead.

The wedding caused some serious ripples in the

community. Nora's brother, John Kennedy, was heard around Lucan uttering threats against William and the Donnellys. But the family barely noticed. After all, John Kennedy was just one more person on the long list of Lucanites with grievances against them.

Chapter 5
A Rival Dispatched

I n late summer, 1875, the stagecoach war between the Donnellys and Patrick Flanagan reached a brutal climax. On a hot evening in August, a group of shadowy figures left the Donnelly homestead and crept towards Flanagan's barn. They snuck up to the barn door and tried the latch to see if the building was locked up. It wasn't. The door was opened and the raiding party stepped inside.

The barn contained a pair of stagecoaches and the horses that pulled them. Both the animals and coaches belonged to the Donnellys' chief rival in the transportation business.

Each man in the raiding party carried a tool. Among

other items, the intruders had brought saws, knives, and hatchets. As Flanagan slept soundly in his nearby farmhouse, the intruders went to work. Methodically and silently, they sawed the stagecoaches apart. And they didn't stop there.

The next morning, Flanagan ate breakfast then stepped out of his house to prepare his coaches for the day's business. As he drew closer to his barn, he heard the sound of whimpering animals. Something was thrashing about the barn in distress.

Flanagan opened the barn door and peered inside. His skin turned icy as he saw the disassembled pieces of his stagecoaches lying in a heap of sawdust. Stagecoach sections were piled on the barn floor like parts of a kit. The air was heavy with the smell of sawdust and blood.

Flanagan cursed then made his way into the barn, his hands balling into fists. The whimpering noises grew louder. Stomach rising, he eased himself to the stalls where his horses were hitched.

The horses were rushing about their stalls, twisting their heads and smashing into the walls. The walls and floors were covered in blood. His horses had been mutilated. Their bodies were covered in cuts and tears and their mouths were streaked with dried blood. Flanagan was a tough man, but this was too much. He screamed.

The commotion drew the attention of John Purtell, a local farmhand who happened to be driving a milk cart on the road outside. Purtell stopped his rig and looked up curiously at Flanagan's barn. A moment later, Flanagan burst through the barn doors, shrieking like a madman about wounded horses and Black Donnellys.

Flanagan had no doubt that the Donnellys were responsible for the atrocity in his barn. Their stagecoach company was in desperate straits, and Flanagan had expected it to go bankrupt any day. The attack on the barn was obviously intended to delay that day of reckoning. Flanagan cursed the Donnellys and invited Purtell to inspect their handiwork.

Purtell walked into the barn and gaped in horror at the bloody horses. He rushed back to his milk cart as Flanagan stepped into his farmhouse in search of a shotgun.

Snapping the reins of his horse, Purtell raced his milk cart down the street, shouting at the top of his lungs. Like a town crier, he bellowed the headlines of the morning's events, describing the butchery at Flanagan's barn and accusing the Donnellys. Lucanites opened their doors and windows and peered outside. Some of them streamed over to Flanagan's barn.

Flanagan, meanwhile, reached into a closet in his house. He removed a shotgun and several shells, and then walked outside. As he stood before the barn door, Flanagan chambered two rounds in his weapon. He snapped the shotgun shut and went into the barn. Breathing heavily, he approached the stalls where his wounded horses were running in circles, maddened with pain. Aiming the weapon at both animals in turn, he gunned them down, one after the

other. He then did a quick examination of his dead horses —
their tongues had been sliced apart.

The sound of the shotgun drew more neighbours to
Flanagan's barn. By the time he stepped outside, nearly 100
Lucanites were standing on his property. Flanagan was slowly returning to his senses. He addressed the people on his
lawn like a politician at a rally. He ranted about the Donnellys
and told the townspeople to go into the barn and see what
the family had done.

Gathering their nerve, a few Lucanites took Flanagan up
on his offer. They gawked in astonishment at the sawed up
stagecoaches and cringed before the blood-splattered horse
stalls. Even farmers who made their living butchering animals shuddered in revulsion.

Lucanites filed out of Flanagan's barn and resumed
their animated conversations. Several residents told
Flanagan he was right to put his animals out of their misery.
The consensus among the crowd was that no one but the
Donnellys would be cruel enough to commit such a crime.
Curses were muttered and vengeance pledged. The crowd
pressed Flanagan, demanding to know how he planned to
exact his revenge.

With his neighbours buzzing around him, a look of
resolve crept onto Flanagan's face. He reloaded his shotgun
then gazed at the crowd. "I'm going to have a chat with the
Donnellys," he announced.

Weapon in hand, Flanagan stepped onto the road. The

crowd let out a cheer, sensing a golden opportunity to attack the hated Donnellys. About 17 men joined Flanagan as he trod down the Roman Line to the Donnelly farm. A larger group, consisting of small boys, old men, and women, followed the posse at a distance.

The mob around Flanagan was quiet but purposeful. Even with their large numbers, the men were leery about confronting the Donnellys. Without Flanagan leading them, it's doubtful they would have made the short march to the Donnelly homestead.

Flanagan's posse trod onto the Donnelly's property. Outside the Donnelly barn, William and James Jr. stood with their shirts rolled to their elbows, preparing their stagecoach for the first ride of the day. There were three passengers — two women and one man — inside their coach.

William and James Jr. were so engrossed in their labours that they didn't see the lynch mob surging towards them. Flanagan called out their names, and finally, the two oldest Donnelly boys looked up. The brothers gazed at their chief rival and grinned. They acted like Flanagan was alone, not at the head of a sizeable mob.

Flanagan cursed the Donnelly family and gave the brothers a graphic report of the carnage in his barn. William and James Jr. shrugged then stepped away from their coach. They reassured their passengers that they would still be leaving on time. Then, William and James Jr. stepped onto the road to meet their angry visitors. Several paces back, a group of onlookers held their breath.

The two Donnelly brothers stood placidly in the road, hands at their sides. Flanagan stared straight at them, flush with confidence. The odds were nine to one in his favour.

Suddenly, a primal bellowing split the air. Startled, Flanagan looked up, only to see a pack of Donnellys marching out of the barn. Old Jim, who was nearing 60, led a procession consisting of his five youngest sons. Robert, John, Mike, Tom, and Patrick all had their sleeves rolled up and were toting clubs, as was their father. James Jr. and William reached into the coach to retrieve their own clubs, which were stashed beneath the driver's bench.

The Donnellys arrayed themselves in a rough formation. Standing shoulder to shoulder in a solid line of flesh, the eight club-wielding, grinning madmen gazed hungrily at their opponents.

Flanagan grunted. Despite the new arrivals, he still felt cocky. Sure, the odds had narrowed, but he still had more men on his side. Plus, there was the shotgun — an equalizer if there ever was one.

Flanagan began to raise his weapon to his eye. In an instant, Old Jim reacted. Moving as quickly as he had in his fight with Patrick Farrell, the patriarch of the Donnelly clan rushed at Flanagan. Jim grabbed the shotgun by the barrels and tore it out of Flanagan's hands. With a vicious shove, he slammed the gun backwards so that its wooden butt crashed into Flanagan's face. Teeth and blood went flying as Flanagan

Robert and Tom Donnelly (seated).
(By permission Ray Fazakas, author, *The Donnelly Album*)

howled in pain. Old Jim bashed him over the head with the weapon for good measure, then tossed the shotgun aside.

While their father brutalized Flanagan, the Donnelly boys charged into action. Uttering bloodcurdling battle cries, they descended on the posse like a pack of wolves.

To the astonishment of the passengers inside the Donnelly coach, the two sides crashed together in a bone-jarring scrum. The men in Flanagan's posse fought back with a desperation borne of fear. They clumsily swung their fists and tried to dodge the Donnellys' hands and clubs. The Lucanites were tough and strong, but they were no match for the rabid family.

The seven Donnelly boys and their father shuffled their feet like professional boxers, kicking, punching, and clubbing as they went. Their quick movements made it almost impossible for Flanagan's men to land any telling blows. They moved through the mob like wraiths, blurry figures doling out pain and destruction.

Thomas, the youngest Donnelly, performed particularly well during the donnybrook. He was already regarded as the best fist-fighter in Biddulph Township, a young man who almost never lost a fight. His vicious fists lashed out at Flanagan's posse, as he joyfully swung at the men around him.

Old Jim also conducted himself nobly. With his strong sons by his side, the elderly Donnelly clubbed his way through the group. His shillelagh crashed down again and again on the skulls of his enemies, leaving them reeling. The onlookers who had followed Flanagan's posse gasped in horror but made no attempt to intervene. They kept their distance as the Donnellys cleaned up.

A Rival Dispatched

Though they took a few blows, the Donnellys easily emerged victorious. Soon, the once confident posse was lying in the dust, groaning from a harvest of bruises, cuts, and fractures. Flanagan lay on his back, just conscious enough to realize he had been humiliated for a second time in less than 24 hours. Unused shotgun shells lay scattered on the ground along with his weapon.

The Donnelly boys applied a few kicks to their prostrate foes, then backed off. They rubbed their sore knuckles and congratulated each other on their fighting prowess. Old Jim whirled his shillelagh like a baton and slapped his boys' backs. The passengers in the Donnelly coach continued to watch with wide eyes and open mouths.

Gradually, Flanagan drew himself to his feet. Glaring at the Donnelly boys and their father with undisguised hatred, he picked up his shotgun, but made no attempt to use it against his vanquishers. Instead, he stood still for several minutes, gulping air and gathering his strength. Slowly, the other men in the posse staggered to their feet. Some of them had to help each other stand up. Aching from his many injuries, Flanagan stumbled away at the head of a limping, groaning mob. It was a humiliating defeat, but at least, Flanagan thought to himself, it was over. He was wrong.

Early in September, the Donnellys paid another visit to Flanagan's residence. They arrived on horseback in the middle of the night, holding torches, which they pressed against the dry wooden sides of Flanagan's barn until sheets of flame rode up its outside walls. Their work complete, the Donnellys rode off, leaving a blazing barn in their wake.

The roaring fire roused Flanagan from a deep sleep. The stagecoach owner stepped to the window of his house and felt his heart sink as he watched his barn burn. The whole structure was ablaze, with angry fingers of flame leaping dozens of metres into the air. It was far too late to try to put the fire out.

His face glowing red from the inferno outside his window, Flanagan uttered a curse under his breath. But this time it wasn't despair he felt seeping through his blood. It was lust for vengeance.

Chapter 6
Law and Disorder

n February 24, 1876, the second floor of Fitzhenry's hotel in Lucan rocked with the sounds of a Donnelly celebration in full swing. The family was out in force, dancing and singing to a traditional Irish band and drinking heavily. The occasion was another wedding reception, this one for Tom Ryder, a friend of the Donnelly brothers.

Tables were packed with baked chicken, apple pie, biscuits, and other treats. Dancers frolicked under oil lanterns as the band played jigs and reels from the Old Country. William joined in on violin; he was an enthusiastic, if not particularly talented fiddle player and loved to perform before his family and friends. The new bride and groom shook hands with their guests and took their turn on the dance floor.

Outside the hotel, a trio of grim-faced men was planning to disrupt the festivities. The trio consisted of three constables named John. There was John Bawden, John Reid, and John Coursey. For reasons known only to them, these lawmen figured a packed wedding reception would be the perfect place to arrest James Donnelly Jr. The eldest Donnelly boy was accused of beating up a fourth constable, Rhody Kennedy, on a previous occasion.

Constables Bawden, Reid, and Coursey swaggered into the hotel, hands on their belts. One of them approached the first-floor bartender. Pointing to the ceiling, the officer asked if the Donnellys were still at the party upstairs. The bartender nodded and the constable hitched up his belt. Like the other two officers, he had a revolver around his middle.

The lawmen made their way up the stairs and barged into the party room. Pushing aside dancers with their shoulders, they marched to the centre of the room then stopped, fingering the butts of their pistols. The band ceased playing and couples stopped dancing. With all eyes upon them, the constables announced they were there to arrest James Jr.

Moments later, the first-floor bartender looked up in surprise to see Constables Bawden, Reid, and Coursey flying down the stairs. They were followed by an angry mob of Donnellys and friends. The constables were shouting that they represented the law, but no one seemed to be listening. The Donnellys and their pals threw vicious punches as the officers scrambled for the exit.

Constable Bawden fumbled for his side arm, only to find that someone had beaten him to it. William Donnelly had lifted the pistol from Bawden's holster, and he waved it haphazardly in the air. Standing on the stairs, William fired a wild shot at Bawden as the constable rushed to the front door. True to form, William missed the officer by a broad margin, even though he was only a few feet away. All three constables scurried through the doorway and outside the hotel, angry, beaten, and bruised.

Standing in the street, the lawmen rubbed their wounds and averted their gazes from each other. They slinked off like injured cats, muttering angry vows beneath their breath.

Once the Donnelly boys had dispatched the lawmen, they went back upstairs to enjoy the party. The band began playing another reel as dancers took to the floor. The wedding guests revelled long into the early morning hours. When the party was finally over, the Donnellys staggered outside, unhitched their horses, and rode off, feeling very light in the saddle.

William rode back to the farmhouse where he lived with Nora, and collapsed on his bed. When dawn broke a couple hours later, he went to breakfast as if nothing out of the ordinary had happened the night before. He was tucking into his eggs and coffee when Constables Reid, Bawden, and Coursey paid a return visit. The three officers had brought several stocky reinforcements with them. All of the lawmen were armed, and none were in the mood for horseplay.

One of the officers knocked loudly on the front door. When Nora opened it, the police poured past her and surrounded William at the breakfast table. William did not go peacefully. When the constables tried to handcuff him, he stood up and thrashed from side to side, swinging his fists. The constables grabbed hold of his arms and trunk, gripping his body like a swarm of angry fish. William struggled his way out of the house and into the yard. But, outnumbered and outgunned, the Donnelly was overwhelmed and forced to the ground, where he was handcuffed and subdued.

William was tossed in jail, charged with shooting at Constable Bawden. His trial took place in March 1876. In the witness stand, William said he was guilty of nothing more than high spirits. He said he fired at Constable Bawden to frighten him and to give his comrades a laugh. The court wasn't impressed, and sentenced William to nine months in jail.

By going to court, William was following in his father's footsteps. Jim Donnelly had set the example for his sons with his criminal trial and subsequent stint in jail. As if trying to emulate Old Jim, all of the Donnelly boys save Patrick appeared in court in the 1870s on a variety of colourful charges. These ranged from arson and highway robbery to poisoning, drunkenness, and brawling.

The Donnellys got away with some of these offences, but not all of them.

John Donnelly, for example, received three months in jail

on an assault charge for his role in the wedding battle. James Jr. got nine months for beating Constable Rhody Kennedy. Tom Donnelly was given two months for participating in a brawl.

Patrick, for his part, continued to be more interested in learning the blacksmith trade than in raising hell. After completing his training in St. Thomas, he settled in the community of Thorold. There, he worked as a smithy and kept out of trouble.

With William in jail, the other Donnelly boys did their best to keep the family stagecoach running. Lacking William's smarts and charm, they fared poorly.

It didn't help that Patrick Flanagan was back in business, taking most of the passenger traffic in Lucan. Having built a new barn and bought new coaches and horses, Flanagan was more determined than ever to bankrupt the Donnellys. He refused to knuckle under, despite the brutal treatment meted out to him.

The Donnellys toyed with the idea of conducting another midnight raid against Flanagan. Perhaps they could burn down his new barn or wreck his shiny new stagecoaches. But they quickly abandoned the idea; Flanagan had taken to posting armed guards on his property. His stagecoach drivers carried guns as well. There was no way the Donnellys could attack their competitor without getting shot in the process.

Then, on the evening of March 17, 1877, the Donnellys received a taste of their own medicine. That night, a mysterious fire broke out at a stable the family was using to house their stagecoach and horse. The fire killed the horse and destroyed the coach. The Donnellys never found out who was responsible.

It was the coup de grâce, as far as William was concerned. After his release from prison, he sold off what remained of his stagecoach company and took up farming as a profession.

The burning of the family stable ignited a wave of arson and destruction in Biddulph Township. In the spring and summer of 1877, the Donnellys regularly rode up the Roman Line, torches in hand.

During this period, Jim Kelly's barn burned down, as did homes and barns owned by Michael Marra and Dan McDonald. Vandals also visited the farms of Ed Sullivan, Pat Dorsey, Jim Corrigan, Jim Toohey, Martin Ryan, and Bill Casey. Poisoned cattle were reported on the farms of Tom Kinsella, John Cain, and John and William Thompson. For good measure, horses owned by Jim Barnes and Martin Darcey were mutilated.

The Donnellys were not responsible for all of these crimes. It's likely that other Lucanites took to arson and vandalism as a way to settle old grievances. And there was also religious strife to consider — animosity between Catholics and Protestants still ran high in Biddulph Township. The Donnellys made convenient scapegoats, however, because of their notorious image.

Lucan was gaining an unenviable reputation as the

wildest town in Canada as major house fires and barn blazes routinely lighted evening skies. Newspapers began referring to the presence of "a Ku Klux Klan in Lucan," confusing the night-riding antics of the Donnellys with those of white terrorists in the southern United States.

The Klan tag was inaccurate, but the spectacular crime wave was not, as the papers regularly reported. "During the last week or two, several thousand dollars worth of property has been destroyed by fire, the origin [being] traced to incendiaries," read a report published in May 1877 in the *London Free Press.* "Some 15 horses have perished, either by burning alive or otherwise. The latest outrage ... caused a great deal of indignation in the neighbourhood, and threats to lynch the miscreants are freely indulged in."

But the Donnellys had bigger problems to worry about than bad press. That spring, James Jr. became deathly ill. An anxious Johannah put him to bed in the Donnelly homestead. The strain of the years had aged Johannah Donnelly enormously; her hair was now snow white, her features grizzled and wrinkled. Her face bore the hint of a beard. She was still fiercely protective of her family, however, and determined to nurse her eldest son back to health.

As with many aspects of the Donnelly saga, the exact nature of James's ailment is unclear. Some Lucanites said that James Jr. simply had a bad case of pneumonia. But according to a more lurid story, he was wounded in an ambush following a night of drinking. It was reported that James made quite a scene of himself, pounding back liquor alone in a local bar. His presence did not go unnoticed.

Singing and carrying on, James Jr. was riding his horse down the Roman Line towards his parents' house when a posse of hooded riders intercepted him. The riders were toting rifles and proceeded to pump James Jr. full of lead. The men allegedly shot James as revenge for his assault on Constable Kennedy.

On May 15, 1877, James Jr. died. Whether his death stemmed from illness or violence made little difference — his surviving kin marked his passing by administering ferocious beatings to anyone who had ever annoyed their big brother during his brief life. Donnelly fists and feet struck out at a wide range of targets as old scores were settled for a now deceased brother. This latest round of fisticuffs came on top of nightly arson parties and other Donnelly specialties.

As far as their long-suffering neighbours were concerned, the Black Donnellys were no longer content with defying the law in Lucan; they were the law.

* * *

Not many Lucanites were content with the Donnellys playing judge, jury, and hangman. So, in the fall of 1877, a new chief constable was appointed in Lucan. The selection was somewhat surprising — Constable Samuel L. Everett enjoyed a drink now and again, and had a reputation for intemperate and unprofessional behaviour in front of the taxpayers. Nonetheless, Everett had two distinct characteristics that made him qualified for the job: he was brave, and he hated the Donnellys.

Shortly after Everett's appointment, a barn belonging to a farmer named Blake burned to the ground. The Donnellys barely knew Blake and had no reason to destroy his property, but Everett wasn't one to be sidetracked by the facts. He promptly found a pair of Donnellys to arrest and charge with arson: William, who was fresh out of jail, and Robert.

Charges against the Donnelly brothers were eventually dropped due to lack of evidence. But while the brothers escaped prosecution, their pride was hurt. It was one thing to be accused of crimes for which they were guilty. It was quite another to be accused of offences in which they had no part.

On the evening of March 18, 1878, Constable Everett was attacked as he tried to enter his own house. The constable had just rapped on the rear door to alert his wife to let him in, when a sharp crack shattered the night's silence. A barrage of buckshot flashed past Everett and embedded itself in the wooden door.

Everett snatched his revolver from his belt and wheeled around, looking for the perpetrator. Scanning the darkness, he saw a bright flash of light coming from a woodpile located roughly 15 metres away. The flash was accompanied by another crack of thunder as more buckshot blasted into Everett's door.

The constable was certain he saw a shadowy figure by the woodpile, possibly holding a gun. He raised his revolver and fired in the general direction of the shadow. He heard a groan, and the sound of a body falling to the ground.

Smoking pistol in hand, Constable Everett bounded over to the woodpile. Cautiously peering behind it, he saw Robert Donnelly lying on his back, clutching his shoulder. Robert had a shotgun with him and he reeked of alcohol. The constable pointed his revolver at the burly Donnelly boy and took him prisoner. Everett savoured the moment. Robert Donnelly would have a hard time hoodwinking a judge this time.

At his trial, the lightly wounded Robert insisted that he didn't mean to kill or injure Constable Everett. Robert claimed he merely wanted to frighten the constable, to punish him for making false accusations against his family. It was the same defence William Donnelly had trotted out at his trial for shooting at Constable Bowden.

There was some merit to Robert's story. As local wits pointed out, Robert wouldn't have fired from so far away if he'd really intended to kill the constable. The Donnellys' reputation as terrible marksmen was as strong as ever. In the end, the court handed Robert a two-year jail sentence. He was lucky — because his target was a law officer, his punishment could have been much stiffer.

The Donnellys' enemies were pleased to see Robert put away. For the first time in many years, they sensed the family was weakening. And with Robert in jail and James Jr. in the grave, there were two less Donnelly boys to worry about.

* * *

In February 1879, a new priest was appointed to St. Patrick's church. His name was Father John Connolly, and he was plump, elderly, and well meaning.

Father Connolly was no ivory-tower theologian who stayed above disputes in the community. He was quick to pick up on issues that concerned his flock. To this end, the good father decided it was time to inject a dose of parochial authority into the running battle between the Donnellys and their neighbours.

The newly appointed priest wrote a petition in his notebook. On a Sunday in the spring of 1879, he took his petition to St. Patrick's and placed it in the front of the church. The petition read:

> *We the undersigned Roman Catholics of St. Patrick's of Biddulph solemnly pledge ourselves to aid our spiritual director and Parish priest, in the discovery and putting down of crime in our mission. While we, at the same time, protest as Irishmen and as Catholics against any interference with him in the legitimate discharge of his spiritual duties.*

That same Sunday, Father Connolly gave a sermon that

addressed the issue of law and order — or the lack thereof — in Biddulph Township. Some parishioners said the priest made a fiery speech in which he blasted the Donnellys by name. Others said he spoke in more opaque terms and didn't single out the Donnelly clan.

Father Connolly kept the petition at the front of St. Patrick's for at least two Sundays in a row. By the time he withdrew it, nearly 100 men had signed his notebook. The priest would later say he merely wanted to test public opinion with regards to the Donnelly family.

As Father Connolly tested public opinion, a semi-secret organization began to take root in Lucan. The organization called itself a "vigilance committee" and modelled itself after similar groups that had sprung up in lawless parts of the United States. Ostensibly established to fight crime, the committee's real mission was to find a way to end the Donnellys' grip of terror on Biddulph Township.

Vigilance committees had a bad reputation in the U.S., where they enforced the law in the absence of adequate police or effective courts. Committee members called themselves "vigilantes" and dished out rough, frontier-style justice. Vigilantes were keen on public lynchings if they felt law and order would be served.

It is difficult to establish when Lucan's vigilance committee was founded. However, 1879 was the year the organization really took off. Fed-up Lucanites flocked to the one group that promised to end Donnelly violence. The vigilance committee started holding regular meetings in a place called the Cedar Swamp Schoolhouse.

Biddulph residents who joined the committee were sworn to secrecy, but that didn't prevent word of the group from leaking out. The Donnellys didn't seem too worried about the organization, despite the fact that their family was the main topic of discussion at committee meetings. The family had always been able to hold their own against hostile attacks from outsiders. Why should a secret committee be any different?

Chapter 7
A Missing Cow

One early September morning in 1879, William Thompson stood in his field, counting and recounting his cows. No matter how many times he counted, he always came up one short. A dark suspicion was beginning to cloud Thompson's mind. Someone had stolen one of his heifers.

Thompson had been a bitter enemy of the Donnellys since William had tried to court his sister, Maggie. It was Thompson's wedding party that the Donnellys and their accomplices had rudely interrupted with gunfire five years earlier. Moreover, there were rumours that the Donnelly clan ran a crooked beef business, selling meat from stolen cows to local hotels. On the basis of these lingering grudges and suspicions, Thompson convinced himself that the Donnellys had absconded with his cow. He stomped into Lucan and loudly informed everyone he met that the Donnellys were a bunch of cattle thieves.

Ordinarily, the disappearance of a single cow from a farmer's field wouldn't have been much cause for alarm. But in the increasingly tense environment of Lucan, residents were receptive to wild rumours, especially if they concerned the Donnellys. A crowd quickly gathered around Thompson as he continued to blast the thieving ways of the Donnelly clan.

The crowd contained several men who had signed Father Connolly's petition. These same men also happened to be members of the vigilance committee. The vigilantes hurriedly called an emergency meeting in the Cedar Swamp Schoolhouse.

At the meeting, Thompson's missing cow was discussed at length. The vigilantes decided to confront the Donnellys, who were the prime suspects. About 40 men, including William Thompson and John Kennedy (William Donnelly's mean-spirited brother-in-law), left the schoolhouse and stepped onto the Roman Line. Some of the marchers carried clubs or sticks. They were determined to find the bovine.

At around 9 a.m., the mob converged on Old Jim and Johannah's home. Jim, who was now in his early 60s, and Johannah, in her mid 50s, met their visitors outside the farmhouse and unleashed a volley of curses on their uninvited guests.

By now, only two Donnelly sons still lived at home: John and Thomas. Old Jim Donnelly was becoming increasingly weak with age and arthritis. Some days, he did little more than sit by the pot-bellied stove to keep warm. Johannah Donnelly, by contrast, had not slowed down at all. While her appearance was clearly that of an old lady, with white hair and a mass of wrinkles, her outlook remained fierce and unbowed. To Johannah, life remained a struggle between the Donnellys and everybody else. If anything, the death of James Jr. had further embittered her against everyone outside of her clan.

Neither John nor Thomas, nor any of the other Donnelly offspring, were around when the mob showed up at their parents' house. As Jim and Johannah scowled, the vigilantes announced that they were trying to locate a missing cow — a cow they were sure the Donnellys had stolen.

Jim and Johannah loudly insisted that there weren't any stolen cattle on the premises. Jim glared at the men with all the intensity his old, gnarled body could muster. The mob glared back. Some members simply laughed at the Donnelly patriarch.

The crowd demanded the right to search the Donnellys' home. Seeing he was vastly outnumbered, Jim reluctantly agreed to let the mob search his property. He and Johannah stepped aside as club-bearing men invaded their farmhouse. The men swaggered about, poking their sticks and clubs into closets, drawers, and other unlikely places where a cow might be hidden.

A small number of vigilantes broke off from the main search party to look inside the Donnelly barn. The group entered the barn with high hopes of locating the bovine at large. Their inspection turned up nothing more sinister than bails of straw, old hay, and rusty horseshoes.

The mob reconvened inside the Donnelly home. No cow was to be found, and the crowd was unsure what to do next. Old Jim and Johannah stood in the centre of their home, loudly demanding that the men leave at once. It began to dawn on the mob that they were in an unparalleled position of power. None of the Donnelly boys were around. Jim and Johannah were the only members of the family present.

As the two aged leaders of the Donnelly clan looked on helplessly, members of the mob began breaking up their home. They used their clubs to shatter windows and their boots and fists to smash up anything else that caught their fancy. The mob tore up all the beds and shattered their frames. They broke dishes, pots, pans, and glasses in the kitchen and pulled shelving off the walls.

Years of pent-up anger against the Donnellys poured out in a frenzy of destruction. By the time the mob was done, the inside of the proud Donnelly home looked like a disaster site. Broken plates, lamps, and shelving littered the floor. Jim and Johannah stood ankle-deep in debris and stared murderously at the intruders.

Someone in the crowd had a new idea: the Donnellys

Johannah and a friend in front of the Donnelly log home, circa 1878.
(Used with the permission of J. Robert Salts, author of *You Are Never Alone*,
from the collection of Joseph Molnar)

had probably hidden the cow at their son William's farm. It was just the sort of crafty thing a Donnelly might do. At the least, visiting William would offer another opportunity to smash up Donnelly property.

Leaving a trail of wreckage behind, the mob left the Donnelly homestead and headed towards William's farmhouse. The houses were separated by roughly five kilometres. After a short march, the vigilantes reached the boundary of William's property.

Nora gazed out the window of her home and saw a pack of angry men coming up the drive. Some of them had sticks and clubs. Crying out in alarm, she alerted her husband. William moved to the window and looked outside. Sure enough, a mass of men stood on his front lawn, calling his name and brandishing weapons. As Nora cringed with fear, her husband casually strolled out of his house to meet the lynch mob.

The crowd seethed and raged as William came into view. The vigilantes accused him of stealing William Thompson's cow. Cries of "devil clubfoot" and "damn Donnelly" rang out.

William said nothing in response. He scanned the crowd with cool, contemptuous eyes. Then, without a word, he turned and walked back into the house, leaving the men to exchange puzzled glances and consider their next course of action.

Moments later, William emerged for a second time. In his hands he held a violin. With a slight grin on his face, William raised the violin to his shoulder and ran the bow across the strings. After scraping out a few notes, he played a tune called "Boney Over the Alps."

The mob stood in place, transfixed by this impromptu concert. They had come prepared for defiance and anger, not a fiddle concerto. William played for several minutes while the crowd milled listlessly about. Members looked at each other and shrugged. Gradually, the mob broke up as individual members walked away from William's farmhouse. Music had soothed the savage beast — for now.

* * *

To everyone's surprise, Jim Donnelly didn't order his sons to beat up the men who had destroyed his farmhouse. Instead, of all places, he turned to the law for justice. In Old Jim's mind, the raid on his house had been such a grievous offence that the police couldn't possibly let the perpetrators go free.

Furthermore, the missing cow that had caused such turmoil eventually turned up in a wooded lot near Thompson's home. The bovine had simply gotten loose and walked away from its pasture.

After considerable prodding from Jim, Lucan authorities arrested 13 men in connection with the home invasion at the Donnellys'. They were charged with trespassing, destruction of property, and assault. John Kennedy was among the baker's dozen that was arrested.

Their trial, conducted in the fall of 1879, proved to be a bitter disappointment for the Donnellys. The defendants insisted that Jim had given them permission to search his house and property. Strictly speaking, this was true, but it should have been clear to all that Old Jim had only agreed to the search under threat of force.

The defendants also insisted they hadn't meant to break anything during their investigation. If the mob's actions had been rough and ready, it was only because the men had been really determined to find the missing cow. A clutch of witnesses, most of them friends of the home invaders, backed these ludicrous statements up in testimony before a magistrate. Charges against the 13 vandals were dropped.

This incident further fuelled the Donnellys' paranoia and rage. The trial proved that the courts and community were united against them. Seeing that the courts weren't interested in their case, the family resorted to a more tried and true form of justice.

Throughout the fall of 1879, various Lucanites were beaten and harassed by the Donnelly boys. A local resident named William Casey was kidnapped and horsewhipped by shadowy avengers, who also took the time to burn his barn down and hamstring his horses. Property on several other area farms was also torched. Cattle belonging to Tom Kinsella were poisoned, while horses belonging to John Kennedy were mutilated.

The Donnellys continued to act true to form — beating, robbing, and torching barns late at night. As in the past, no one seemed capable of standing up to the wild clan and ending their reign of terror.

* * *

About the time the Donnellys were conducting their fall rampage, Constable Everett was sizing up his prospects as chief of the Lucan constabulary. He didn't like what he saw. The township was out of control, and Robert Donnelly was due to be released from jail. Samuel L. Everett was no coward, but he wasn't a fool either. After tallying the odds, he decided to step down as chief constable.

The most unpopular job in Lucan was available. While no experienced lawman would go near the position, Lucan did find an eager recruit in the form of James Carroll, a farm equipment salesman from Perth County. Carroll didn't bring much experience to the job, but like Everett, he possessed the two essential qualities that would endear him to the residents of Biddulph Township: he was tough as nails, and he wasn't afraid of the Donnellys.

Carroll was six feet tall and weighed nearly 200 pounds. He had straight black hair and a huge jaw, which was covered in a thick, dark beard. No one would ever call him handsome, but that was fine with Carroll. He was more interested in gaining people's respect than their affection.

Carroll was familiar with the town's running feud against the Donnellys, and the inability of the local constabulary to keep the family in line. He assured Lucanites that he was the man to put the rogue family in their place.

As far as the Donnellys were concerned, it was business as usual. In October, Tom Donnelly caught up with Patrick Flanagan, the clan's old rival in the stagecoach business, and beat him to a pulp. New constable or not, Tom wanted to maintain the Donnellys' reputation as the most feared family in Biddulph Township.

Chapter 8
Bad Moon Rising

One fall evening in 1879, four men on horseback trotted up the Roman Line. Oblivious to the November cold, they laughed, sang, and jousted with each other, buoyed by the bottles of whisky they passed between them. Old Jim Donnelly led the pack, with Michael, John, and Thomas in tow.

In spite of the recent mob actions against them, the Donnellys still liked to raise hell whenever the mood hit them. Riding slowly in the dark, the three young men and their father felt invincible. They stayed close together, sharing slugs of whisky and ribald songs.

Around nine o'clock, Old Jim suggested the family get their fortunes read. It seemed like as good an idea as any to the Donnelly boys. They followed their father as he steered his horse towards the residence of one Grandma Bell.

Grandma Bell was an elderly African American woman who lived in a dilapidated shack outside of Lucan. She was one of the last remaining occupants of an African American settlement that had thrived in the area in the 1820s. When all her friends and neighbours left, Grandma Bell stayed put. She acquired a reputation as a soothsayer, telling fortunes for a fee.

The Donnellys clambered over to the old lady's log house. They stopped their horses outside and tied their reins to some trees. Laughing coarsely, they bounded over to Grandma Bell's shack.

Grandma Bell was surprised to hear someone pounding on the door so late in the evening. Curious, but cautious, she made her way to the door. She opened it a crack and asked who was there. Old Jim replied for his sons. He said it was the Donnellys, and that they were there to have their fortunes read.

Aware of the Donnellys' vicious reputation, Grandma Bell wasn't eager to let them inside, but figured it was the wisest course. The old woman opened the door and the Donnellys staggered in, stomping their feet and shouting with excitement.

They swaggered into Grandma Bell's tiny, cluttered kitchen and made themselves at home. Under their impatient stares and smirks, Grandma Bell boiled some water and made tea. She drew herself a cup, drank its contents, and then sifted through the tea leaves at the bottom with her finger. Scrutinizing the sodden leaves, she tried to discern glimpses of the future through patterns and shapes at the bottom of her cup.

Old Jim and his boys gazed at the fortuneteller with undisguised amusement. Their grins became ever bigger when Grandma Bell suddenly pulled back in horror. Turning to her uninvited guests with bulging eyes, she said she had gleaned evil tidings from the tea leaves. More specifically, she foresaw violent death stalking the Donnelly clan.

The Donnellys laughed heartily at this prediction. Since when hadn't death and violence stalked them? Death and destruction were things the Donnelly men scoffed at. They made their own way through life, fate be damned.

Old Jim slapped his thigh then rummaged through his pocket. He took out a few coins and tossed them on Grandma Bell's kitchen table. He thanked her for the good chuckle then told his boys it was time to leave. The group made their way out of Grandma Bell's shack, singing and laughing raucously. They mounted their horses and rode off to find new amusements.

Grandma Bell stepped outside to watch the Donnellys depart. Shivering in the fall cold, she looked up at the dark sky. The big November moon was blood red. The soothsayer shuddered. If only she had noticed the moon before. It was another sign of trouble to come for the Donnelly clan.

* * *

A few weeks after his visit to Grandma Bell, Michael Donnelly, the rail man, found himself in Waterford — 110 kilometres southeast of Lucan — on a stopover. More to the point, he found himself in front of Slaght's Hotel, rubbing his moustache thoughtfully. Would he continue on to his boarding house for the evening, or stop in for a quick drink? Rummaging through his pockets, he found he had enough for a round or two. A drink it would be, then.

The warmth of Slaght's Hotel was a welcome contrast to the harsh December cold. And truth be told, Michael wasn't looking forward to another night away from his wife, Ellen, and their two young children. They lived in a home in St. Thomas, a small community outside London, Ontario. Michael had managed to overcome his youthful propensity for laziness. He worked hard at his job as a railway brakeman, and was looking forward to spending the holidays with his family.

The hotel saloon was crowded, with men drinking at tables and talking loudly. Michael ignored them as he made his way to the bar. The Donnellys were used to drinking alone. Michael ordered a shot of spirits, paid the bartender, then gazed around the inside of the hotel.

Reports differ on what happened next. According to the most reliable accounts, Michael spotted a man who was being cruel to a dog. This anonymous person had brought the dog inside the hotel and was busy abusing the animal by his table.

Such rough handling outraged Michael's sense of fair play. Beating up people was one thing, but beating up animals wasn't sporting as far as he was concerned. In a booming voice, he suggested that the man might want to treat his pet a little more gently.

A second man in the bar, William Lewis, chimed in that the dog owner was a friend of his. In a sneering tone, he urged the Donnelly boy to mind his own business. Lewis had lived in Biddulph Township and knew very well what kind of man he was addressing.

Michael wasn't one to stand down from a challenge. He stood six feet tall and loved to brawl as much as his brothers. He weighed Lewis's words and concluded a beating was in order. Michael tore off his thick winter coat and tossed it aside as he approached Lewis, fists outstretched. The other clients in Slaght's Hotel stepped back to clear the way. Some of them got up from their chairs to watch the action.

Lewis jumped to his feet and kicked his own chair aside. He held out his balled fists and prepared to meet Michael, while the abused dog cringed under a table. The two men tangled in a whirl of muscle and brutal fists. Both opponents were evenly matched. They pummelled each other, seeking any advantage. The other men in the hotel cheered them on.

Michael pushed Lewis into a corner then pulled back

his hand to deliver a knockout punch. It was a fatal mistake. As Michael retracted his arm, Lewis reached into his pocket and took out a knife. In a flash, Lewis plunged the blade deep into his opponent's solid frame. The knife struck home near Michael's groin.

Michael gasped and staggered backwards. The men around him made no attempt to impede his progress. He walked to the end of the bar on unsteady feet, hands gripping his blood-soaked wound. Crying out, he collapsed into a stranger's arms. Several bar patrons eased Michael onto the floor. They tore open his clothes and examined his wound. Some of them tried to staunch the flow of blood with their hands. Most of the men inside Slaght's just stood around, gaping at the dying man in their midst.

Even without a doctor present, it was obvious that Michael's wound was serious. No one could stop the bleeding. There on the beer-soaked floor, Michael died a few minutes after being stabbed. He was 29.

Two days after the altercation, a jury inquest in Waterford named William Lewis as Michael's killer. Lewis was never sentenced, however, nor did he suffer any consequences for his offence.

Such suspicious behaviour on the part of authorities fuelled rumours about Michael's death. Some thought Lewis was a member of the vigilance committee, and that Michael had been set up. The committee, whispered Lucanites, intended to pick off the Donnellys one by one. Others said

Michael was the victim of nothing more heroic than a bar fight; it was his mistake to pick a quarrel with someone who knew how to use a knife.

On December 12, 1879, a funeral service was held for Michael Donnelly at St. Patrick's church. Father Connolly preached the sermon to Michael's dazed family and grieving widow.

Old Jim and Johannah were shattered by the second death of a second son within two years. Jim remembered Grandma Bell's warning and cursed. It was not right that a man's sons die before him. After the service, Michael's body was lowered into the frozen earth. He was buried in a cemetery plot next to his brother James.

Residents in Lucan braced themselves for the violent retribution they were sure would come from Michael's surviving brothers. Such vengeance had washed over Biddulph Township after James Jr. had died, and Lucanites expected a repeat performance.

To everyone's astonishment, the Donnellys did nothing. In the days following Michael's death, the remaining members of his family seemed sullen and uncertain. Perhaps for the first time, they sensed their enemies were gaining on them. Indeed, the vigilance committee was reaching its peak of power.

Under the guidance of Constable James Carroll — who had taken a leadership role, if not command, of the committee — the organization had topped 150 members. Their meetings at the Cedar Swamp Schoolhouse were becoming increasingly belligerent. Anyone who wanted to join the committee was now required to take an oath:

> *I do solemnly swear, before Almighty God and his holy evangelists, never to divulge the business that may be discussed or transacted by the Biddulph Vigilance Committee, and in case I should be arrested or captured for taking part in said business, I hereby declare I will never reveal the names of my associates, even though I should be tortured or sent to the gallows for refusing to do so.*

This wasn't just fraternal order foolishness; the vigilance committee was gearing up for war.

* * *

In mid January 1880, the vigilance committee struck. Committee members burned down the barn of Lucan resident Patrick Ryder then tried to pin the crime on the Donnelly boys. Surely, they reasoned, the community would be so outraged by this latest atrocity that it would be roused to action against the Donnelly clan. At the very least, they hoped the Donnellys might be tossed in jail for a while.

Unfortunately for the vigilance committee, the Donnelly boys were at a dance the very evening Ryder's barn was set ablaze. Dozens of witnesses testified to seeing the brothers dancing jigs and reels through the night.

Old Jim laughed when he heard of the committee's accusation. As his boys had solid alibis, Jim felt confident he could sue the members of the committee and win. He brazenly announced his intention to counter-charge the vigilance committee in court.

Jim planned on introducing his counter-charge in the nearby Granton, Ontario Court House on the morning of February 4. Figuring the process would take all day, he hired a local boy named Johnny O'Connor to take care of the morning chores. Johnny's duties included feeding the pigs and digging a path through the snow from the road to the farmhouse. While they inspired terror in most of their neighbours, the Donnellys still maintained a few friends and acquaintances who occasionally did odd jobs for the family.

Expecting a snowstorm on the night of February 3, Jim invited Johnny to stay over at the Donnelly residence. That way, Johnny wouldn't have to fight through snowdrifts and freezing temperatures to make his way to the Donnelly farm in the morning.

Johnny was the second guest in the farmhouse. The other guest was Bridget Donnelly, a 21-year-old relative from Ireland. Bridget, Jim's niece, was visiting Canada from the Old Country. That made a total of five people in the Donnelly homestead: Old Jim and Johannah, Johnny, Bridget, and Tom.

That evening, the Donnellys indulged in a late-night snack of apples and chatted about their upcoming court case. At about 11 p.m., the family went to bed. Jim was now sleeping in the downstairs bedroom off the parlour. When it was time to turn in, Johnny bunked with Old Jim, in the same bed. Upstairs, Bridget, Johannah, and Tom settled in.

At another farmhouse a few kilometres away, William Donnelly and his wife Nora were also bedding down for the evening. William and Nora had a guest of their own, in the form of John Donnelly. John took a bedroom near the front of his brother's house.

As the Donnellys slept, a group of men gathered at the Cedar Swamp Schoolhouse. The men carried clubs, hatchets, knives, and rifles, and they were dressed warmly against the bitter cold. They represented the hard core of the vigilance committee. Jim Donnelly's threatened lawsuit had inspired the more aggressive committee members to gather for what might be their last meeting. The time had come for action.

Constable James Carroll nodded as the vigilantes entered the building. Some of them nodded in return. Others avoided the officer's gaze. Many of the men brought bottles of liquor with them. These were opened and passed around. Even men who didn't regularly drink took big slugs. A portion of those present had been drinking for hours. As the vigilantes waited at the schoolhouse, they continued to drink. Few men spoke as the bottles passed from hand to hand.

The group inside the Cedar Swamp Schoolhouse included several of the Donnellys' most bitter enemies. Besides

Constable Carroll, there was John Kennedy and John Purtell.

Thomas Ryder and his brother James were also in attendance. It was Thomas's wedding reception where the fracas had broken out between the Donnelly boys and the three Constable Johns. Some reports suggest that Thomas Ryder was still friends with the Donnellys and wanted to warn them of the committee's intentions. Other accounts indicate that Ryder had grown weary of the Donnellys' antics in the years following the incident at his wedding.

In total, about 30 vigilantes gathered at the school. When he decided no one else was likely to arrive, Constable Carroll addressed the group in a low, harsh voice. He went over the evening's plan and urged any faint-hearted members to leave. No one did. The officer looked over his posse and then announced it was time to go. It was just after midnight on the morning of February 4.

Constable Carroll led the heavily armed vigilance committee out of the schoolhouse. It was very cold, and the men adjusted their coats and stomped their feet. The constable grunted an order, and the men mounted the horses that were waiting outside.

Some said a series of faint moans could be heard above the wind that night. It was the banshee, they insisted, a dismal female spirit familiar in Irish folklore. According to the Irish immigrants of Biddulph Township, the banshee's cries foretold death and destruction.

Perhaps the vigilantes thought the banshee was on

their side, for on a signal from the constable, they steered their horses onto the Roman Line and made for the old Donnelly farmstead.

Chapter 9
A Dirge for the Donnellys

J ohnny O'Connor was fast asleep in the big bed he shared with Old Jim Donnelly when the sound of someone pounding on the door woke him up. At first he thought it was a nightmare. But then Old Jim started to grunt and swear, and Johnny knew it wasn't a dream.

Blinking sleep from his eyes, Johnny watched Jim lift the heavy covers from the bed and sit up. Jim put on his boots, still cursing under his breath. Johnny could barely make out his form in the darkened room. Jim stood up and stepped through the open bedroom door and into the parlour. A moment later, a bright flame illuminated Jim's face. The head of the Donnelly clan had lit a candle so he could see.

Candle in hand, Jim trudged towards the door. "Who is it?" he demanded, as the pounding increased in volume. The words spoken from the other side of the door were muffled, and Johnny couldn't make them out. Jim muttered something about "a fine time to visit a hard-working family" then opened the front door.

In the flickering candlelight, Johnny saw Constable Jim Carroll standing in the doorway. The young boy could feel the cold wind from outside brush against his face. He kept his body under the warm covers, sticking his head out of the sheets like a turtle.

Jim greeted Constable Carroll with a few gruff words. The constable grunted in return and barged past the old man and into the kitchen. Johnny could hear the officer talking about "new criminal charges" against the Donnelly clan. The accusations were vague and Jim expressed rude amazement that the constable would bother him on such trivial grounds so late at night.

The ruckus in the parlour woke up the rest of the household. One by one, Johannah, Thomas, and Bridget filed into the room to see what was going on. Johannah and Bridget were both wearing long-sleeved flannel nightgowns. Thomas had bare feet and wore long underwear.

More candles were lit, giving Johnny a good view of the strange scene that was unfolding. Old Jim insisted that the constable read the arrest warrant he had presumably brought with him. Carroll offered only excuses as to why he couldn't produce the document.

At one point, Carroll took Thomas aside. The constable and the youngest Donnelly son moved out of view. Johnny could hear the two men arguing, but he couldn't see them. Thomas and his father began cursing at the constable. Old Jim asked his son if Constable Carroll had placed him in handcuffs.

"Yes. He thinks he's smart," Tom sneered.

Thomas moved back into Johnny's view. The little boy saw it was true: Thomas's powerful wrists were encircled with steel. A wave of fear washed over Johnny — he sensed something terrible was about to happen. As quietly as he could, he slipped out of the covers and took up a position beneath the bed. It was cold on the hard wooden floor, but Johnny felt safer there.

From his new hiding place, he continued to watch the action in the parlour. The Donnellys and Constable Carroll were still bickering and shouting. No one noticed the boy beneath the bed.

Suddenly, Constable Carroll stopped talking and moved across the parlour so that he was directly in front of a window. He lifted a hand and made a gesture that Johnny didn't recognize.

Old Jim demanded to know what the officer was up to. Before he could finish his sentence, 20 men surged through the door and swarmed around the Donnellys. The men carried clubs, knives, and axes. Before Jim could protest, the men raised their weapons and brought them to bear on their stunned prey. Someone tossed a club to Constable Carroll and the officer joined in the fray. Within seconds, the Donnellys were engulfed in a sea of blows and blood as their neighbours sought to avenge decades of violence and bullying.

Johnny froze in terror as the war whoops of the intruders mixed with the angry, panicky screams of all four Donnellys. It was the first time he had ever heard a Donnelly cry out in pain.

Thomas swung his imprisoned arms desperately, trying to strike at the wolf pack around him. His manacled fists smashed against the jaw of one of the intruders. It was a sharp blow that sent the vigilante staggering backwards in pain, but it made little difference to the fight's outcome. As the one injured vigilante stepped away, half a dozen others moved forward to bash Thomas with heavy clubs. Killers besieged the youngest Donnelly boy on all sides.

With a defiant scream, Thomas thrust out his brawny shoulders and raced forward, knocking his assailants aside. Carving a path through the frenzied intruders, he made it out the open door. He ran madly, bare feet slamming against the snow.

But there were vigilantes outside the house, guarding against just such an escape attempt. Before Thomas had gone five paces, he was knocked down and savagely beaten, his blood staining the white snow. Still struggling, he was dragged back into the house.

A Dirge for the Donnellys

Johnny couldn't see Thomas's face, but rather his feet, lying on the bloodstained farmhouse floor. The Donnelly boy's screams turned into whimpers as his muscular body was pierced, mangled, and torn. At one point, a committee member slammed a spade over the prostate Tom's head. His feet twitched briefly, then lay still once and for all.

Old Jim and Johannah suffered the same fate. The vigilantes smashed the two elderly Donnellys with their clubs and stabbed them repeatedly with knives. Johannah screamed and cursed with all her might. She condemned the men's souls and said they would be damned to hell for their actions. Then she too was knocked senseless and cut to pieces. Someone placed the muzzle of a rifle against her chest for good measure, and pulled the trigger. Johannah's body flopped in the air as the bullet passed through her.

Jim fought back with a fury born of fear. He screamed and swung his fists at the gibbering faces around him. Some of his punches connected and sent men reeling. Bellowing like a wounded bull, the Donnelly patriarch grabbed a chair and held it out in front of him. He bashed the chair over his enemies' heads until it splintered to pieces. Some of the vigilantes dropped back, bruised and injured. The mob continued to press their attack, however, and forced Jim up against a wall. The remnants of the chair were knocked from his hands as the oldest Donnelly was punched, bludgeoned, and stabbed.

Mortally wounded, Jim staggered around his kitchen,

hands limp at his sides, blank eyes staring from a blood-smeared face. The elderly man, who once killed a blacksmith in a fight, fell to the floor. The butchers circled around him for a final kill. They laughed and whooped as their clubs and knives came down on Jim's dying body. One of the vigilantes said he was going to cut Jim's head off. His comrades cheered and urged him on.

Johnny suddenly heard a hysterical female voice screaming from the second floor of the house. Bridget — whose only crime was being called Donnelly — had raced upstairs when the vigilantes had burst into the kitchen. With Thomas, Jim, and Johannah dead or dying, a group of armed men bounded up the stairs after her. One of the vigilantes shouted he was going to "bash the sow's head in."

Bridget's screams turned into cries of pain and then faded altogether, as the last Donnelly standing fell silent. The only sounds Johnny could make out were the rough voices of the men, laughing and boasting.

Johnny held his breath in terror as one of the vigilantes entered the room where he was hiding. The man was carrying a metal canister in his hands. He dumped the contents of the canister over the bed and furniture. Johnny immediately recognized the scent of inflammable coal oil. The oil was set on fire as the men filed out of the house, whooping and swinging their clubs. Amidst the killing and chaos, they hadn't noticed Johnny.

The bedroom rapidly filled with smoke as long tongues

A Dirge for the Donnellys

of flame lapped up the walls of the Donnelly residence. Johnny waited for as long he could, then dashed out of his hiding spot. Ducking so no one could see him through a window, he made his way through the blazing kitchen. He could see Tom and Johannah lying on the floor, horribly battered and mutilated, their bodies wreathed in smoke and flame.

The terrified boy raced out of the burning farmhouse into the freezing night. Numb with fear, he stumbled barefoot over the frozen ground to the nearest farmhouse. Behind him, the Donnelly residence was spouting huge flames. The vigilantes had left several minutes earlier. There was no one in sight save one petrified boy, dashing through fields of snow.

In the darkness, Johnny swore he heard the banshee singing a dirge for the Donnellys. Desperate to escape the death house, he ran on. In the distance, framed against the night sky, he could see the farmhouse of Patrick Whelan, the Donnellys' closest neighbour. Johnny raced towards the house, weeping from fright and cold.

* * *

After leaving the Donnellys' farmstead, the vigilance committee began to break up. A few of the men had been seriously injured and required medical attention. The wounded committee members rode home, along with a few other vigilantes who wanted to call it a night. The combination of cold air and savage butchery had sobered many of the men to the point of nausea.

About a dozen committee members remained behind. Sitting on horseback, Constable Carroll gathered the remaining men around him. He said it was time to put the second part of the vigilance committee's plan into effect. With Carroll in the lead, this small group directed their horses to the nearby residence of William Donnelly.

John Kennedy was one of the few men who stayed with Carroll. He was eager to settle scores and kill the clubfooted demon who dared defile his sister.

With Constable Carroll riding point, the vigilantes approached William's residence, their horses' hooves crunching through the snow. Some of the men had brought rifles or shotguns with them. When they were close enough to William's house, they dismounted and tied their horses to some trees. They approached the farmhouse on foot, rifles at the ready.

Inside their home, William and Nora were sleeping, oblivious to the stealthy advance of the vigilantes. John Donnelly, who was staying at his brother's house for the evening, was fast asleep in the spare bedroom near the front door. William and Nora slept in another bedroom nearby.

The three people inside the farmhouse were suddenly awakened by a series of frantic cries from outside. A man was shouting "Fire! Fire!" over and over again. "Open the door, Will!" yelled the man. It was roughly 2:30 a.m.

William lurched out of bed and rubbed his eyes. He couldn't smell smoke and he couldn't place the voice of the man shouting. Was his farmhouse on fire? William couldn't tell. He got up anyway to check on the racket outside. The same thought occurred to John Donnelly. He too got out of bed and headed to the front door.

John made it there first. With William behind him, John swung open the heavy farmhouse door. Peering out into the cold, dark night, John could make out maybe a dozen men standing only a few steps away. Some of them had guns in their hands. Before John could speak, the vigilantes fired and his body was ripped apart by bullets.

* * *

Johnny O'Connor banged frantically on the front door of Patrick Whelan's farmhouse. Awakened by the noise, Whelan and his wife got up to investigate. Whelan lit a lamp and went downstairs. As he did so, Johnny burst into the house through the unlocked door. The Whelans found him standing in bare feet in the middle of their kitchen, sobbing uncontrollably. He was white with fear, his skin nearly frozen.

The Whelans wrapped Johnny in warm blankets then lit a fire in their wood stove. Johnny gazed into the flames with dull eyes as he stammered an account of the evening's events. He said the Donnellys were dead, that a mob of men had killed them. He also said that Constable Carroll had led the mob, and that it had included Tom Ryder, John Purtell, and other members of the community.

Whelan watched Johnny with incredulous eyes. The boy sounded like he'd been reading too many dime-store cowboy novels. Mob lynchings were something that happened in Texas, not Ontario.

Without averting his gaze from the wood stove, Johnny continued his grim tale. He said the vigilantes had set the Donnelly house on fire before they left. Still sceptical, Whelan moved to the window. He looked out across the darkened fields to the Donnelly place. In the distance, he could see fingers of light reaching towards the sky. "Jesus Christ," he thought. "The boy was right." The Donnelly place was burning.

* * *

John Donnelly screamed and flew backwards, his chest a mass of gaping holes. He collapsed in the doorway, gurgling blood and gasping in pain. William pulled his brother inside the house then slammed the door shut. With Nora looking on in horror, William tended to his dying brother. He cradled John in his arms as the men outside laughed and boasted about their kill.

William could hear the voice of his brother-in-law, John Kennedy. John was congratulating himself on finally getting rid of "that devil clubfoot." William looked at his wife, his face white with shock. The vigilantes had been after him.

A Dirge for the Donnellys

They'd shot John by mistake.

William made a move to grab his rifle, but Nora stopped him by seizing his wrist. She pressed a finger to her lips. "If they know you're alive, they'll kill us both," she whispered. William stared at his wife. She was right. He shuddered, and then knelt down to tend to his dying brother. William held John in his arms and spoke to him softly as he died. The oldest living Donnelly continued to whisper encouragement to John, even when it became apparent he was no longer breathing.

Outside, the vigilantes watched and waited. With dawn breaking, they finally mounted up and left, satisfied their evening's work was done.

Chapter 10
Requiem

The four surviving Donnellys sat in the front pew at St. Patrick's church as Father John Connolly conducted a funeral service for their murdered family. Jennie Donnelly sobbed while Patrick, Robert, and William stared numbly at the altar.

There were two coffins in the centre aisle of the church. The first contained the remains of John Donnelly. The second was filled with bits of bone and burnt flesh recovered from the ashes of the Donnelly family homestead. Presumably, these were the remains of Jim, Johannah, Thomas, and Bridget.

The church was packed with town residents. Most of them were genuinely shocked at the terrible crime that had taken place two days earlier. Others were relieved to see the Donnelly family torn apart.

Among the many mourners was Johnny O'Connor. He sat in a pew with his sister and elbowed her in the ribs when John Purtell came into the church. "He was there the night the Donnellys were killed," Johnny whispered. Other killers were also present in the church that day, including Constable James Carroll.

Johnny's sister urged her brother to keep quiet. A funeral was no place to be making accusations, especially when the Donnellys' killers were still at large.

It's likely that William, Patrick, and Robert were aware that some of the men who had killed their family members were seated behind them. But the brothers were too shattered to make a scene or utter threats of retribution. They sat glumly through the service, gazing blankly as Father Connolly led mass.

Several reporters from Canada's biggest newspapers attended the funeral service. The Donnelly murders had become national news. "At 12 o'clock precisely, Mass was celebrated by the Rev. Father Connolly," wrote a reporter from *The Toronto Telegram*. "[He] undertook to address the congregation, with which the church was crowded to suffocation. [At one point,] his reverence completely broke down, being overcome by the intensity of his feeling ... Then, with his handkerchief over his eyes, and staggering back against the altar, he threw himself upon it and wept like a child."

Father Connolly managed to pull himself together to finish the service. During his sermon, the priest spoke highly of Jim and Johannah Donnelly. He described the Donnelly boys as "hard characters," but insisted they hadn't deserved the fate that had befallen them.

"I cannot understand how this has taken place," said Father Connolly. "I did not believe that there was a man capable of doing anything like that in Biddulph. I believed that there were men who would give a man a clout when half drunk, or waylay him upon the road, but I never thought that they could commit such a butchery as this."

To some, the priest's grief seemed exaggerated; there were rumours he was part of the vigilance committee, or at the least supported the group's cause.

Once the service was over, the coffins containing the five Donnellys were taken outside for burial. They were placed in the Donnelly family plot in the cemetery behind St. Patrick's church.

While William, Patrick, Robert, and Jennie grieved, police launched a huge investigation into the massacre. Most of the constables and lawmen involved lived outside Biddulph Township. "Detectives fell upon Lucan in great numbers to investigate what happened the morning of February 4, 1880," reported *The Toronto Globe*. "They knocked on doors, pulled doorbells and interviewed, interviewed, interviewed."

The police questioned Johnny O'Connor at length. Once they gathered sufficient evidence, authorities detained over a dozen members of the vigilance committee. Some of these members were soon discharged, leaving only six men to face trial for the Donnelly murders. The six consisted of Constable Carroll, John Kennedy, Martin McLaughlin, John Purtell, and James and Thomas Ryder. Police considered them the ringleaders.

Not everyone in Lucan was pleased to see justice served. The surviving Donnellys had to endure a degree of low-level harassment in the months following the funeral. A few days after he put his parents in the ground, William Donnelly received an anonymous letter. It read:

> *You and your relatives have been a disgrace and a curse to our country. Your chances are favourable to leave now. If you delay our friends will assist you. So take warning. If your brother Patrick remains at Lucan he will take his chances with our friends ...*
> *Yours truly,*
> *ONE THAT SAW YOUR FATHER AND MOTHER FALL.*

William Donnelly made no attempt to strike back after reading this letter. His spirit had been shattered. He accepted such harassment with a sense of stoic resignation and hoped the guilty would be punished for the crimes they committed against his family.

The criminal trial for the Donnellys' killers began in October 1880, at the Middlesex County Courthouse in London, Ontario. Constable Carroll was tried separately from the other five defendants.

Johnny walked the court through the murders, from the first appearance of the constable in the Donnellys' doorway, to the flames that engulfed the farmhouse once the killing was over. But in spite of this eyewitness account, the jury claimed it couldn't reach a verdict. The prisoners were taken back to their cells in preparation for a second trial, which began in January 1881.

The second trial proved as desultory as the first, with the jury declaring Constable Carroll "not guilty." The crown prosecutor was ready to throw in the towel. If the court couldn't convict Carroll, the mastermind behind the massacre, there was little hope they could convict the remaining men in the prisoners' dock. The prosecutor announced that he was giving up. With this pronouncement in mind, the judge declared that the prisoners were free to leave on bail.

The release of the Donnelly defendants caused a sensation. When the six returned to Lucan, they were met with bugles and drums. Banners on buildings hailed the vigilantes as heroes. Grateful townspeople cheered lustily as the core members of the vigilance committee waved and bowed. The six were paraded to a hotel, where a dinner and dance were held in their honour. Local dignitaries described them as "redeemers of the community."

The hero's welcome afforded the accused killers left the three remaining Donnelly brothers even more embittered against their neighbours. During the summer of 1881,

William, Patrick, and Robert left Lucan, where they had been staying throughout the trials. Patrick went back to his blacksmith trade in Thorold, and William and Robert settled in nearby villages.

In the years that followed, the Donnelly killings began to take on a mythical status. Layers of rumour and gossip were added to the core facts of the case. According to one particular legend, Johannah Donnelly's ghost could be seen riding on a spectral horse late at night. She supposedly haunted the back roads of Biddulph Township. The wailing of a banshee accompanied her apparition.

It was said that many of the men involved in the Donnelly massacre died unusual deaths. Indeed, one vigilante, named Joe McIntyre, went mad with grief and committed suicide. Before he hung himself, he allegedly confessed to cutting off Tom Donnelly's head.

In truth, most members of the vigilance committee succumbed to nothing more exotic than farm accidents or old age.

For the remaining Donnellys, life went on without much more drama. William Donnelly sired a total of four children with his wife Nora. To commemorate family members, the children were named James, Johannah, John William, and Hanora. James Donnelly died shortly after his birth, but the other children survived into adulthood.

As a further way to commemorate his family, William also built a home on the site of his parents' original

The Black Donnellys

farmhouse. At one point, a theatrical promoter asked him to narrate a stage play about the Donnelly murders. The promoter offered William $100 a week — a large fee in the 19th century — but William turned it down.

William died on March 7, 1897, remembered by all as the cool-headed leader of the wild Donnelly boys. He was buried next to his parents in the cemetery of St. Patrick's Church.

Robert Donnelly and his wife, Annie Currie, had one child who died while still an infant. Robert was enormously affected by the murder of his family members. According to Lucan lore, he became a fixture at funerals held for members of the vigilance committee. It was said that he liked to spit on the coffins of the men who had murdered his family.

Robert died on June 14, 1911. The same year marked the death of Father John Connolly in Ingersoll, Ontario. Towards the end of his life, the priest would cry copiously whenever anyone asked him about the Donnelly murders. His role in the vigilance committee remains a mystery.

Patrick Donnelly married twice. His first wife, Mary Ryan, bore him one child who died at age two months. Soon after, Mary herself died. Patrick's second wife, who was also named Mary, gave birth to five children: Jenny, Annie, Mary, John, and Matthew.

Patrick continued to work as a blacksmith after the death of his parents. He lived around Thorold for the rest of his life, and died on May 18, 1914. Always somewhat aloof, Patrick remained apart from his family even after death.

Requiem

While his brothers were buried alongside their father and mother at St. Patrick's church, Patrick was buried in Thorold. After Patrick's funeral, Jennie Donnelly went back to the quiet, domestic life she had been leading with her husband, James Currie. Jennie and James lived in a farmhouse located in St. Thomas, Ontario. They produced a huge brood of 12 children. Among their ranks were boys and girls named Robert, Johannah, James, John, Michael, and Patrick.

The graceful, much-loved "Irish pixie" of the Donnelly family outlived all of her brothers, dying on September 3, 1917.

Thomas Ryder, the ambiguous friend of the Donnelly family, died on November 17, 1918. One of his contemporary relatives, Earl Ryder, wrote an essay suggesting that Ryder and Constable Carroll had been trying to protect Old Jim Donnelly (by arresting him) when the vigilance committee had stormed into the Donnelly residence and wreaked havoc.

Constable Carroll ended up working and living in lumber camps and rough frontier towns in British Columbia. It was said he bore a guilty conscience for the remainder of his years. Legend had it that Carroll would get highly emotional whenever anyone mentioned Father Connolly's name.

Today, London is a major southern Ontario city with nearly half a million people. The village of Lucan and the Township of Biddulph amalgamated in 1999 to form the municipality of Lucan Biddulph. Its population remains small, under 5000 people.

One side of the original tombstone erected by William Donnelly in 1889.
(By permission Ray Fazakas, author, *The Donnelly Album*)

Lucan Biddulph is still a farming community. The Roman Line still exists, as does the home that William built on the site of his parents' ill-fated farmhouse. Old Jim's barn also remains on the property. Tourists from across North America flock to the Donnelly place, and the current owner is happy to play tour guide to the hordes of visitors.

St. Patrick's church is still standing as well. The small cemetery behind the church has also become a popular tourist destination, though in a peculiar twist, the Donnelly tombstone is no longer there. Church authorities removed it in 1964, uneasy with the message it imparted.

William Donnelly had installed the original tombstone in the late 1880s. The grave marker he selected was dark, and shaped like a multi-tiered wedding cake. It had a square base, on top of which were three layers inscribed with the names of the dead. William made sure that the inscriptions were short and to the point. They read as follows:

JAMES DONNELLY, BORN MARCH 7, 1816. MURDERED FEBRUARY 4, 1880.
JOHANNAH DONNELLY, BORN SEPTEMBER 22, 1823. MURDERED FEBRUARY 4, 1880.
NATIVES OF TIPPERARY, IRELAND.

JOHN DONNELLY, BORN SEPTEMBER 16, 1847. MURDERED FEBRUARY 4, 188Q.
THOMAS DONNELLY, BORN AUGUST 30, 1854. MURDERED FEBRUARY 4, 1880.
NATIVES OF MIDDLESEX, ONTARIO.

BRIDGET DONNELLY, BORN MAY 1, 1858. MURDERED FEBRUARY 4, 1880.
A NATIVE OF TIPPERARY, IRELAND.

Epilogue

London, Ontario, 1920s

It's a slow day in the district office of the London Police Station. The desk sergeant looks up to see an old lady shuffling towards him. He sighs.

Year after year, for as long as London, Ontario, police can remember, the lady has come in around February 4, requesting action on a very cold case. It may be the 1920s, but she is obsessed with a crime that was committed before the desk sergeant was born.

The elderly woman makes her way to the desk. The sergeant greets her politely, then asks how the police might help her. She looks up at him and inquires whether the police could "do something" about the Donnelly murders. She insists justice has not been served in the case.

The desk sergeant assures the woman that the police will "look into it." Request made, the elderly woman leaves the station, not to return for another year.

It's a story they still tell around Lucan, and the tale hasn't become any less poignant in the telling. According to residents of Lucan, the old lady in the story is none other than Maggie Thompson, William Donnelly's long-lost love.

Epilogue

Maggie never lost her passion for the second-born son of Canada's wildest family, nor the sense of injustice that haunted her to the very end.

Bibliography

Crichton, William. *The Donnelly Murders.* PaperJacks Ltd., 1977.

Fazakas, Ray. *The Donnelly Album.* Macmillan of Canada, 1995.

Kelley, Thomas. *The Black Donnellys.* Firefly Books, 1954.

Kelly, Thomas. *Vengeance of the Black Donnellys.* Pagurian Press Limited, 1962.

Miller, Orlo. *The Donnellys Must Die.* Macmillan of Canada, 1962.

THE
PARENT'S GUIDE
TO THE
U.S. NAVY

THE
PARENT'S GUIDE
TO THE
U.S. NAVY

THOMAS J. CUTLER

NAVAL INSTITUTE PRESS
Annapolis, Maryland

Naval Institute Press
291 Wood Road
Annapolis, MD 21402

Library of Congress Cataloging-in-Publication Data
Names: Cutler, Thomas J., date, author.
Title: The parent's guide to the U.S. Navy / Thomas J. Cutler.
Description: Annapolis, Maryland : Naval Institute Press, [2017] | Includes
    bibliographical references and index.
Identifiers: LCCN 2016051449 (print) | LCCN 2016052258 (ebook) | ISBN
    9781682471753 (pbk. : alk. paper) | ISBN 9781682471760 (ePDF) | ISBN
    9781682471760 (epub) | ISBN 9781682471760 (mobi)
Subjects: LCSH: United States. Navy—Sailors' handbooks. | Families of
    military personnel—United States—Handbooks, manuals, etc. | United
    States. Navy—Military life—Handbooks, manuals, etc.
Classification: LCC V113 .C87 2017 (print) | LCC V113 (ebook) | DDC
    359.00973—dc23
LC record available at https://lccn.loc.gov/2016051449

Figures 8, 13, 14, 15, 16, 17, 18, 19, 20, and 22 and the ratings specialty
    marks in Appendix E created by Jim Caiella.
Figure 3 created by Chris Robinson.
All other images are officially released Navy Department photos or are
    from the U.S. Naval Institute photo archive.

♾ Print editions meet the requirements of ANSI/NISO z39.48-1992
(Permanence of Paper).
Printed in the United States of America.

25 24 23 22 21 20 19 18 17   9 8 7 6 5 4 3 2 1
First printing

CONTENTS

ILLUSTRATIONS

PHOTOS

TABLES

THE
PARENT'S GUIDE
TO THE
U.S. NAVY

INTRODUCTION

Welcome aboard! These words carry a world of significance to those who have chosen to serve in the United States Navy. If your son or daughter has made that choice, or is considering making that choice, it is one of the biggest decisions a young person can make. By raising her or his right hand and taking the oath of enlistment, your child becomes a member of one of the most important military services in the world and joins one of the biggest businesses in the United States. Whether choosing to stay for only one enlistment or deciding to make the Navy a full career, your son or daughter will be contributing to the well-being of this great nation through hard work and sacrifice while being fairly paid and enjoying the many benefits that come with military service.

To the average citizen, military ways are quite enigmatic, an alien world where acronyms often replace words and where "1330" is a time of day. Add to that, the Navy is not only military, it is nautical, which means that centuries of seagoing terminology and practices are added to the confusion, such that you might have better luck understanding a Klingon on a *Star Trek* rerun than deciphering what your son is trying to tell you about life at his first duty station. While your son or daughter will be *uniformed*, you are likely to be *uninformed*.

This book is the antidote to that debilitating disease of "uninformity." In these pages you will find many of the mysteries of the Navy explained. While it is a translation guide, to be sure—helping you to understand the many new terms you will be hearing—it is also a cultural guide, an explanation of your son's or daughter's chosen new world that includes high standards and a level of dedication not found in most walks of life. For example, to a Sailor the concept of "shipmate" means much more than "friend" or "co-worker"; it is something that true Sailors understand and value highly, containing an element of obligation as well as belonging.

You may already have detected a bit of bias in this book. I am a *Sailor* in every sense of the word—having served as both an officer and enlisted—and I make no apologies for holding this Navy of mine in very high esteem. But this "bias" is born not of some mindless devotion; it is instead something *gained* by way of experience and a hard-earned education. Not everything went my way all the time in the Navy, and there were times when I very much wanted to find an easier way of life, but I have absolutely no regrets for having served and honestly cannot imagine my life without it. I am convinced that I would be a lesser person had I not been privileged to serve in this demanding, rewarding way.

My love for the Navy does not mean that I see it as perfect or that I cannot at times laugh at it. An organization that is steeped in centuries of tradition, that bears the scars of bureaucracy, and that is subject to congressional whim, sometimes requires the salve of laughter to avoid succumbing to tears of frustration. Take, for example, the Navy's rank system, where silver outranks gold some of the time (but not always) and where the word "petty" has a completely different meaning from what you might expect. Such things must be met with patience and the occasional chuckle. So, please know that I view the occasional absurdity as a small price to pay for this vital and very successful Navy of ours.

You may find this book much more than you need at times, and at others, you may wish I had included more detail. I have tried to include enough material to satisfy those parents who want to wade far out into the ocean of naval knowledge, while keeping it from turning into a tome more suitable for doorstopping than reading. Because some of the things covered are subject to periodic change (such as pay scales), I have chosen to alert you to their existence while assuming you can find up-to-date information on the Internet once you know what to look for.

When all is said and done, I sincerely hope that this book will serve you as intended, that it will give you a better understanding of what your child will be doing as he or she leaves your nest for a very different way of life. Come away reassured that your child is in good hands, that your understandable fears and concerns are offset by the knowledge here offered. Take pride as you realize that your son or daughter is serving in the world's finest Navy, helping to protect this great nation of ours.

—*Thomas J. Cutler*

1 JOINING THE NAVY

I am a United States Sailor.
I will support and defend the Constitution
of the United States of America and
I will obey the orders of those appointed over me.
I represent the fighting spirit of the Navy
and those who have gone before me to
defend freedom and democracy around the world.
I proudly serve my country's Navy combat team
with Honor, Courage, and Commitment.
I am committed to excellence and fair treatment of all.

These are the words of *The Sailor's Creed*, and they guide all Sailors who serve in the United States Navy. As the words make clear, joining the Navy is serious business. If your son or daughter decides to take that momentous step, he or she will be embarking on a great adventure that will prove extraordinarily challenging and immensely rewarding.

Today's Navy is a massive and complex organization, a far cry from the makeshift fleet that opposed the British in the Revolutionary War. Hundreds of ships, thousands of aircraft, hundreds of thousands of people, and an annual budget in the billions of dollars go together to make the U.S. Navy a powerful and important component of the American defense establishment, playing a vital role in maintaining our national security, protecting us against our enemies in time of war, and supporting our foreign policy in peacetime.

Through its exercise of sea power, the Navy ensures freedom of the seas so that merchant ships can carry the vital raw materials and consumer goods we import and export. Sea power makes it possible for us to use the oceans when and where our national interests require, and denies our enemies that same freedom. Sea power permits us to take the fight to the enemy when necessary, rather than waiting for the enemy to attack us in our homeland.

As a Sailor, your daughter or son becomes a part of all that—a *vital* part, for the ships and aircraft of the Navy are only as good as the people who operate them.

Taking the oath of enlistment into the world's greatest Navy behind home plate on U.S. Cellular Field during the twenty-eighth annual Chicago White Sox Navy Night

The World's Greatest Navy

ENLISTED OR OFFICER?

People serving in uniform in the Navy are either "enlisted" or "officers." Consequently, there are different paths into the Navy that your daughter or son may take, depending upon whether she or he will be enlisting or joining through an officer accession program. The difference between the two is largely determined by education.

In earlier times—before the United States of America changed the world with its successful democracy—if a man were born into the so-called nobility and entered military service, he would become an officer, and as a result of good performance, or too often because of *whom he knew*, he could aspire to reach the levels of command and perhaps go beyond to achieve the highest ranks of general or admiral. If an individual were of so-called common birth, his only choice was to enter the army or navy as a foot soldier or deckhand, and while he might be promoted, there was a ceiling he could never penetrate because of his social class.

In America, even though our Army and Navy were originally modeled after the armies and navies of Europe, this class system was obviously not going to work in a democracy. Various means of keeping this basic system but tailoring it to American ideals were tried—including the election of officers—but what eventually evolved was a system based primarily upon education. A reasonable way to look at the system that evolved—and is still basically in effect today—is to think of enlisted Sailors as those who enter the Navy without a college degree and officers as those individuals who enter the service with college degrees. There are exceptions and variations, but it is a reasonably accurate way to begin to understand the system. Another way of looking at it, that is not entirely accurate but may be helpful in understanding the differences, is to think of enlisted personnel and officers as roughly equivalent to labor and management respectively in civilian life.

An enlisted Sailor aboard ship

Officers (an ensign and a commander) salute on the missile deck of a guided-missile destroyer

As mentioned, there are exceptions to the education model described above. One exception is that a person may enter the service with a college degree but may prefer to be enlisted rather than become an officer. Another exception is that some young men and women who have demonstrated the appropriate potential may be accepted into one of the Navy's special programs that provide a college degree while simultaneously preparing them for service in the Navy as officers. The U.S. Naval Academy and the Naval Reserve Officer Training Corps (NROTC) are examples. There are also many ways that an enlisted Sailor can become an officer partway through his or her career.

PEOPLE TERMINOLOGY

People who enlist in the Navy are generically called "enlistees" or "enlisted personnel" and serve specifically contracted periods of time called "enlistments." People who enter the Navy as officers (or later become officers) are referred to generically as "officers" and are said to be "commissioned." Their commissions come from the president of the United States and are open-ended in time, ending only when the officer resigns, or is retired, or is dismissed from the service. Although officers do not sign on for specific enlistments as enlistees do, they do often incur periods of obligated service—as "payback" for going to the Naval Academy or flight school, for example—that prevent them from resigning before that obligation is met.

Although there are different terms used to distinguish officers and enlisted personnel, all people serving in the Navy on active duty or in the Navy Reserve are known as "Sailors," just as all members of the Marine Corps are referred to as "Marines," regardless of their rank.

The Secretary of the Navy has directed that the terms "Marine" and "Sailor" should be capitalized. Not everyone adheres to that practice, including some newspapers and book publishers, so don't be surprised or offended if you see these terms used without capitalization. It is merely a matter of style, not judgement.

Today, you can never go wrong calling anyone in a Navy uniform a "Sailor," but this was not always the case. In the past, the term "Sailor" was often used to describe only enlisted people. In more recent times, Sailor applies to all Navy personnel in uniform—although you may encounter a "dinosaur" who still makes the old distinction.

In older books and articles about the Navy, you may see the phrase "officers and men" used, when describing a ship's crew or a list of casualties, and so forth. This is no longer appropriate in today's Navy where women play an increasingly important role.

One holdover remains, athough it may eventually go away: when making a distinction between enlisted and officer personnel, the term "enlisted Sailor" is sometimes used, but "officer Sailor" is not. So you may encounter phrases like "Many enlisted Sailors were there, but not many officers attended the seminar."

CAUTION!

Joining the Navy can be one of the best things a young person can do. Serving the nation as a Sailor can bring a great deal of pride—to both the Sailor and his or her parents—and it can lead to greater maturity, present opportunties for personal development, and provide many tangible benefits, including pay, health care, and professional growth and advancement. But it can be prove to be a *terrible* decision if the would-be Sailor is not sufficiently motivated to take on the challenges that come with all those benefits.

Life in the Navy is more regimented than most civilian occupations, which means less control of one's time. It can be a great way to see the world, but travel can also mean separation from family and friends. While safety is paramount in the Navy, there are dangers. With those challenges as very real considerations, it is imperative that a young person be personally motivated to make this important decision.

The bottom line—and this is absolutely essential: your son or daughter must be the one to make the ultimate decision to join the Navy. Not you!

You may encourage your child and help him to consider the pros and cons. But you must not "push" her to join. If you do, you may invite great disappointment—for both of you.

ENLISTING IN THE NAVY

Your son's or daughter's introduction to the Navy will probably start at a local recruiting station, with interviews and processing conducted by a Navy recruiter. Recruiters are specially trained to compare desires with individual qualifications and with the needs of the Navy to establish the terms of service. This "contract" with the Navy is officially called an enlistment, but you will sometimes hear it described more informally as a "hitch." It begins when your daughter or son takes the oath of enlistment, and it will last from two to six years, depending on the terms agreed upon.

Potential recruits must be at least seventeen to join the Navy but must have your permission. If they are eighteen or older, parental permission is not required.

RECRUIT TRAINING COMMAND

All Recruits begin their naval careers in what is officially called Recruit Training Command (RTC), but is more traditionally referred to as "Boot Camp." Currently the Navy is operating only one RTC, located at the Naval Station Great Lakes in Great Lakes, Illinois, as part of the Naval Service Training Command. This 1,628-acre training facility, on the shore of Lake Michigan about forty miles north of Chicago, has been training Sailors since July 1911. During World War II, nearly a million Sailors were trained there.

While at Boot Camp, your son or daughter will be known as a "Recruit" (officially a "Seaman Recruit"). Once they have completed training at RTC, Recruits are usually promoted to "Seaman Apprentice" and become "Sailors" from then on.

Your Recruit will make the transition from civilian to military life—known as "Sailorization"—in the time spent at RTC, typically seven to nine weeks. Nearly every minute of every day will be filled with military drills, physical training, hands-on experiences, and a busy schedule of

Recruit Training Command ("Boot Camp")
at Great Lakes, Illinois

classes on naval history, traditions, customs, operations, and regulations. Recruits will probably find the transition initially quite challenging—having completely changed their environment, diet, sleep patterns, climate, clothes, and companions—so do not be surprised if your Recruit calls (when permitted) and tells you that he is not sure he made the right decision by joining the Navy. As a parent hearing your child say such things as "I want to come home" can be very difficult, but rest assured that this is a common occurrence and is in nearly every case a passing phase. Your understanding and reassurance will go a long way in helping your Recruit through this transition. Within a relatively short period, nearly all Recruits make the necessary adjustments and find a great deal of pride to replace their initial anxiety.

Besides a great deal of training while at Boot Camp, your Recruit will also receive a military-style haircut, extensive medical examinations, dental care, and a full "seabag" of Navy uniforms. Every Sailor in the

Recruit uniform inspection—part of the "Sailorization" process

Navy is paid twice a month. Pay is provided by electronic transfer of funds through the direct deposit system to the banking institution of his or her choice. While at RTC, Recruits will of course be paid, but they do not need money while in training, so they will be issued a special Navy Exchange (NEX) card that they can use in the Navy Exchange, which is essentially a Navy shopping mall, for toilet articles, sewing kits, shoeshine gear, notebooks, and pens and pencils.

What Recruits *Must* Bring to Boot Camp

- ✓ Photo identification/Driver's license
- ✓ Social Security card
- ✓ Marriage certificate (if applicable)
- ✓ Divorce decree (if applicable)
- ✓ Copies of dependents' birth certificates (if applicable)
- ✓ Complete civilian and military immunization records
- ✓ Direct deposit form with bank account and routing number information

What Recruits *May* Bring to Boot Camp

- › Wrist watch, wedding ring
- › Religious medallion (no larger than the size of a dog tag)
- › Writing material (no bottled ink)
- › Pocket dictionary
- › Pocket bible or other similar religious devotional
- › Small address book
- › Hairbrush and comb
- › Pre-paid phone cards
- › One pair of prescription glasses, reading glasses, or contacts (with one week of cleaning solution)
- › A small amount of cash (i.e., less than $10)

Note that the above list does *not* include cell phones and other electronic devices that young people today often consider essential. Those items will be waiting for them after Sailorization but are not permitted during Boot Camp.

Women Recruits may also retain the following personal items:

> › Feminine sanitary items
> › Conservative cosmetics (one of each): face powder, blush, lipstick, eye shadow, and mascara (non-aerosol or glass). Makeup will be authorized for division photos and graduation weekend only.
> › Barrettes (must match hair color)
> › Birth control medications

Because they will be issued complete uniforms, Recruits should report with a minimum of civilian clothing. Once they have received their uniforms, Recruits must either mail their civilian clothes back home or donate them.

Boot Camp Life

Not all of the Recruits' time at RTC is spent in training. There will be administrative periods during which they make pay arrangements, are fitted for uniforms, complete their medical and dental work, and make known their desires for future assignment. Based upon their Armed Services Vocational Aptitude Battery (ASVAB) test scores and their classification interviews, their initial career path in the Navy will be determined.

They will be given the opportunity to attend the religious services of their choice. Facilities are available for the conduct of religious services by Navy chaplains, who are also available for pastoral counseling and religious education. Recruit choirs are organized and often sing at the services.

Underlying all the training that Recruits receive at RTC is a focus on self-respect, respect for others, and the Navy's core values of *Honor, Courage, and Commitment.* These are not just words but interrelated concepts that Recruits must take to heart to guide them in virtually everything they do as Sailors. Before they make a decision or do something, they must consider whether their action will reflect a loss of honor, a failure of courage, or a lack of commitment. If it does, then they must not do it. They should keep in mind that honor includes the honor of their nation and their Navy as well as their own, and that maintaining honor will often require courage and commitment. They should remember that courage can be physical or moral—sometimes having to make a decision that is not easy and may not result in their getting what they want, but because it is the right thing to do, they must find the courage to do it. And they must be committed to doing what they know is right, what is honorable, what is courageous.

(See Appendix B for additional discussion of these core values.)

Contacting Recruits

Because of the structured nature of the training at Boot Camp, your Recruit will not be able to contact you except on specified occasions.

Upon arrival, Recruits are assigned to a special barracks that is called a "ship" and will have a name that reflects the Navy's heritage, such as "USS *Pearl Harbor*" or "USS *Constitution*." They will begin receiving their mail there, usually around the second or third week. To help avoid delays, you should wait until you receive your Recruit's official address via mail. While you can write to your Recruit every day, your Recruit can only write to you a few evenings each week and during "holiday routine," meaning Sundays and federal holidays.

Recruits can receive anything that can fit into a standard-sized envelope. Do not write on the outside of the envelope except the recipient and return addresses, and do not send "care packages."

Recruits are generally allowed only three phone calls during their time at RTC. The first call is permitted when they arrive to notify a family member or friend that they have arrived. This is a single call only, and it will be up to the Recruits whom they call, so try not to be disappointed if your Recruit chooses a boyfriend or girlfriend to call instead of you.

Recruits will be given the opportunity to place a second call midway through their training. There is no set schedule and no way to know if or when these calls will come.

Calling home

The final call you will (hopefully) receive is the call letting you know that your daughter or son is no longer a Recruit, but is a Sailor in the world's finest Navy! This call comes during the final week of training. As you can probably imagine, this is often an emotional call for the Sailors and their families.

There is one additional call that you do not want to receive but that may be necessary. If your Recruit fails a training requirement or becomes injured or ill, he or she will be allowed to call.

If you have an emergency situation that requires you to contact your Recruit, you will need to contact the American Red Cross at (877) 272-7337. The Red Cross will relay to your Recruit urgent messages containing accurate, factual, complete, and verified descriptions of an emergency such as the death or serious illness of an immediate family member.

Graduation

Recruit graduation is known as "Pass-in-Review." It is a formal military ceremony—a parade of sorts—that honors your Recruit's hard work and dedication to a new way of life. It is a ceremony that ties together the future of the Navy with long-held naval traditions and customs.

You may attend this special ceremony, but only your Recruit can place names on the guest list. The number of guests permitted will be limited to three or four, depending upon the size of the graduating group, and anyone three and older must be on the guest list. Children under two years of age may attend and do not have to be on the list. Guests eighteen and over will be required to show a photo ID, such as a driver's license, passport, or military ID. The restricted number of guests is necessary because the ceremony is held indoors and the space available for guests is limited.

Graduation "Pass-in-Review"

Your Recruit will be given the opportunity to send home an information letter from the commanding officer, along with very important information regarding graduation. This letter will notify you of the graduation date, and will provide you a password for the vehicle gate pass. **Take care to not misplace this password; you will use it to download your parking pass from this website: www.bootcamp.navy.mil /upcoming_grads.html.** Keep in mind that Recruits mail this information themselves, so RTC does not know where the information was sent and cannot send additional information.

It is important to know that your Recruit's graduation date might change or be delayed based on his or her performance. For that reason, you should purchase refundable travel tickets if at all possible.

As mentioned, RTC is located approximately forty miles north of Chicago on Lake Michigan near the Wisconsin border. RTC is conveniently located near three major international airports, so you may want to check fares into all three to find the best rate:

> Chicago's O'Hare International Airport is thirty miles from RTC.
> Chicago's Midway International Airport is forty-five miles from RTC.
> Milwaukee County's General Mitchell International Airport is fifty miles from RTC.

If you are utilizing a Global Positioning System (GPS), input the following address for best results: 3355 Illinois Street, Great Lakes, IL 60088.

Be sure to be seated in the ceremonial drill hall before the Pass-in-Review begins. Once the doors close, no one will be allowed to enter until the ceremony is completed.

After Pass-in-Review

After the ceremony, your Sailor may have additional responsibilities but then will be given "liberty," which is the Navy way of saying "free time to go ashore." This is a time for family members and friends to spend some leisure time with these brand-new Sailors and to share their pride in their achievement. Be aware that this newly acquired freedom comes with some important restrictions. Your new Sailor:

> may not travel more than fifty miles from base during liberty, meaning no further than downtown Chicago
> may not use alcohol or tobacco products
> may not drive a vehicle
> must remain in uniform at all times
> must allow ample time to get to his or her ship (barracks) before the expiration of liberty
> may not bring civilian items (clothes, mobile phone, MP3 player, etc.) or food back to RTC

Most Sailors will attend a Class "A" School after leaving RTC. These specialized schools provide occupational training that will vary in length depending upon your Sailor's rating. (See Chapter 6 and Appendix E for an explanation of ratings.)

Once your Sailor has successfully completed "A" School, she or he will likely report to her or his first operational duty assignment, such as a billet on a ship or in an aircraft squadron. This assignment could be virtually anywhere in the world. It is at this point that your Sailor will begin to play a vital role in the defense of this great nation. The importance of this cannot be overemphasized and should be realized with a degree of gratitude as well as pride.

BECOMING AN OFFICER

A Navy officer must be able to assume a variety of duties at sea, in the air, and ashore. Navy officers must have at least a bachelor's degree and must be U.S. citizens, physically fit, and at least nineteen years old. As explained earlier, your son or daughter may qualify to enter the Navy to become an officer. There are two commissioning programs that lead to a college degree as well as a commission—the U.S. Naval Academy and the Naval Reserve Officers Training Corps (NROTC). There are also other commissioning programs, such as Officer Candidate School (OCS), for those who already have a degree.

U.S. NAVAL ACADEMY

The United States Naval Academy (USNA), located in Annapolis, Maryland, provides a four-year undergraduate education leading to a bachelor's degree and a commission as a Navy or Marine Corps officer. Applicants must be single with no children, be of good character, and must meet rigorous academic and physical requirements.

Unlike other colleges with daunting tuition costs, students attend for free and are actually paid a monthly salary. But there are other "costs" for this unusual opportunity. Graduates must serve on active duty for at least five years after graduation—the actual length of obligated service depends on follow-on training and designation. While many graduates make a career in the Navy or Marine Corps, many others do not, going on to other careers after meeting their "payback" service obligation.

Admission to the Naval Academy is made through nominations from United States senators, representatives, the president and vice president of the United States, or the Secretary of the Navy. It is a complicated—but worthwhile—process. **A good place to start is to visit www.usna.edu/Admissions.**

Once your son or daughter has been accepted for admission to the Naval Academy, another useful website to visit is www.usna-parents.org. There you will find much useful information, including a "Parent Survival Guide."

Naval Academy Preparatory School

Some applicants who are not quite up to full eligibility for admission to the Naval Academy may be given the opportunity to attend the Naval Academy Preparatory School (NAPS) in Newport, Rhode Island. At NAPS, your son or daughter will receive ten months of instruction in English Composition, Mathematics, Chemistry, Physics, and Information Technology. Demanding military, physical, and character development programs complement the academic preparation to fully prepare students for the challenges of life at a service academy. As part of the physical development program, NAPS offers a varsity athletic program that competes against other preparatory schools, junior colleges, and college junior varsity teams.

A Word of Caution

The earlier warning in this book about parents "pushing" their child to join is every bit as important here. Because of the prestige of a Naval Academy education, and because of the free tuition and the guaranteed post-education employment, you may be tempted to exert some extra encouragement (i.e., "push") to your daughter or son to go to the Academy. But it is imperative that she or he *wants* to go to USNA. Young people who go to the Academy because their parents want them to, but who do not share that commitment, are virtually guaranteed to be very unhappy and are not likely to succeed. To gain admission, they will have been very thoroughly vetted in terms of academic credentials, physical abilities, and leadership potential, but they must also have the requisite desire to be there.

Not Your Typical College

Attending the Naval Academy is a very different college experience. Students are called "Midshipmen" (often abbreviated to "Mids") and all live on board the campus—called "The Yard"—in a huge dormitory named Bancroft Hall. They eat most of their meals together in King Hall and participate in mandatory athletics and military drill, including colorful parades. As freshmen, they are known as "Plebes" and as sophomores they are called "Youngsters." They will have ranks, starting with Midshipman Fourth Class in their Plebe Year, Midshipman Third Class as Youngsters, Midshipmen Second Class, culminating in their "First Class" (senior) year. While they will have the opportunity for some leave (vacation) during their four years, large parts of their summers will be taken up by additional Academy programs, including spending time in the Fleet.

Plebe Summer

It all begins with "Induction Day," which occurs in the summer before their first academic year, roughly around Independence Day. This marks the beginning of what is known as "Plebe Summer," an experience that your daughter or son will not forget. Designed to be a challenging and transforming experience, Plebe Summer is in many ways much like

Naval Academy Midshipmen under way in the
Severn River—an unusual college experience

Induction Day at the U.S. Naval Academy begins when the incoming Plebes
(freshmen) are issued uniforms, are given medical examinations, receive haircuts,
and learn basic military drill. Here a group of Plebes study *Reef Points*,
a handbook that helps them transition from civilian life to the Navy.

"Boot Camp" described above. Many mental and physical demands are made on the Plebes that will test their mettle to make sure they have the qualities and abilities to eventually serve as leaders in the Navy.

Plebe Summer introduces neophyte Midshipmen to the basic how-tos of the Navy. Saluting and marching are accompanied by the basics of small-arms safety and marksmanship. Sailboats are used to teach the basics of seamanship and navigation, and leadership training begins with the experience of good followership. Plebes also learn about the high standards of honor, courage, and commitment that are elemental to the Academy and the Navy.

Parents may accompany their Plebes on Induction Day, but will soon be separated from them once they begin the induction process, when they will be busy getting haircuts, receiving uniforms, and adjusting to their new military life. Parents may attend the formal swearing-in ceremony later in the day—an experience that most parents describe as a real mix of emotions that include pride and a realization that their child has taken a huge step in "departing the nest."

The formal swearing-in ceremony in Tecumseh Court

Whether you accompany your Plebe to Induction Day is a personal decision—*for you and your Plebe*. Some people find it a once-in-a-lifetime experience not to be missed, while others prefer to handle the inevitable emotions of "letting go" in privacy back home.

Just as with Boot Camp, there are many restrictions on what your Plebe can bring with them when reporting and, once there, there will be limitations on communications. Phone calls are few and "snail mail" is the primary means of communication during Plebe Summer, so plan on writing often. It will likely play a significant role in your Plebe's morale.

The aforementioned Parent Survival Guide warns that your Plebe will likely develop a "love/hate relationship" with USNA that will result in days of jubilation and days of despair. The guide wisely warns that parents are likely to "follow a similar pattern."

Parents' Weekend

Near the end of Plebe Summer, the Naval Academy hosts a "Parents' Weekend" that is designed to offer family members and guests an opportunity to visit with their Midshipman prior to the start of the fall term to experience a taste of the traditions, academics, and atmosphere unique to the Naval Academy.

There are several airports (Baltimore-Washington International Thurgood Marshall, Washington Dulles International, and Ronald Reagan Washington National) that serve the Annapolis area, and AMTRAK trains also can get you to the area.

If you are able to attend, it is a worthwhile experience. But not all parents are able to come to Annapolis for Parents' Weekend. The Parent Survival Guide advises that "if there are 'orphans' in your Mid's company that do not have family there, invite them along! The more the merrier! Extra Mids are an asset. You will hear more stories with extras around."

"Four Years Together by the Bay"

The student body at USNA is known as the "Brigade of Midshipmen." The Brigade is approximately 4,400 strong and is divided into 6 battalions, each having 5 companies of approximately 150 Mids, for a total of 30 companies.

The company is central to Midshipman life. Company mates eat, sleep, study, drill, play, and compete as teams together. The company experience provides an idea of how things work in the Navy and Marine Corps, where small-unit cohesion, teamwork, and morale are as important in peacetime operations as in combat.

The Naval Academy's mission is "to develop Midshipmen morally, mentally and physically and to imbue them with the highest ideals of duty, honor and loyalty in order to graduate leaders who are dedicated to a career of naval service and have potential for future development in mind and character to assume the highest responsibilities of command, citizenship and government."

Guiding them as they fulfill this mission is an "Honor Concept" that states:

> *Midshipmen are persons of integrity: They stand for that which is right.*
> *They tell the truth and ensure that the truth is known.*
> **They do not lie.**
> *They embrace fairness in all actions. They ensure that work submitted as their own is their own, and that assistance received from any source is authorized and properly documented.*
> **They do not cheat.**
> *They respect the property of others and ensure that others are able to benefit from the use of their own property.*
> **They do not steal.**

Like most colleges, USNA has an alma mater. The lyrics to "Navy Blue & Gold" are:

> Now colleges from sea to sea may sing of colors true,
> But who has better right than we to hoist a symbol hue:
> For sailors brave in battle fair since fighting days of old
> Have proved the sailor's right to wear the Navy Blue & Gold.

> Four years together by the Bay, where Severn joins the tide,
> Then by the Service called away, we're scattered far and wide;

But still when two or three shall meet, and old tales be retold,
From low to highest in the Fleet, we'll pledge the Blue & Gold.

So hoist our colors, hoist them high, and vow allegiance true,
So long as sunset gilds the sky, above the ocean's blue.
Just let us live the life we love, and with our voyage through,
May we all muster up above, a-wearing Navy Blue.

Commissioning Week

Graduation for Midshipmen takes place in the latter part of May each year and is marked by the better part of a week of exciting and unique activities. For the Midshipmen, it is more than receiving their baccalaureate degrees; they also are being commissioned as officers in the Navy or the Marine Corps.

Parents are invited and encouraged to attend. You should of course make every effort to do so. Your Midshipman will give you the details. Be sure to make reservations for travel and lodging well in advance.

Graduation and commissioning at the Naval Academy

NAVAL RESERVE OFFICERS TRAINING CORPS (NROTC)

Differing from the Naval Academy in a number of ways—most prominently by its taking place on civilian college and university campuses—the NROTC Program is the largest single source of Navy and Marine Corps officers and plays an important role in preparing mature young men and women for leadership positions as commissioned officers in the Navy and the Marine Corps.

NROTC is offered at 63 colleges and universities throughout the United States, and nearly one hundred other schools have "cross-town" enrollment agreements with host units. Through a highly competitive process, those applicants who are selected for the NROTC Scholarship Program receive full tuition, books stipend, educational fees—even a monthly spending allowance—for up to five years of college.

Students selected for the NROTC Scholarship Program make their own arrangements for college enrollment and room and board and take the normal course load required by the college or university for degree completion.

Full information concerning the NROTC Scholarship Program is available from any of the colleges and universities with NROTC units, from Navy and Marine Corps recruiters, and online at www.nrotc .navy.mil.

Life as an NROTC Midshipman

While there are some differences at each university's NROTC unit, certain things are common to all. Your daughter or son should report to orientation in good physical condition, and there will be things to learn and do—such as marching and saluting, military organization, and uniform issue—that other students at these same schools will not encounter.

In addition to classes required for their particular degree program, NROTC Midshipmen must take naval science classes each semester and will periodically wear their uniforms at least once weekly. There will likely be opportunities for extracurricular activities related to NROTC, such as participating in drill teams or color guards. Summers will include additional NROTC training at sites away from the college, including going to sea, the possibility of nuclear power or aviation training, and opportunities for foreign exchange.

Upon graduation, NROTC Midshipmen are commissioned as officers and will incur a service obligation that varies with their individual program.

OTHER OFFICER ACCESSION PROGRAMS

If your son or daughter already has, or is about to earn, a college degree, he or she may apply for Officer Candidate School. Located in Newport, Rhode Island, this twelve-week program provides candidates the requisite training to prepare them for leadership in the Navy. It is a competitive program to get into and a demanding program to complete.

An applicant must be at least nineteen years old and must be able to be commissioned prior to his forty-second birthday. She must be of

Midshipmen about to be commissioned as ensigns at one of the many civilian universities that hosts NROTC units

good moral character and conduct with no record of felony conviction; she also must not have been convicted of any misdemeanors other than minor traffic violations during the three years preceding her applying.

An "Officer Aptitude Rating" (OAR) will be administered, and while there is no minimum passing score, applicants are judged relatively, and a score of less than thirty-five is generally not competitive. Physical requirements include meeting specified height, weight, and body fat standards. Eyesight must be correctable to 20/20 and defective color vision is disqualifying.

OCS is a program of intensive officer training and indoctrination. The OCS course has been designed by Navy officers and educators to give selected individuals a basic knowledge of the high-tech naval establishment afloat and ashore and to prepare them to assume the demanding responsibilities they will face as officers in the Navy. Military training is conducted by Navy Recruit Division Commanders and Marine Corps Drill Instructors.

Candidates should expect a training environment similar to that encountered by recruits at Boot Camp. Marching, drilling, inspections,

A newly commissioned ensign receives his first salute from his drill instructor at Officer Candidate School in Newport, Rhode Island.

and intense physical training accompany the rigorous academic training, and there is limited "free time" and few opportunities for "liberty" (leaving the base to participate in local, outside activities).

The OCS course is designed to prepare members to become commissioned officers by providing basic knowledge of the naval profession and its related military, academic, and nautical subjects. It provides moral, mental, and physical development and emphasizes the highest ideals of duty, honor, and loyalty. The training that candidates receive is divided into thirteen units of instruction: naval history, naval orientation, seamanship, navigation, damage control, engineering, military law, administration, military training, physical fitness, Navy 3rd class swim course, naval leadership, and various special emphasis programs. In most cases, graduates receive specialized follow-on training after OCS to further prepare them for their initial fleet assignments.

Graduates of OCS serve in the fields of Surface Warfare, Aviation, Submarines, Special Warfare, Special Operations, Intelligence, Information Dominance, Supply, and Civil Engineering. They serve aboard ships, with aircraft squadrons, and at shore bases around the world.

There are also other, specialized ways to earn a commission in the Navy—and in many cases receive financial assistance toward college expenses—including the Civil Engineer Collegiate Program (CECP), the Nurse Candidate Program (NCP), and the Nuclear Propulsion Officer Candidate Program (NUPOC).

Although there is some information available online, a local Navy recruiter is probably the best source of information for these programs.

Joining the Navy is an important decision that will likely have a major impact on your Sailor's life. Whether Sailors remain in the Navy for a full career or merely use the experience to transition to another phase of their lives, they will benefit from the experience in many ways. And beyond the personal, their service will help to keep this great nation safe, which is no small accomplishment by any definition. Through your Sailor's service you also will be indirectly serving your nation as well. **Be proud!**

2 SAILOR CARE
The Benefits of Serving

Serving in the U.S. Navy is something that will likely be a source of pride for your Sailor. But no one expects your son or daughter to survive or thrive on pride alone. Just as in any profession, Sailors are paid for their work. And just as there are special demands and sacrifices that go with life in the Navy, there are also benefits that come with the job.

The Navy provides a growing number of apps—such as "New to the Navy"—that have some information on pay and benefits, but the best source of information about these benefits for your Sailor is his or her command career counselor. These are trained specialists who have all the latest information on the benefits available to Sailors.

As a parent, you cannot take advantage of a career counselor. If you are looking for detailed explanations of the benefits available to your Sailor, an excellent source of information is the latest edition of *The Military Advantage: The Military.com Guide to Military and Veterans Benefits*, written by Terry Howell and published by Naval Institute Press.

Following is a less-detailed but useful summary to give you a good general idea of what the Navy provides to its Sailors in pay and benefits.

PAY AND ALLOWANCES

Sailors receive two kinds of financial remuneration while they are in the Navy: *pay* and *allowances*. There are certain legal and economic distinctions between the two, but the most practical way to distinguish them is that pay is much like the salary a civilian would receive in her or his job and is, therefore, subject to federal income tax. Allowances are extra payments designed to help Sailors meet certain expenses of Navy life. Some allowances are not subject to federal income tax while others are.

Because there are these two types of remuneration in the Navy (some taxable and some not), when comparing how much money Sailors make with how much their civilian counterparts make, a dollar-for-dollar comparison is not entirely accurate.

When discussing pay and allowances, I may provide examples just to give you an idea of approximately what is being discussed, but be aware that these amounts change often, so it is best to refer to the latest edition of *The Military Advantage* or to check online for the latest amounts.

BASIC PAY

Basic pay depends on your Sailor's paygrade and years of service. It is the same for every Sailor in that same paygrade with the same amount of time served. It is the largest single part of a Sailor's paycheck.

Those "paychecks" are paid twice a month, usually on the first and the fifteenth, through the direct-deposit system (DDS). Pay and entitlements are electronically transferred to the banking institution of the Sailor's choice. With DDS, no matter where a Sailor is—aboard ship, on shore, at an overseas station, in a travel status, or on leave—when payday rolls around Sailors will have immediate access to their money because their pay will be in their accounts, on time.

BASIC ALLOWANCE FOR SUBSISTENCE (BAS)

All Sailors receive Basic Allowance for Subsistence (BAS) to cover their meals. When serving in a capacity where meals are provided, such as aboard ship, BAS will be deducted from their pay.

BASIC ALLOWANCE FOR HOUSING (BAH)

This allowance is complicated with a lot of variables. The amount varies considerably, depending upon the Sailor's paygrade, the number of family members ("dependents" in military jargon), availability and use of government quarters, and a number of other possible variables,

based on the individual's situation. Geographic location has a significant effect on the amount; living in southern California is considerably
more expensive than living in portions of the South, and the government takes that into consideration when determining the amount of
BAH your Sailor is to be paid.

CLOTHING ALLOWANCES

Your Sailor may receive clothing allowances at various times during
his or her service, depending upon whether he or she is an officer or
enlisted and whether the Sailor's specific duties require special kinds
of clothing. These include *Initial Clothing Allowances, Cash Clothing
Replacement Allowances, Extra Clothing Allowances*, and *Clothing
Maintenance Allowances.*

FAMILY SEPARATION ALLOWANCE (FSA)

If your Sailor has dependents (is married with or without children), he or
she may be entitled to some additional money when separated as a
result of government assignment, such as an unaccompanied tour overseas or on a ship on overseas deployment. There are specific requirements
and restrictions, depending upon marital status, length of separation,
whether or not accompaniment is authorized, and some other considerations.

OTHER FORMS OF PAY AND ALLOWANCES

There are ways that your Sailor's paycheck may be increased. There
are travel and transportation allowances, cost of living allowances
(COLA), hostile fire/imminent danger pay, special duty assignment pay,
hardship duty pay, reenlistment bonuses, and a number of others that
your Sailor may or may not be eligible for.

LEAVE AND EARNINGS STATEMENT (LES)—A KEY DOCUMENT

Sailors should review their monthly *Leave and Earnings Statements*
(LES) to keep track of their pay and allowances. **The Defense Finance
and Accounting System provides the MyPay system online (mypay.dfas
.mil) where Sailors may review their pay and other benefits as well as
make discretionary changes (such as allotments) without having to resort
to paper forms.**

ALLOTMENTS

Through allotments Sailors may assign part of their pay regularly, for example to a spouse, parents, a bank, or an insurance company. Once the appropriate forms have been filled out, the specified monthly amount is automatically deducted from the Sailor's paycheck and payments will automatically be made by the Navy.

GENERAL BENEFITS AND SERVICES

There is no doubt that the pay in today's Navy is one of the real benefits. There are others, such as commissary (grocery store) and exchange (department store) privileges, medical and dental care for Sailors and their dependents, and an extensive educational program.

FAMILY HOUSING

The family housing program includes public quarters (government rental units), mobile-home parks, government-insured privately owned projects, and leasing of privately owned units. The Navy tries to make sure adequate housing facilities are available for Sailors and their families at a reasonable cost and within reasonable commuting distance.

Because on-base housing is a popular benefit, being more convenient and less expensive than renting or buying a place to live off base, there is usually a waiting list. When Sailors are preparing to transfer to a new duty station, they should contact the housing office at their new location as soon as possible to see what the housing situation is and to get on the list as soon as they are eligible.

Where Navy housing is not available, housing referral offices will provide assistance in locating private housing in the community.

HEALTH BENEFITS

Under the Uniformed Services Health Benefit Program (USHBP), care is provided in Uniformed Services Medical Treatment Facilities (USMTFs) when possible. Other care is provided in civilian facilities at full or partial expense to the government when necessary.

Active-duty members must be provided all necessary medical care. The primary source of care for all eligible beneficiaries is the USMTF.

Family housing at Trumbo Point, an annex
of Naval Air Station Key West

When care is not available from the USMTF for an active-duty member, it may be provided at government expense under the Non-Naval Medical Care Program and must be preauthorized. Each USMTF can provide acute medical and surgical care to varying degrees. Since not all USMTFs have the same medical capabilities, the health benefits advisor (HBA) should be contacted to determine what services are available.

Dependents and retired personnel are provided care at a USMTF if space, facilities, and proper medical staff are available.

SERVICEMEMBERS GROUP LIFE INSURANCE (SGLI)

Your Sailor is eligible for a special life insurance policy provided by the U.S. government. Currently your Sailor may elect to take up to $400,000 of life insurance coverage. The monthly cost to your Sailor is 7 cents per every $1,000 of coverage, with an additional mandatory $1.00 per month for "Traumatic Injury Protection." Sailors may opt out or take less than the maximum amount of coverage, but they must choose to do so. If they do nothing, they will automatically be enrolled at the maximum amount. They must also specify who will receive the money if they opt in, and it will be a part of their official service record.

DEATH BENEFITS

If your Sailor should die while on active duty, his or her next of kin will receive a death gratuity (currently $100,000) tax free. If he or she has dependents, they would be eligible for certain benefits to help them financially, including housing and health care assistance, as well as additional Social Security benefits. Death benefits would also occur if your Sailor should die within 120 days after leaving the Navy and if the death is determined to be service-related.

LEAVE

All personnel on active duty, from seaman to admiral, earn vacation time just as civilians do, but in the military it is called "leave." If Sailors want some time off to go back to their hometown to visit friends and relatives, they must submit a request, using the chain of command, specifying the exact days they want to be away. Because of the operational needs of the Navy, your Sailor cannot take leave whenever he or she feels like it. Your Sailor will be an important member of the crew of a ship or station, so his or her absence will have to be carefully planned in order to keep things running smoothly while he or she is gone. A Sailor should not make airline reservations or other firm plans until the leave request has been approved.

Earned at the rate of two and a half days each month, this amounts to a total of thirty days a year. The only exceptions are time spent in the brig or if your Sailor is absent without authorization for twenty-four hours or more. "Earned leave" is the amount credited to your Sailor on the books at any given date. Under certain circumstances, Sailors may be permitted to take more leave than they are entitled to. This is called "advance leave" and will give them a negative balance. Advance leave is paid back as your Sailor earns it through continued service.

As leave accumulates, it is carried over from one fiscal year to the next. Except for special circumstances involving extended deployments or hostile conditions, no more than sixty days can be carried over on the books. This means that if your Sailor has sixty-seven days of leave on the books on September 30 (the end of the fiscal year), she or he will lose seven days of leave. For this reason, your Sailor should watch the leave balance on his or her LES and plan accordingly.

Persons discharged under honorable conditions with leave still on the books are paid a lump sum equal to the daily rate of basic pay they are earning at time of discharge for each day. The most leave a Sailor can "sell back" in a military career is sixty days. Those discharged with a negative leave balance will pay back approximately a day's pay for each day's leave owed.

Your Sailor's commanding officer has the authority to grant all earned leave on a yearly basis, plus up to forty-five days' advance leave. Personnel lacking enough earned leave during an emergency can be granted advance leave up to sixty days.

Convalescent leave is an authorized absence while your Sailor is under medical care and treatment. It must be authorized by her or his commanding officer on orders of a medical officer, or by the commanding officer of a military hospital. It is usually granted following a period of hospitalization and is not charged as leave.

Maternity leave of up to twelve weeks and *paternity leave* of up to two weeks is available to Sailors having children while on active duty. Also, twenty-one days of *adoption leave* is available to Sailors who adopt a child under a qualifying adoption.

Occasionally, a death in the family or some other serious consideration will require a Sailor to need leave in a hurry. This is called *emergency leave*, and the procedures are, of course, different from those of routine leave requests. **As indicated earlier, the best way to get in touch with your Sailor in an emergency is to notify the American Red Cross by calling (877) 272–7337; after verifying the situation, the Red Cross will immediately notify the Navy.**

OVERSEAS SCHOOLS FOR FAMILY MEMBERS

The Department of Defense (DOD) operates many educational facilities for minor family members of all U.S. active-duty military and DOD civilian personnel stationed overseas. There are many DOD schools overseas with a portion Navy-sponsored. Army and Air Force schools in many countries are open to Navy family members. From first grade through high school, family members can receive an education overseas at the government's expense.

CHILD CARE

The Navy operates child-development centers at almost all naval installations. This program provides high-quality child care in conveniently located child-development centers at moderate cost to the Sailor (fees are based on paygrade). Additionally, at naval installations having government housing, family child care is provided in government housing and is run by government-certified child-care providers. Commanding officers of installations that have child-care centers may establish priority of access in child-development centers (for example, single parents, dual military couples).

COUNSELING ASSISTANCE

The Navy has human relations experts ready to advise and help Sailors with difficult personal and family affairs. Navy chaplains, like ministers or priests at home, can offer counseling as well as perform religious ceremonies like baptisms, marriages, and funerals.

Personal help is available through Fleet and Family Support Centers (FFSC), where program specialists and clinical counselors assist with adaptation to Navy life and provide services and skills for self-sufficiency and personal success. These specialists offer a wide variety of programs and services, including counseling for problems relating to alcoholism and drug abuse, the effects of discriminatory practices in and out of the Navy, and family and personal affairs, including the successful management of the challenges of deployment. They can help Sailors with debt management, estate planning, and other financial services.

A legal-assistance officer can help your Sailor draw up wills, powers of attorney, deeds, affidavits, contracts, and many other documents. She or he also can advise your Sailor on transfers of property, marriage and divorce, adoption of children, taxation, personal injury, and other legal problems. The advice is free and may help your Sailor avoid a lot of trouble. All matters are treated confidentially.

The Navy's Sexual Assault Prevention and Response program (SAPR) provides both prevention programs and victim assistance. Fleet-wide training programs aim at eradicating sexual assaults, while special reporting procedures and professional counseling services tend to the needs of those who have been victimized.

CARING FOR FAMILIES

The Family Advocacy Program provides help with problems of child and spouse abuse. Services include prevention classes and individual help for victims and offenders, as well as working closely with military and civilian agencies in dealing with these issues.

The Exceptional Family Member (EFM) program ensures that the special needs of family members are met by making sure that the service-member's assignments are compatible with those needs. Because special needs cannot be met at every duty station throughout the world, EFM enrollment is mandatory for active-duty sponsors who have family members with chronic illness or incapacity, mental illness, or learning disabilities.

Relocation assistance services help Sailors and families adjust to new duty stations. Typical services include destination area information, intercultural relations training, settling-in services, and help in finding a home.

Help is available for civilian spouses in locating and obtaining local employment. Workshops are offered on how to search for a job, plan a career, write a résumé, have a successful job interview, and network.

New parents may take advantage of programs of identification, screening, home visitation, information, and referral for new and expectant parents. Prevention education programs and referrals to community support services are also offered.

MILITARY ONESOURCE

This service is available twenty-four hours a day and serves as a "one-stop" place to go whenever servicemembers or their family members need assistance of any kind. **This program can be accessed by calling 1-800-342-9647 or by visiting the Military OneSource website: www .militaryonesource.mil/.**

MORALE, WELFARE, AND RECREATION

Morale, welfare, and recreation (MWR) programs provide many different recreational, social, and community support activities for all Navy personnel and their dependents.

Sports and fitness programs are designed to provide the Navy community with facilities and programs that enhance the overall quality of life and contribute to physical and mental readiness. The base-level sports and fitness program consists of informal or recreational sports (where individuals participate for fun and fitness) and organized (intramural) sports (i.e., individual, dual, team, and meet events) where the element of competition is included for events within and between individual commands. Some MWR programs also offer "Captain's Cup Field Day" competitions that are designed to build morale and teamwork while providing a means to have a great deal of fun.

The higher level sports program (armed forces sports program) is for active-duty members who demonstrate exceptional athletic abilities. Competitive forums for the higher level sports program include Navy trial camps, which are used to evaluate and select athletes for Navy teams and the armed forces championships. These two competitive forums provide a pathway for athletes to represent the armed forces in competition at the international level.

Outdoor recreation facilities may include outdoor equipment rental centers, parks, picnic areas, archery ranges, recreational vehicle (RV) parks, skeet and trap ranges, campgrounds, stables, marinas, beaches, swimming pools, cabins, cottages, off-base recreational areas, outdoor obstacle/challenge courses, paintball competition courses, and climbing walls. Instructional classes, outdoor equipment rentals, specialty equipment sales, organized group activities, special events, self-directed activities, and seasonal/geographic activities are also provided in various areas.

An information, tickets, and tours (ITT) program is located on virtually every shore installation in the Navy. ITT serves the military community with local recreation information (on and off base), entertainment tickets, and local tour services. Additionally, a hotel reservation system is available to assist travelers in finding quality, low-cost accommodations while on vacation.

Auto-Craft skills centers at some bases provide automotive enthusiasts with a quality, value-based program for the repair and maintenance of their vehicles. These are not service stations, but are facilities where patrons can work on their vehicles and learn automotive skills.

The Navy golf program is offered at over forty bases, providing course play, snack bars, pro shops, driving ranges, and cart rentals, as well as classes and personalized lessons.

The Navy bowling program offers open and league bowling, and special youth programs at many shore facilities.

The Navy Club System provides food, beverage, entertainment, and recreation programs at most bases.

Young bowlers at a Navy bowling alley on the base in Yokosuka, Japan

SERVICE ORGANIZATIONS

Many organizations provide assistance and services to Sailors and their families. Three of the most important are the Navy–Marine Corps Relief Society, the USO, and the American Red Cross.

Supported entirely by private funds, the Navy–Marine Corps Relief Society assists Sailors/Marines and their families in time of need. Though not an official part of the Navy, this society is the Navy's own organization for taking care of its people. It is staffed and supported largely by retired and former naval personnel and provides financial aid to those in need in the form of an interest-free loan, a grant, or a combination of both.

The United Services Organization (USO) provides programs, entertainment, and services at more than 180 USO locations worldwide, including Afghanistan, Djibouti, Kuwait, the United Arab Emirates, Germany, Italy, Japan, Iraq, South Korea, and the United States. Since 1941 the USO has attended to servicemembers' morale by bringing entertainment to forward deployed forces, often hosting comedians, musicians, and athletes who voluntarily support those who defend.

The American Red Cross supplies financial aid to naval personnel, does medical and psychiatric casework, and provides recreational services for the hospitalized. It also performs services in connection with dependency discharge, humanitarian transfer, emergency leave, leave extensions, and family welfare reports.

EDUCATIONAL BENEFITS

Your Sailor's professional education begins with recruit training and continues throughout his or her naval career, whether it lasts for four years or thirty. Your Sailor may attend one or more Navy vocational/technical schools, may be able to receive college credit for military training and experience, and may also qualify for specialized training (such as nuclear engineering or diving school).

But the Navy also places very high value on personal development, recognizing that additional education is not only a potential morale booster but that it can make for a better Sailor for reasons that should be obvious.

Men and women who have the desire and the ability to expand their personal educational horizons will find a number of programs offering correspondence courses, tuition assistance, college opportunities, high school equivalency, and other ways to improve themselves. Your Sailor will discover that there is never a shortage of educational opportunities in the Navy.

THE GI BILL

One of the best educational opportunities for servicemembers is the so-called GI Bill. This first came into existence after World War II and has gone through several iterations since, the most recent one being the Post-9/11 GI Bill. Providing significant financial benefits to servicemembers—including tuition costs, a monthly housing stipend, and additional money for books and other expenses—the amounts available vary according to your Sailor's state of enrollment (full- or part-time), number of units taken, and the amount of active-duty service. **Too complicated to explain in detail here, this outstanding benefit is explained online at a number of websites—including www.benefits.va .gov/gibill/.**

One important expansion of the post-9/11 GI Bill is that some benefits can be transferred to dependents. This transferability option allows eligible servicemembers to transfer all or some unused benefits to their spouse or dependent children. The Department of Defense (DOD) determines whether or not you can transfer benefits to your family. Once the DOD approves benefits for transfer, the new beneficiaries apply for them at the Veterans Administration (VA). **More information is available at www.benefits.va.gov/.**

DEFENSE ACTIVITY FOR NON-TRADITIONAL EDUCATION SUPPORT (DANTES)

Despite the rather labored acronym, this program helps servicemembers pursue their education goals and earn degrees or certifications while continuing to serve. DANTES maintains three online catalogs that list distance learning courses and programs:

- An "Independent Study Catalog" lists more than six thousand high school, undergraduate, graduate level, and examination preparation courses from regionally accredited institutions.
- An "External Degree Catalog" lists academic programs available from regionally accredited colleges and universities that have little or no residency requirements for degree completion.
- A "Catalog of Nationally Accredited Distance Learning Programs" lists courses and degree programs from various national accrediting bodies. Subjects range from "Appliance Repair" to "Zionism and Judaism in Israel."

NAVY COLLEGE PROGRAM (NCP)

This program helps Sailors earn college degrees by providing them academic credit for Navy training, work experience, and off-duty education. NCP also enables Sailors to obtain a college degree while on active duty. While the NCP is primarily geared toward enlisted Sailors, officers have access to some NCP components.

A petty officer first class receives a master of science degree during Southern Illinois University and Navy College's thirty-sixth annual graduation ceremony at Naval Base Coronado. The mission of Navy College is to provide academic support for Sailors across the Fleet seeking technical and college education.

Navy College Program for Afloat College Education (NCPACE)

Part of the Navy College Program, NCPACE allows Navy and Marine Corps servicemembers to pursue education while on sea-duty assignments. In many cases an instructor will be assigned to a ship or unit to provide on-site instruction. Both undergraduate and graduate courses are available through NCPACE.

NAVY KNOWLEDGE ONLINE (NKO)

The Navy Knowledge Online Learning Portal involves a systematic process for acquiring, creating, integrating, sharing, and using information, insights, and experiences to achieve organizational goals and to help Sailors and Marines pursue their educational and career goals.

THE SEAMAN TO ADMIRAL PROGRAM

Also known as "STA-21," this is a commissioning program that provides selected active-duty Sailors a full scholarship to attend a top-notch university. Through this program, enlisted personnel move on to careers as naval officers.

SERVICEMEMBERS OPPORTUNITY COLLEGES (SOC)

The Navy version of this degree program is known as "SOCNAV" and consists of colleges that offer associate's and bachelor's degree programs on, or accessible to, Navy installations worldwide. Each college in the network accepts credits from all the others. SOCNAV guarantees that Sailors can continue toward completion of a degree even though the Navy may transfer them to various locations.

THE NAVY TUITION ASSISTANCE PROGRAM

Helping to cover up to 100 percent of the cost of an active-duty Sailor's education, this benefit is available to Sailors who meet the following qualifications:

- Must have served one year on board in his or her *first* permanent duty station (this requirement may be waived by commanding officer).
- Will serve on active duty through the last day of the academic course.

- Has passed the most recent physical fitness assessment or received a waiver.
- Has taken her or his most recent advancement exam, if applicable, and is recommended for advancement or promotion.
- Has not received a non-judicial punishment (NJP) within six months, or is not pending administrative separation.
- Is not under instruction in initial skills training or in a duty under instruction training status.

NAVY–MARINE CORPS RELIEF SOCIETY'S EDUCATION ASSISTANCE PROGRAM

Offering interest-free loans and grants for undergraduate/post-secondary education at an accredited two- or four-year education, technical, or vocational institution in the United States, this financial assistance is available for children of active-duty, retired, or deceased Sailors and Marines and for spouses of active-duty and retired Sailors and Marines. This program offers interest-free loans and grants ranging from $500 to $3,000 per academic year to cover tuition, books, fees, room, and board. The money is paid directly to the student's academic institution and repayment of these interest-free loans must be by military payroll allotment.

THE NAVY COLLEGE FUND

Also known as a GI Bill "kicker," this financial resource is available to those who sign up for the GI Bill. Qualified applicants can receive, upon enlistment, more than $15,000 in addition to their GI Bill education funding.

STUDENT LOAN REPAYMENT PROGRAM (LRP)

College students or graduates who qualify will receive, upon enlistment, up to $65,000 toward student loans.

MILITARY PROFESSIONAL STUDIES AND POSTGRADUATE PROGRAMS

The Department of Defense operates several graduate schools for military officers seeking to earn their postgraduate degrees. These include the following schools:

- Naval Post Graduate School
- Naval War College
- Air Force Institute of Technology
- The Judge Advocate General's School of the Army
- National Defense Intelligence College
- School of Advanced Air and Space Studies
- Uniformed Services University of Health Sciences

STAYING OR LEAVING

The Navy is not forever. Sailors may stay for only one enlistment or may choose to make a full career of the Navy, remaining until it is time to retire. The processes for staying or leaving the service are different for enlisted and officers.

REENLISTMENT

An enlisted Sailor who completes an enlistment in the Navy may be eligible to reenlist—sometimes called "shipping over." Reenlistment is not a right; it is a privilege. To earn that privilege, Sailors must be recommended for reenlistment by their commanding officer, be physically qualified, and meet certain standards of performance. Another consideration will be the "needs of the service"—how much your Sailor's particular specialty is needed. In cases where the need is significant enough, your Sailor may be offered a sizable reenlistment bonus.

Sailors may ask to reenlist for anywhere from two to six years. In cases where a reenlistment bonus is available, the more years your Sailor ships over for, the more money she or he will receive.

In some cases, Sailors may ask to extend their current enlistment rather than reenlist. Extensions may be granted at any time during an enlistment for special circumstances, such as wishing to qualify for advancement, or to make an upcoming cruise or deployment, or to gain entry into a service school or a special program. Extensions are executed in increments of one or more months, not to exceed a total of forty-eight months on any single enlistment.

Reenlistment ceremonies can be done virtually anywhere that is safe. The Navy gladly accommodates unusual venues to enhance the memorable experience.

An unusual reenlistment ceremony taking place in the Gulf of Aqaba

SEPARATION OF OFFICERS

Officers do not "enlist," so if your Sailor is an officer, leaving the Navy is a bit different. There is no term of enlistment for officers—and they continue to serve until they either resign or retire—but there may be a term-of-service obligation of a specified number of years that they must complete before deciding to leave the Navy. As already explained, graduates of the Naval Academy or other officer accession program are required to serve a number of years before they can leave the Navy. Additional service obligations can be incurred by entering certain specialized programs, such as flight school or nuclear power training.

Officers who have fulfilled their obligated service may submit a letter of resignation from active duty if they choose. Subject to the needs of the Navy, separations are normally approved when the officer has completed minimum time on station for the particular type of assignment. This is not a speedy process so, when requesting separation, officers should submit their letter of resignation nine to twelve months in advance of the date they desire to separate.

Under current rules, officers may be involuntarily separated for twice failing to be selected for promotion. In addition, administrative separations "in the best interest of the service" may be awarded to officers under certain circumstances, and courts-martial may award punitive dismissals for violations of the Uniform Code of Military Justice.

Just as enlistments can sometimes come with incentive bonuses, officers in certain specialties may be offered monetary incentives to remain on active duty, depending upon the needs of the Navy.

NAVY RESERVE

One other option—between active duty and separation—is service in the Navy Reserve. This is a way that your Sailor—officer or enlisted—can leave active duty but continue to serve and receive certain benefits, while also pursuing a civilian career. Although fewer and modified, there are many benefits that come with reserve service. But it is very important to realize that with those benefits come obligations, including the possibility of being called to active duty in times of need.

DISCHARGES

When Sailors leave the Navy, whether voluntarily or involuntarily, they receive a formal discharge, and the type of discharge they receive can have a significant effect on their eligibility for continued benefits. Certain discharges eliminate some veterans' rights and benefits, and many employers will reject a former military person who cannot produce an honorable-discharge certificate.

An *honorable discharge* means what it sounds like: separation from the service with honor. It is given to Sailors who have performed well and are leaving the service voluntarily at the end of their obligated service or are being asked to leave for reasons of disability or for the convenience of the government (fewer Sailors authorized, for example). To receive an honorable discharge, the final average of a Sailor's performance marks must meet minimum specifications and he or she cannot have been convicted by a general court-martial, or convicted more than once by a special court-martial.

General discharges are given under honorable conditions for those whose conduct and performance, though technically satisfactory, has not been good enough to deserve an honorable discharge.

The discharges your Sailor especially does not want are (in order of increasing severity), the *undesirable discharge* (UD), *bad conduct discharge* (BCD), and *dishonorable discharge* (DD). The UD is given by administrative action for misconduct or breach of security, the BCD only by approved sentence of a general or special court-martial, and the DD only by approved sentence of a general court-martial.

RETIREMENT

Although it is unusual for young people to think seriously about such things, the retirement benefits of military service are something your Sailor should consider before leaving the Navy. Too complicated to go into in detail here—and frequently up for review for possible changes— retirement from military service has always been worthwhile, occurring

A master chief and his wife and daughter are "piped over the side"—a long-standing Navy tradition that is part of the retirement ceremony.

earlier than most civilian occupations and generous enough to warrant serious consideration. No one should use this benefit as the sole reason for remaining in the Navy, but if your Sailor is considering the pros and cons of remaining in service or leaving the Navy, this should be one of the considerations. Sailors should talk with their career counselor to get the latest information about this important benefit.

Thrift Savings Plan

Another thing to consider is the Thrift Savings Plan offered by the Navy. This is an added benefit that your Sailor can choose to supplement her or his retirement income. The plan allows them to have some of their pay automatically deducted and invested. There are several options available, and a visit to the Command Financial Specialist (CFS) is the best way to find out the details.

ADJUSTING

Whether your Sailor leaves the Navy after only one "hitch" or eventually retires from service, there will be a period of adjustment. There is a certain amount of social and psychological shock that comes from leaving military society, where rules and paths are well defined. Even though your Sailor was a civilian before he or she joined the Navy, going back to the civilian world will take some adjustment. Even though they always looked sharp in their uniforms and passed every inspection with flying colors, Sailors may find that dressing themselves for a new job is a real challenge. They will probably be surprised at how missing a little sleep is a much bigger deal to civilians than it is to them. They may find that what is early morning to their civilian coworkers is midday to them. They will probably get some quizzical looks the first time they ask a coworker where the scuttlebutt is or explain that they are "going topside for a minute."

Don't expect this transition to happen overnight. It may take weeks, months, or even longer. The important thing to remember is that it is perfectly normal and that your Sailor is not the first who has had to make this adjustment.

It is important to bear in mind that a Sailor's years of service in the Navy have strengthened him as a person, taught him a great many things, and prepared him to handle many of the challenges of life. She will likely have learned the importance of leadership and followership, and she will know the importance of self-discipline and a strong work ethic. He should not be cocky, but he should be confident. As a former Sailor, there isn't much he or she can't handle.

WHAT YOU CAN DO

If you are old enough to have a child who is old enough to join the Navy, you know that parenting never completely stops—it only evolves. The fact that you are reading this book indicates that you probably recognize that because young people do not always look out for themselves with the same vigilance that we, as parents, might prefer, it is not a bad idea for us to be aware of benefits that are there for your Sailor.

Reading this book will not only make you better able to communicate with your Sailor, it can equip you for the task of watching out for your Sailor's well-being by being aware of the benefits and opportunities that this chapter describes. *Without pushing*, some well-timed queries (such as "Have you thought about taking advantage of the GI Bill?" or "I've heard that Military OneSource is a pretty good service; have you or Sally had occasion to use it?") might stimulate your Sailor to investigate further.

Perhaps posting the following emergency numbers on your refrigerator where your Sailor will see them when visiting will remind her or him that they exist and that you are aware of them:

American Red Cross	1-877-272-7337
Military Crisis Hotline	1-800-273-8255
Sexual Assault Crisis Support	1-877-995-5247
National Domestic Violence Hotline	1-800-799-7233
National Suicide Prevention Lifeline	1-800-273-8255

Ideally, your Sailors will be on top of things, aware of the many benefits and opportunities their Navy offers. But it cannot hurt for you to be "in their corner," ready and able to discuss these things in an informed and understanding manner. In their newfound service there is no limit to the number of shipmates they may acquire—but parents are a finite quantity, and sometimes only a parent will do.

THE GREATEST BENEFIT

Perhaps the single greatest benefit that Sailors receive while serving in the U.S. Navy is the satisfaction of knowing that they are serving their nation. By being a part of the finest Navy the world has ever seen, whether in the throes of combat or carrying out the daily routine, they are helping to preserve freedom in the United States of America, and that is a special satisfaction not found in many walks of life.

Another benefit that most Sailors enjoy is the opportunity to travel, to do for free what other people pay significant sums of money to do. But there is another, more significant, aspect to travel as well. Your sons and daughters will likely return from their travels raving about the sights they have seen or the experiences they had; they may say they wish they could have spent more time at one of their port stops; or they may even say they wish could live on that tropical island they visited; but they will most likely also come home to America with a much deeper appreciation of what they have here in this great nation.

Seeing other parts of the world enlarges our vision, offers unique insights into different cultures, and makes clear that we are privileged to be inhabitants of this wondrous planet. But it also allows us to compare and contrast, and with few exceptions, the end result is a great surge of gratitude that *we are Americans*!

We are incredibly fortunate to have vast resources at hand and a standard of living that is the envy of most of the world. We have a form of government that cannot solve every problem and may not always make the best choices, but it is rooted in the soil of individual freedom and human rights, and has a long record of striving to do what is right. One does not have to go far beyond our borders to realize how fortunate we are, to compare how others live and what many must endure, and your Sailor is likely to have that opportunity.

To enjoy such privileges is a pleasure; *to defend them is an honor.*

3 A TRANSLATION GUIDE

Parents often find that they have some difficulties knowing what their Sailor is talking about. Military people talk very differently from civilians—often using acronyms, abbreviations, and cryptic terms to speed up their conversations—and Sailors go even further by having many more unique terms that are the result of centuries of seafaring tradition. You probably will not be bewildered when your Sailor refers to the floor as a "deck" or refers to the bathroom as the "head," but you may get lost when he says he will be home at 1300 or you may wonder why the scowl when you referred to her guided-missile cruiser as a "boat."

In the pages that follow we will provide some information that will help you to understand what your Sailor is saying and to better appreciate the Navy's strange vocabulary. To do this completely would likely require a book twice the size of this one—military and naval acronyms alone could fill the pages allocated for this book—but we can get closer to naval fluency by explaining a select few of the more common terms that your Sailor might use.

NAVY TERMINOLOGY

Just as doctors, lawyers, baseball players, engineers, artists, and police officers have their own language when communicating within their professions, the Navy too has its own special terminology. Doctors speak of contusions and hemostats, baseball players have their own meanings for "in the alley" or "ahead in the count," and police officers use special words like "perp" and "SWAT." In the Navy, special terms used aboard ship include *helm* (steering wheel), *screw* (propeller), and *forecastle* (deck area on the front part of a ship—pronounced "*FOHK-sul*," by the way). Everyday items also take on new names in the Navy, where bathrooms are *heads*, floors are *decks*, walls are *bulkheads*, stairways are *ladders*, and drinking fountains are *scuttlebutts*. A Sailor goes *topside* instead of upstairs and *below* instead of downstairs. The Navy also uses short abbreviations (also known as acronyms) in place of long titles, such as OOD for officer of the deck, QMOW for quartermaster of the watch, and USW for undersea warfare. You might also encounter longer ones, such as COMNAVSURFLANT for "Commander Naval Surface Forces Atlantic." It helps to know that there are quirks as well, such as LANT meaning "Atlantic" and SURF referring to "Surface Forces" while SUW describes "Surface Warfare."

Many of these terms will seem strange at first—even comical or irritating—but your Sailor is using them because she or he is now a member of a special profession that uses its argot as a means of identification and a point of pride. Remember that many of these terms come from a long history of seafaring and nautical traditions and were used (and still are) by some rather extraordinary individuals who contributed to the nations' defense and well-being.

The best way to deal with this new—often confusing—terminology is to be patient, absorb what you can through context, and do not hesitate to ask for explanations.

Appendix A of this book is a glossary of some of the more common terms and abbreviations you might encounter while conversing with your Sailor.

SHIPBOARD TERMINOLOGY

No doubt you already have some knowledge of shipboard terminology even if you have never set foot on a deck. Many nautical terms have found their way into everyday usage, and the mere fact that I used the word "deck" without explaining it in the previous sentence is an indication of that.

What follows is a basic introduction to shipboard terminology. It will not make you an "old salt," but it may allow you to understand more of what your Sailor is talking about.

Structural Terms

Although the terms are different and there are certainly significant structural differences, a ship is in some respects like a building. There are floors (called *decks*), ceilings (*overheads*), corridors (*passageways*), and stairs (*ladders*).

Walls are a little more complicated. Generally, you will be fine if you call what looks like a wall a *bulkhead*, but technically a bulkhead is a wall that is structurally significant (supports decks and is watertight, for example). If a "wall" is only there to divide one space from another and is otherwise not structurally significant, it is more properly called a *partition*.

What would be "rooms" ashore are generally called *compartments*, but they are also sometimes called *spaces* (as in *engineering spaces*) and sometimes even "rooms" (as in *fan room* or *wardroom*). Which word is used when does not lend itself to rules, except that either *compartment* or *space* can be used generically (as in, "A lot of those compartments need painting," or, "Most of those spaces up forward belong to first division"), and "room" is never used alone but is always attached to another word as in the examples above.

Whereas ships have *storerooms*, and the items that are kept in them are generically called "stores," things are *stowed* rather than stored about ship, as in, "Those cables are stowed in the forward storeroom." And the word *stowage* is more nautical than "storage."

Doors are doors on ships just as in buildings, but there are technically two kinds. *Watertight doors* are just what they sound like—doors that are specially designed to keep out water. They are strongly built and equipped with rubber gaskets around the edges to seal tightly when closed, and they have heavy-duty clasps called *dogs* to keep them tightly shut. *Non-watertight doors* are used inside the ship to separate compartments much as doors are used ashore.

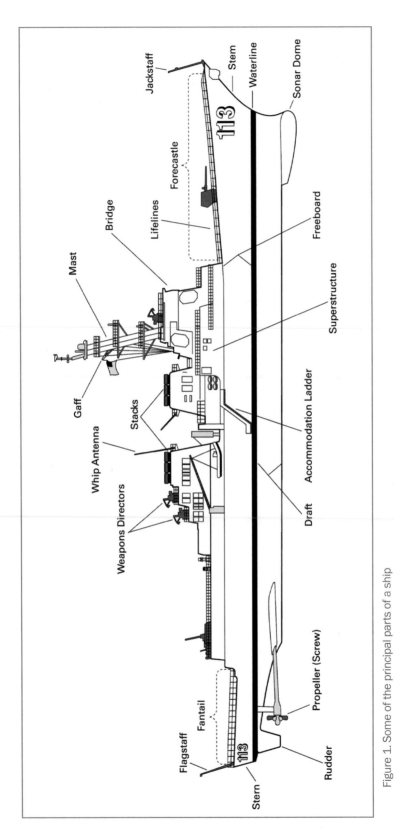

Figure 1. Some of the principal parts of a ship

One mistake you will see many people make—even some Sailors—is to call a door a "hatch." The two are not synonymous: hatches refer to horizontal openings in ships that allow you to go from one deck to another; doors are vertical openings in bulkheads or partitions that allow you to pass from one compartment to another on the same deck. To be really precise, the opening in a bulkhead or partition is a doorway and the object that closes it off is a door; similarly, the opening in a deck is a *hatchway,* whereas the cover for it is the *hatch*—and it is sometimes called a *hatchcover.* But you will often see "hatch" used as I have here, as in, "To get to the berthing compartment below, use that hatch over there."

Windows (of which there are very few on most Navy ships) are usually called *ports,* but you will also hear the term *bridge windows* used for those that are located on the bridge.

The uppermost deck that runs the entire length of the ship from bow to stern is the *main deck.* An exception to this rule is the aircraft carrier, whose main deck is actually considered to be the hangar deck, not the flight deck, which would seem to fit the normal definition of main deck. "Floors" below the main deck are called *decks,* but those above the main deck are called *levels.*

The outside parts of a ship (which come in contact with wind and waves) are collectively known as the *skin* of the ship. The major part of the ship that is topped by the main deck is known as the *hull.* Those decks that are exposed to the elements are called *weather decks.*

To keep people from falling off the ship (*overboard*), ships have *lifelines* made of strong cable that are rigged all around the edges of the deck similar to railings on balconies ashore. If they are solid (instead of made of cable) they are more properly called *rails.*

The structures above the main deck looking somewhat like houses or huts are collectively referred to as the *superstructure.* Different kinds of ships have different types of superstructure; some may be one continuous mass, others may be split into separate groups; the superstructure projecting above the flight deck on an aircraft carrier is called *the island.*

View looking up from the flight deck of an aircraft carrier. The ship's superstructure (also called "the island") is silhouetted against the sky somewhere in the Arabian Sea.

Often, the superstructure is topped off by one or more *masts*. At its simplest, a mast is a single pole extending vertically above the rest of the ship. Masts often are fitted with a horizontal crossbar, called a *yardarm*, which is used to attach flag *halyards* (lines used to hoist the flags) or support navigational and signal lights and various antennas and electronic devices. If the ship has two masts, the forward one is called the *foremast*, the after one the *mainmast*. Modern ships do not normally have three masts, but in the days of sail, when masts also played a role in the propulsion of the ship by supporting her sails, some ships had a third mast, called the *mizzen*, which was mounted after the mainmast. On single-masted ships, the mast is usually part of the superstructure and is simply called *the mast*.

The *stack* of a ship serves the same purpose as the smokestack on a power plant ashore. It carries off smoke and exhaust gases from boilers on steam-powered ships and from gas turbines and diesel engines on ships with those forms of propulsion. Nuclear-powered ships do not need stacks because their reactors produce no smoke or gas. Some diesel-powered vessels release their exhaust from vents on their sides. On some ships, the masts and stacks have been combined to form large towers called *macks*.

Ships are steered by a *helm*, which is also called a *"ship's wheel"* or simply *the wheel*. That wheel moves a *rudder*, the simplest design being a flat board or blade that extends perpendicularly into the water beneath the vessel's stern. In an open boat, a *tiller* can be attached directly to the rudder to turn it, but larger vessels have more complex steering systems—often using hydraulics, duplicate electrical cable systems, etc.—that culminate with the helm that is used by a helmsman to steer the vessel. Naval ships often have more than one rudder, but in the case of multiple rudders the rudders do not act independently but are controlled together.

Ships are driven through the water by propellers, and though this term is acceptable, you will more often hear them called *screws,* which avoids any confusion with aircraft propellers.

One of the two propellers—also known as "screws"—of a large amphibious ship, seen here in drydock for repairs

Ships or boats with two screws can be steered fairly well without a rudder by using the engines. If one screw turns faster than the other, the bow will swing toward the slower screw. If one screw goes ahead while the other goes astern, the bow of the ship will swing toward the backing screw; boats, and even very large ships, can turn within the diameter of their own lengths using this method, which is appropriately called *twisting*.

Directions on a Ship

The front (forward) part of a ship is the *bow*; to go toward the bow is to *lay forward*; something that is located closer to the bow than something else is said to be "forward of" (as in, "Place that pallet forward of the others because it contains anchor parts"). The back (after) part of the ship is the *stern*; to go toward the stern is to *lay aft*. Something located farther aft than another object is said to be *abaft* the other. You will also encounter the term *fore*, which is usually used in conjunction with another word to indicate its relative position, such as the foremast; it is also occasionally used more generically as in, "Give the ship a clean sweep down fore and aft."

In a building you would go upstairs or downstairs; in a ship you *lay topside* or *lay below*. If you go extra high up in a ship, like climbing the mast, you would be *going aloft*. If something is located high up on a ship (above the superstructure) it is said to be *aloft*.

As you face forward on a ship, the right side is *starboard* and the left side is *port*. Note that this does not mean that port and starboard are synonymous with left and right—if you are facing aft on a ship, starboard is now on your left and port is to your right.

Now it's time for some shipboard "relativity." Fortunately, you do not have to be an "Einstein" to understand it. We've already seen that objects are said to be forward or aft of each other depending upon their positions relative to the bow and stern—such as, "The mainmast is aft of the foremast," or, "The anchors are located forward of the super-structure." Now imagine a line running full-length down the middle of the ship from bow to stern; although you will never see one, it helps to know that it is theoretically there and is called, appropriately, the *center-line*. An object that is closer to the centerline than another is said to be *inboard*; one that is farther from the centerline is said to be *outboard*— such as, "The lifelines are outboard of the mast," or, "The mast is inboard of the lifelines." This terminology is also sometimes extended beyond an individual ship, such as when ships are *nested* (moored along-side one another at a pier)—one closer to the pier than another is said to be inboard, and vice versa.

Someone or something going from one side of a ship to the other is moving *athwartship*. This term also applies to something located in such a way as to run from one side to the other, as in, "An electrical

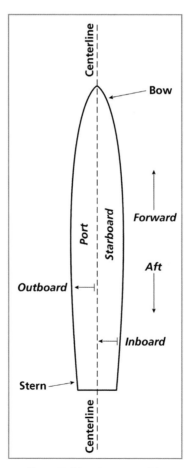

Figure 2. Directions on a ship

cable has been rigged athwartship from the starboard side to the port." Something running in a direction perpendicular to this is said to run *fore and aft*, as in, "Run a line fore and aft from the bow to the top of the mast."

Something located in the middle of the ship—neither forward nor aft—is *amidships*, as in, "Two of the inspectors headed for the bow, two others for the stern, and the rest remained amidships."

Under Way and Other Conditions

Ships are considered *under way* when they are free-floating (i.e., not tethered to a pier or anchored to the bottom). You will see this term technically misused fairly often—even by some Sailors—when it is used to describe a ship moving through the water, as in, "The ship was under way at fifteen knots." Though this statement is correct in that a ship cannot be moving through the water without being under way, confusion can result if one does not realize that a vessel can be under way without moving. Movement through the water is properly described as *making way*. "The ship got under way at dawn and began making way at low speed once the signal to proceed was received," would be correct usage of these two terms.

In simplest terms, when ships are not under way, they are *moored* or *anchored*. Ships are moored to piers using *mooring lines*. To anchor, a ship uses her *ground tackle* (anchors and their associated equipment, such as chains and *windlasses* to haul them in).

When a ship gets under way from an anchorage, she hauls in on her anchor until it leaves the bottom; at this point—with the anchor dangling from its chain—it is said to be "aweigh." From that the Navy's service song gets its name "Anchors Aweigh" (NOT "Anchors Away"!).

"Parking" Ships—Dock vs. Pier vs. Jetty vs. Wharf vs. Quay

There are a number of terms that deal with where ships are moored when not under way or anchored. These can be a bit confusing and are often misused or misunderstood by "landlubbers" (non-sailors).

Dock—the water area where a ship is floating when moored; analogous to a "parking space" ashore.

Pier—a structure mounted on pilings that extends outward (perpendicularly) from the shore.

Jetty—similar to a pier except that is based on fill rather than pilings.

Wharf—similar to a pier (i.e., on piles) but parallel to the shore, rather than perpendicular.

Quay—parallel to the shore and built on fill rather than pilings.

Important Locations Aboard Ship

The forward area of the main deck (about one-fourth to one-third the length of the ship, usually that area of the main deck forward of the bridge) is called the *forecastle* and the after part is the *fantail* (usually the deck area aft of the superstructure).

In port, the *quarterdeck* is a formal area on a ship that serves as the point of entry or exit for people coming aboard or going ashore. It is manned by a watch team twenty-four hours a day when the ship is not under way and its location can change depending on how a ship is moored (it will be on the port side of the ship if she is moored port side to the pier, for example).

The *bridge* is the primary control station for the ship when she is under way and the place where all orders and commands affecting the ship's movements and routine originate. It is roughly analogous to the driver's seat in a car or the cockpit of an aircraft, but it is large enough for a team of people to function as they steer, control the engines, watch radar scopes, talk on radios, etc. For obvious reasons, the bridge is positioned such that it affords a good view of the world beyond the ship.

The *combat information center* (CIC) is the nerve center of the ship, where information is collected, processed, displayed, evaluated, and disseminated to other parts of the ship (or to other ships) for use in decision making and in properly employing the ship. Sometimes it is known by other names (such as *combat direction center*). A wide range of electronic equipment is installed in the CIC to process information received from a wide variety of sources, including radio, radar, sonar, electronic-warfare intercept receivers, IFF (identification friend or foe) transponders, visual communications, satellites, fathometers (depth

The bridge is the primary control station on ships that are under way.

gauges), and networked computers. The CIC is the place where the ship's tactical operations are controlled. Such operations include the evaluation of targets, weapons firing, the control of friendly aircraft, surveillance operations, navigational assistance, submarine tracking, and many others.

The *engineering spaces* in a ship contain the propulsion machinery of the vessel as well as various types of equipment that supply the ship with electricity (generators), fresh water (evaporators), and so on. Steam-powered ships will often have both boiler rooms and engine rooms, but gas-turbine-powered ships only have engine rooms. The primary control station for the engineering plant is usually called *main control.*

Damage control central (DCC) serves as the central information and control site for matters affecting the safety of the ship. By monitoring conditions aboard ship and maintaining control of vital systems

Combat Information Center (CIC) is the nerve center of the ship, where information is collected, processed, displayed, evaluated, and disseminated.

A Sailor checks lube-oil levels in the forward diesel engine room of an amphibious assault ship.

such as those used in firefighting and flooding control, and by maintaining careful records, damage-control charts, and liquid-loading diagrams, DCC sees that the ship is kept safe and stable during routine conditions and coordinates damage control operations when emergencies arise.

Magazines are special storerooms used for the stowage of missiles, rockets, and gun ammunition. For obvious reasons, these important but potentially dangerous areas aboard ship are kept locked and under close control. They also are protected by various alarm and firefighting systems and are usually located in spaces well below the waterline so that, in case of fire, they can be flooded.

The living spaces aboard ship are essential to accommodate the needs of the crew. Generally, enlisted crew members sleep in *berthing compartments*, whereas officers sleep in *staterooms*. The commanding officer's living area is called the "captain's cabin." Other living spaces include *heads* (lavatories), *wardrooms* (living and dining areas for officers), *messes* or *mess deck* (where enlisted personnel eat), and *galleys* (kitchens). The medical clinic aboard ship is called *sick bay*. Larger ships may have other spaces for the health and comfort of the crew, such as tailor shops, libraries, barber shops, chapels, weight or aerobic rooms, and crew lounges. Virtually all ships have a *ship's store* that carries toiletries, uniform items, *gedunk* (snacks), and so on.

Shops and offices can be found on virtually every Navy ship. The number of each depends upon the size and the purpose of the ship. An aircraft carrier will have more than you can count; a patrol craft may have only one or two.

Vital Ship's Systems

A number of systems are essential to every Navy ship and, in many ways, are analogous to the nervous, circulatory, respiratory, and excretory systems of the human body.

The electrical system is essential for running complex weapon and communications systems, computing the solutions to a vast spectrum of tactical problems, powering ammunition hoists and aircraft elevators, detecting incoming enemy missiles and aircraft, running shipboard

School children try out the bunks in a
shipboard berthing compartment.

television systems for entertainment, and so on. These, and hundreds of
other functions, make electricity as vital to a modern vessel of war as
ropes were to a sailing vessel.

Ships generate their own electricity and have backup systems to
provide power when the primary system fails. Vital electrical circuits
are also frequently duplicated so that power can continue to flow after
battle damage occurs.

The ventilation system supplies fresh air where it is needed and
carries off unwanted exhaust. Supply ventilation brings fresh (external)

air into the ship and in cold weather heats the air by means of preheaters installed in the ducting. Exhaust ventilation carries away the air that has served its purpose and needs to be replaced. In those spaces containing equipment that generates heat or humidity or both (such as main engineering spaces, galley, or head facilities), the exhaust system is particularly vital. *Recirc ventilation* is provided to spaces containing electronic equipment (which requires a cool environment for proper operation), as well as to berthing, messing, and office spaces. As its name implies, this system recirculates internal air to prevent stagnation and, when necessary, draws the air through a cooling system to maintain the proper temperature.

In the event of fire, flooding, or some other danger requiring the isolation of a space or spaces, ventilation systems can be secured by de-energizing the fan motor and can be segregated by closing valve-like devices in the ducting (often found where the ducting penetrates decks, overheads, and bulkheads).

The potable water system provides water for drinking, personal hygiene, and cooking. Potable water is made in the ship's distilling units (*evaporators*) from saltwater taken from the sea, and it is stowed in tanks specifically designated for potable water only. Piping systems carry the water from the tanks to the heads, galleys, and drinking fountains (*scuttlebutts*) where it can be used.

The saltwater system covers other water needs. Drawn directly from the sea through underwater intakes and pumped throughout the ship using a different piping system from the one used for potable water, this water is available for firefighting when needed and is used on a routine basis as flushing water for the heads. Saltwater is also is used as cooling water for certain items of machinery and electronic equipment and can be piped into tanks for *ballast* (to stabilize the ship). Special sprinkler heads mounted all over the outside of the ship can be opened to allow a wash down of the ship to rid her of contaminants in the event of a chemical, biological, or radiation (CBR) attack.

The drainage system includes the piping, valves, and pumps that discharge water from the ship. It is used routinely for pumping a ship's bilges (the lowest parts of the ship's hull where water collects) and in emergencies to remove seawater that has entered the hull because of damage, collision, or heavy weather. It is also coupled with the saltwater system so that water can be shifted around to maintain proper *trim* (stabilize the ship).

Because weather-deck drains collect natural rain and seawater, the drains connected to these areas are piped directly overboard. But internal drains (from sinks, showers, galleys, toilets, and urinals) are carefully controlled for environmental reasons. Drainage from these sources is collected in specially designed tanks for appropriate disposition.

The fuel system includes fuel-stowage tanks, pumps, filling lines, transfer lines, and feed lines to the ship's boilers, engines, and generators. Like the other liquid systems aboard ship (potable water, saltwater, and drainage) the fuel system is also constantly monitored and moved about to help maintain proper trim (stability).

The compressed air system is used to charge torpedoes, operate pneumatic tools, run messages through pneumatic dispatch tubes, power automatic boiler controls, eject gases from guns after they have fired, and so on. Compressors create the compressed air, and special piping carries it where it is needed in the ship.

AIRCRAFT TERMINOLOGY

Because aircraft are such an important component of the Navy, familiarity with certain basic terms concerning the structure of aircraft and helicopters is useful.

The *fuselage* is the main body of the aircraft. The wings are strong structural members attached to the fuselage. Their airfoil shape provides the lift that supports the aircraft in flight. Wings are fitted with controllable *flaps* for increased lift and may be fitted to carry guns, rockets, missiles, and other weapons, as well as fuel tanks, engines, or landing gear. Besides fixed-wing aircraft, there are "rotary-wing aircraft," more commonly called "helicopters"; instead of having wings in the traditional sense, they have *rotors* (which are actually wings that rotate).

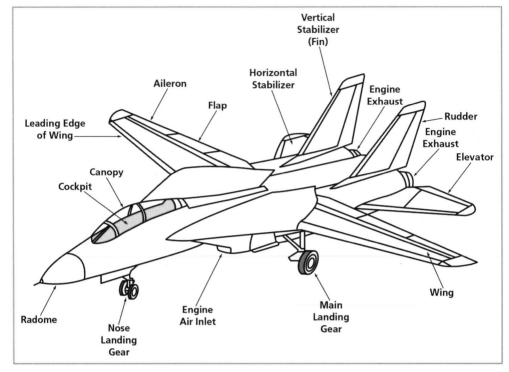

Figure 3. Aircraft terminology

The tail assembly of a fixed-wing aircraft usually consists of vertical and horizontal stabilizers, rudder(s), and elevators. These components are key elements in the flight controls of the aircraft. Helicopters often have a tail rotor that keeps the helicopter from spinning like a top.

The *landing gear* usually means the wheels, but in certain specialized aircraft these may be replaced by skids, skis, or floats.

Fixed-wing aircraft that land on aircraft carriers have *tail hooks*, which are designed to catch a cable stretched across the flight deck, allowing the aircraft to land in a very short distance.

The *powerplant* develops the thrust or force that propels the aircraft forward, providing mobility and—in combination with the wings— the lift necessary to keep the aircraft aloft. In the case of helicopters, the powerplant provides the power to keep the rotors spinning, which keeps the aircraft aloft and allows it to hover as well as move through the air. The powerplant may consist of reciprocating (piston) engines that drive propellers, jet engines that develop thrust (turbojet and turbofan), or turbine engines and propellers or rotors in combination (turboprop or turbo shaft).

Another useful aircraft term is *Mach*, which is commonly used to measure the speed capability of an aircraft or missile. Formally defined as the ratio of speed of an object to the speed of sound in the surrounding atmosphere, it is used as follows. An aircraft traveling at Mach 1 would be moving at the speed of sound. One going Mach 2 would be going twice the speed of sound, and Mach 1.5 would be one-and-a-half times the speed of sound. Depending upon the altitude, temperature, and some other variables, the speed of sound varies, but a rough figure to use for approximation is 650 miles per hour. So an aircraft flying at Mach 2 would be moving at a speed of approximately thirteen hundred miles per hour. An aircraft that is able to fly faster than the speed of sound (Mach 1) is said to be *supersonic* and one that cannot is called *subsonic*. A *hypersonic* aircraft flies at Mach 5 or greater.

Stealth technology has changed the appearance and actual structure of aircraft considerably. Stealth is accomplished by incorporating different materials and designing an aircraft's outer surface at various angles that will deflect a radar signal rather than return it to the transceiver from which it came, thereby making the aircraft virtually invisible to enemy radar.

DATES AND TIME

In the Navy, you will find that dates are stated differently. Whereas the civilian convention is month-day-year (as in "December 7, 1941" or "September 11, 2001"), in the Navy the format is day-month-year (as in "7 December 1941" or "11 September 2001"). Further, you will often see an abbreviated version, such as "07AUG41" (note the use of the zero when the day of the month is less than ten) or "11SEP01."

You may see exceptions to this, as when a computer-friendly system is being used ("30 August 2007" becomes "20070830" for example) or other special circumstances, but the most frequently used format in the Navy is day-month-year.

One can argue about the relative merits of many of the strange habits one encounters in the Navy, but nowhere does the military trump the civilian world more than in the telling of time. The "a.m." and "p.m." system that we grew up using is familiar and therefore comfortable, but *dumb!* The twenty-four-hour system makes so much more sense because it does not lend itself to confusion. Note that it is not only used by all the military services but also by police forces, in hospitals, by air-traffic controllers, and in every other profession where the telling of time is important.

This system may be unfamiliar at first, but it is not difficult to learn. Very simply, instead of starting the twelve-hour cycle over again at noon, the twenty-four-hour system just keeps going, so that instead of 1:00 p.m., we say 1300 (pronounced "thirteen hundred"). Instead of 2:00 p.m., the time is 1400, and so on, until we reach midnight. How you get used to this is up to you. Some people remember it by subtracting two (or two hundred) from the strange times to get to their more familiar "p.m." time, so that 1500 minus two (hundred) becomes 3:00 p.m. Others just think in terms of a twenty-four clock and the times are rather logical. Whatever system you use at first, eventually it will become second nature, and unless you are very stubborn, you will come to appreciate the logic and simplicity of it.

Times other than the actual hour are virtually the same as in the twelve-hour system, so that 1:05 p.m. becomes 1305, 11:47 p.m. becomes 2347, and so on. Note that there are no colons used as there are in civilian time.

One other thing you must get used to is that zeros are used so that time is always expressed in four digits. This means that the "a.m." hours are virtually the same in both systems, but are said a little differently in the twenty-four-hour system, so that 10:00 a.m. becomes "1000" (pronounced "ten-hundred") and 7:00 am becomes 0700 (pronounced "oh-seven-hundred" or "zero-seven-hundred"). Likewise, 3:38 a.m. becomes 0338 ("oh-three-thirty-eight" or "zero-three-thirty-eight").

Midnight in the twenty-four-hour system is a little odd in that it can be expressed as 2400 *or* 0000, but one minute after midnight is always 0001, not 2401.

One final area of confusion. You may hear someone say "1300 hours" ("thirteen-hundred hours"). Technically this is not correct in the sea services (Navy, Marine Corps, and Coast Guard). The Army and Air Force append the word "hours," but Navy, Marine, and Coast Guard people should not. To be honest, this is one of those traditions that may be dying, so you may in fact hear Navy people saying "1722 hours" ("seventeen-twenty-two hours") instead of simply "1722." You may also encounter the term "zero-dark-thirty" when talking with military people. This is just unofficial slang for "very early."

Studying Table 1 should help you become more familiar with the twenty-four-hour system and help you to understand this strange but actually very logical system.

UPPERCASE VERSUS LOWERCASE

You will see capitalization used more liberally in the military than in the civilian world. For example, a newspaper may refer to the "secretary of the navy" but a Navy directive will usually write "Secretary of the Navy."

Though there may be little or no logic to it (and little or no parallel in the civilian world—except perhaps the capitalization of "God" and associated pronouns, such as "He" and "Him"), there is an understood convention in the military that capitalization confers importance. In military culture, one instinctively capitalizes (1) whenever someone or something seems or is important, and (2) whenever in doubt! This latter tendency is the opposite of the conventions usually used in the civilian world, where capitalization is more often avoided. Consequently, from across a room you can usually identify a document as military because of the proliferation of uppercase letters on nearly every page.

The proliferation of acronyms does not help. Though our society in general is more and more prone to the use of acronyms, the military still holds the lead—by a wide margin—in the use of these efficient, but sometimes cryptic or exclusionary, "words."

And because some military communications systems archaically used all caps, you will sometimes find yourself reading a document that is written entirely in capital letters.

Table 1. Navy Time

CIVILIAN TIME	24-HOUR CLOCK	SPOKEN AS
Midnight	0000 or 2400	
1 a.m.	0100	"Zero-one-hundred" or "Oh-one-hundred"
2 a.m.	0200	"Zero-two-hundred" or "Oh-two-hundred"
3 a.m.	0300	
3:30 a.m.	0330	"Zero-three-thirty" or "Oh-three-thirty"
4:00 a.m.	0400	
5:00 a.m.	0500	
6:00 a.m.	0600	
6:15 a.m.	0615	"Zero-six-fifteen" or "Oh-six-fifteen"
7:00 a.m.	0700	
8:00 a.m.	0800	
9:00 a.m.	0900	
10:00 a.m.	1000	"Ten-hundred"
11:00 a.m.	1100	"Eleven-hundred"
11:47 a.m.	1147	"Eleven-forty-seven"
12 Noon	1200	
1:00 p.m.	1300	"Thirteen-hundred"
2:00 p.m.	1400	
3:00 p.m.	1500	
3:59 p.m.	1559	"Fifteen-fifty-nine"
4:00 p.m.	1600	
5:00 p.m.	1700	
6:00 p.m.	1800	
7:00 p.m.	1900	
8:00 p.m.	2000	"Twenty-hundred"
8:01 p.m.	2001	"Twenty-oh-one"
9:00 p.m.	2100	
10:00 p.m.	2200	
11:00 p.m.	2300	"Twenty-three-hundred"
12 Midnight	2400 or 0000	"Twenty-four-hundred" or "Zero-zero-zero-zero"
12:01 a.m.	0001	"Zero-zero-zero-one"

PHONETIC ALPHABET

When talking on a radio circuit, on a sound-powered telephone aboard ship, and even on a standard telephone, a person's voice does not have the same clarity that it does when speaking face to face with someone. That is one of the reasons why the Navy insists upon standardized terminology when communicating and has devised some unusual ways to avoid confusion.

Using the phonetic alphabet prevents confusion when speaking on a radio.

One of the most valuable tools in maintaining clarity and avoiding confusion in communications is the phonetic alphabet. C, D, E, P, V, T, and Z all sound very much alike on a telephone, for example. By using phonetic equivalents (Charlie, Delta, Echo, Papa, Victor, Tango, and Zulu) there is no chance of someone misunderstanding what letter is meant. If someone says, "We need part number six Alfa," instead of "six A," there is no chance that someone will confuse that with part six K (which would be "six Kilo"). The phonetic alphabet can also be used to spell out unfamiliar words that someone is having difficulty understanding: "Echo-Xray-Echo-Golf-Echo-Sierra-India-Sierra" works a lot better on the telephone than "ee-ex-ee-gee-ee-ess-eye-ess"; unfortunately, the phonetic alphabet will *not* tell you what that word means!

The phonetic alphabet has been around for a long time, but has not always been the same. Back in the days of World War II, the phonetic alphabet began with the letters "Able, Baker, Charlie," K was "King," and S was "Sugar." After the war, when the NATO alliance was formed, the phonetic alphabet was changed to make it easier for the people who speak the different languages found in the alliance. That version has remained the same, and today the phonetic alphabet begins with "Alfa, Bravo, Charlie," K is now "Kilo," and S is "Sierra."

As you look over the phonetic alphabet, you will notice certain idiosyncrasies that you must accept. For example, the letter "Alfa" is spelled with an F instead of "ph." This is because some of our allies do not have a "ph" in their language. Also note that "Whiskey" ends in "key," not "ky," and "Juliett" ends in two Ts.

Note the pronunciations in the table provided, each word is accented on the syllable in capital letters. This is no time for individuality—it is essential that everyone say these words as much the same as is possible to avoid any confusion, which is the whole purpose. The letter P is pronounced *pah-PAH*, not *POP-ah* as most Americans are more likely to say. L is *LEE-mah*, not *LYE-mah*, and Q is *kay-BECK*, not *QUEE-beck*.

a	Alfa	*AL-fah*
b	Bravo	*BRAH-vo*
c	Charlie	*CHAR-lee*

d	Delta	*DELL-tah*
e	Echo	*ECK-oh*
f	Foxtrot	*FOKS-traht*
g	Golf	*GOLF*
h	Hotel	*hoh-TELL*
i	India	*IN-dee-ah*
j	Juliett	*JEW-lee-ett*
k	Kilo	*KEY-loh*
l	Lima	*LEE-mah*
m	Mike	*MIKE*
n	November	*no-VEM-ber*
o	Oscar	*OSS-ker*
p	Papa	*pah-PAH*
q	Quebec	*kay-BECK*
r	Romeo	*ROW-me-oh*
s	Sierra	*see-AIR-rah*
t	Tango	*TANG-go*
u	Uniform	*YOU-nee-form*
v	Victor	*VIK-ter*
w	Whiskey	*WISS-key*
x	Xray	*ECKS-ray*
y	Yankee	*YANG-key*
z	Zulu	*ZOO-loo*

RADIO TALK

Because many Sailors have to talk on radios as part of their profession, you may note that some of that radio jargon appears in normal conversation. Don't be surprised if someone says "affirmative" and "negative" instead of "yes" or "no." You will also hear "Roger" (or "Roger that") as a means of acknowledgement. You may well begin to emulate this kind of talk, which is fine, as long as you do it correctly. Hollywood loves to imitate military talk but absolutely refuses to get it right most of the time and thereby instantly loses credibility among military viewers. A few quick definitions (in layman's terms) will avoid much embarrassment:

- "ROGER" means, "I heard what you said."
- WILCO" means, "I heard and understood what you said and I will do what you say" (*will* comply).
- "OVER" means, "I am finished talking and now it's your turn to talk."
- "OUT" means, "I am finished talking and no response from you is necessary (in other words, "This conversation is over").

Because "over" says one thing and "out" says something entirely different, you should *never* hear these two words used together (yet you often do). To say "over and out" is to say "I am finished talking and now it's your turn to talk and I am finished talking and you should say nothing."

And because the meaning of "ROGER" is included in the meaning of "WILCO," only the uninformed and a Hollywood star would say "Roger, Wilco" together.

Sad to say, there are times when someone who wants to sound military will say "roger, wilco, over, and out." Like nails on a chalkboard!

BRAVO ZULU

This is not a hybrid version of two famous movies. It is the Navy's unique way of praising someone, of saying, "Well done." Remembering the phonetic alphabet explained above, you might be tempted to ask, "Why not 'Whiskey Delta?'"

The origins of the term can be found in the practice of using codes to convey information or orders at sea. Before radio was invented, ships needed some means of communicating, so a set of signal flags representing letters and numbers was created so that messages could be created and hoisted by one ship and read by other ships within visual range. But trying to spell out a message of very many words would require a lot of halyard space, so signal books were devised with simple codes that assigned longer meanings to short combinations of letters. For example, if all ships in a squadron had the same signal book that assigned the code letters "DCV" to mean "Engage the nearest enemy from windward," the squadron commodore could order that for all his ships at once, simply by hoisting those three flags. This had the added advantage that, without the same signal book, the enemy would not know what the commodore was intending.

When radio was invented, the same codes could still be used to convey longer messages in shorter terms (over longer distances), simply by broadcasting the code letters by Morse code or voice. As explained above, for voice radio a phonetic alphabet was created to prevent a commodore intending to tell his ships to "engage the enemy" (DCV) from accidentally telling them to "return to port" (TCE). If they heard the letters wrong, such a mistake could hardly be career-enhancing.

The signal books, assigning specific meanings to different combinations of letters and numbers, have changed at times to keep enemy forces from becoming familiar with the codes and to reflect changes of technology. The codes also grew, incorporating administrative as well as tactical information. One of the signals included along the way was one that allowed a commander to send his approval for a successful evolution, to say, "Well done." During World War II, "Tare Victor George" was listed in the codebook with that meaning.

When a new codebook, called the Allied Naval Signal Book (ACP 175), was adopted after the creation of NATO in 1949, "Tare Victor George" was replaced by "Baker Zebra" for no other reason than randomness. It remained that way until 1957 when the new phonetic alphabet changed it to "Bravo Zulu."

One can presume that the Navy was doing a lot of things well through the years, because Sailors became used to (and coveted) the words "Bravo Zulu." It became so familiar and so traditional that subsequent changes to the signal book retained that one code when everything else changed. It remains today; so if your Sailor happens to say "Bravo Zulu" to you, you should smile and pat yourself on the back for a job *Well Done*.

LIBERTY AND LEAVE

Even time off from your job is referred to differently in the Navy. At the end of a normal work day when your Sailor's ship is in port, or if he or she is stationed ashore, your Sailor may be allowed to leave the ship or station to spend some time doing what he or she enjoys, such as going to a movie, visiting local friends, eating at a restaurant, going home to visit family if they live nearby. This time off is called *liberty,* and may last until the next morning, or for an entire weekend, or it may end at midnight or some other designated time, depending upon the circumstances. Liberty overseas when your Sailor's ship is visiting a foreign port is one of the great advantages of being in the Navy. Most people would have to spend thousands of dollars to take a trip to Italy or Japan, but Sailors often find themselves visiting such places as part of their jobs.

For longer periods of time—a "vacation" in civilian life—your Sailor may take *leave* as explained in the previous chapter.

By now, it should be clear that the Navy has a virtual language of its own. While you will never be as conversant in that unusual argot as your Sailor is, having some understanding of the Navy's terminology may improve your communications with your Sailor. And that is never a bad thing.

Sailors on liberty in Marseilles, France

4 NAVY MISSIONS AND HERITAGE

Since the Revolutionary War, the Navy your son or daughter is now part of has had a long, proud history of successfully carrying out its missions, when Sailors have been called upon to contribute to the defense and well-being of our nation. Now, your Sailor will be called upon to do the same.

MISSIONS

The United States, fourth largest nation in the world in terms of land area, has always been a maritime nation. Throughout the nation's history, interaction with the sea has played an important role in America's economy, defense, and foreign policy.

During the colonial period and in the early days of the Republic, it was much easier to travel from colony to colony or state to state by ship or boat than by horse or on foot. Fishing, whaling, and overseas trade were among the fledgling nation's most important businesses.

The War of 1812, fought just a few decades after the Revolution, was in no small part decided by a series of stellar U.S. naval victories over ships of the British Royal Navy, then the world's foremost sea power. A naval blockade and riverine warfare were essential elements in the Civil War. The war with Spain at the end of the nineteenth century began with the sinking of battleship *Maine* and was decided by American naval victories in Manila Bay and the waters off Cuba.

A Sailor watches the USS *Constitution*—the Navy's oldest ship still in commission—as she makes way on her two-hundredth birthday. Technology changes, but the fighting spirit exhibited by "Old Ironsides," this War of 1812 veteran, remains intact.

American commerce would never have thrived—and would not *today*—without open sea lanes. Two world wars could not have been won without the lifelines maintained across the world's oceans, and American control of the sea was an essential element in the triumph over the Soviet Union in the Cold War. Today, the United States of America continues to look to the sea for these same things and relies upon its Navy to preserve and further the nation's maritime interests.

Being a maritime nation means having a comfortable relationship with the sea, using it to national advantage, and seeing it as a highway rather than as an obstacle. World War II provides an excellent example. By 1941 Hitler had conquered much of the land of Europe, but because Germany was not a maritime power, he saw the English Channel (a mere twenty miles across at its narrowest point) as a barrier, and England remained outside his grasp. Yet the Americans and British were later able to strike across this same channel into Europe to eventually bring Nazi Germany to its knees. And in that same war, the United States attacked Hitler's forces in North Africa with ships, Sailors, and embarked Soldiers sailing across the Atlantic Ocean—a distance of more than 3,000 nautical miles.

The navy of a maritime nation must be able to carry out a variety of strategic missions. Currently, the U.S. Navy has six important missions, all of which have been carried out effectively at various times in the nation's history and continue to be as important as ever in today's challenging world:

- All Domain Access
- Sea Control
- Deterrence
- Forward Presence
- Power Projection
- Maritime Security

ALL DOMAIN ACCESS

When the U.S. Navy first began defending the nation, the sea's surface was the only naval domain. Armed ships capable of moving about on the waters of the world to defend the nation's interests carried out the Navy's missions. But as technology advanced, new domains opened up, requiring Sailors to go beyond the realm of the sea's surface into equally challenging new environments under the sea and above it. Today's Navy must maintain access to all of these domains in order to be able to carry out its vital missions.

Forward Presence is one of the Navy's vital missions. Here, USS *Porter* (DDG 78), an *Arleigh Burke*–class guided-missile destroyer forward-deployed to Rota, Spain, transits the Suez Canal en route to the Red Sea.

As early as the American Revolution, Sailors were experimenting with vessels that could go under the water to take advantage of being unseen by the enemy. As time went on, this capability was more and more developed, and by World War I at the beginning of the twentieth century, submarines were a major part of the war at sea. By the end of that same century, submarines had become formidable weapons, powered by nuclear energy and able to remain hidden and to deliver devastating nuclear-tipped missiles to virtually anywhere on earth.

In that same twentieth century, the Navy took to the air, mastering the ability to fly aircraft from ships as well as from naval air stations around the world. Propeller-driven, fixed-wing aircraft pioneered the way into the skies and were eventually joined by incredibly fast jets and by helicopters that have the ability to hover in one place and land on relatively small ships. No longer limited to the range of shipboard weapons, Navy ships could now project power across vast expanses of ocean and far inland.

Jet technology was accompanied by the development of guided missiles. These in turn reached greater and greater heights and eventually into outer space, where satellites today give the Navy vastly improved navigation, reconnaissance, and communications capabilities, as well as greatly improving our ability to effectively control weapons and other vital systems.

As Sailors—aided by civilian scientists and engineers—ventured into the domains of sea, undersea, air, and space, these explorations and achievements led to further developments in other, less tangible, realms: the electromagnetic spectrum and cyberspace, impressive names associated with more familiar things like radios, radars, and computers.

In little more than two hundred years the Navy has gone from sailing ships with limited capabilities to vastly more powerful ships, submarines, aircraft, missiles, satellites, electronic systems, and computers that carry out our nation's vital missions around the world.

The Navy extends its reach into the domain of outer space as a Navy "Mobile User Objective System" (MUOS) satellite is launched at Cape Canaveral.

SEA CONTROL

Because navies are expensive, the newly created United States tried to do without one in the years immediately following the American Revolution. Within a year after the termination of hostilities with England, Congress ordered all naval vessels sold or destroyed. The men who had fought for independence as Sailors in the Continental Navy during the Revolution were left high and dry by the new government's decision. Even John Paul Jones, our most famous naval hero during the American Revolution—recognized by many as the "father of the U.S. Navy"—left America and served as an admiral in the Russian navy. No money was allocated to the building of naval vessels in the first ten years following the Revolution, and George Washington, who had shown a keen understanding of the importance of naval power during the war, relied as president upon his secretary of war to oversee both the Army and the limited Navy we had retained. Thomas Jefferson viewed a navy as not only expensive but provocative and, when he became the nation's third president, relied on an inexpensive fleet of defensive gunboats to guard the nation's shores.

But these frugal measures did not last. World events and human nature conspired to prove that a maritime nation cannot long endure without a navy. Almost immediately, the so-called Barbary pirates, sponsored by North African petty despots—the sultan of Morocco, dey of Algiers, bey of Tunis, and bashaw of Tripoli—began preying on defenseless American merchant shipping in the Mediterranean Sea. Additionally, the ongoing struggle between France and England made American ships and their crews tempting targets, and both nations began taking advantage of the helplessness of the Americans by seizing merchant ships and sailors on flimsy pretexts. Under these provocations, the cost of not having a navy soon outweighed the cost of having one. Spurred to reluctant action by these costly and insulting blows to U.S. sovereignty, Congress approved the reestablishment of a navy and the building of several ships.

In a series of engagements on the high seas in the next two decades, the fledgling U.S. Navy successfully defended the nation's right to use the world's oceans. During the Quasi War with France (1798–1800), the frigate *Constellation* defeated 2 French frigates in separate engagements, and other American ships, including the feisty little schooner *Enterprise*, managed to capture more than 80 French vessels of various sizes and descriptions. In the War with Tripoli (1801–5), a band of American Sailors and Marines led a daring raid into the enemy's home harbor that earned them respect throughout much of the world. At the beginning of the War of 1812, the U.S. Navy had only 17 ships while the British had more than 600, yet the Americans won a number of ship-to-ship battles that contributed to the favorable outcome of the war. Considering the relative inexperience and small size of this new navy, American Sailors fought far outside their weight class. Naval leaders such as Bainbridge, Perry, and Decatur, and warships such as *Constitution*, *Essex*, and *Niagara*, achieved enduring fame, and the motto "Don't Give Up the Ship" was etched into history. The new nation secured its rights and proved its ability to use the oceans of the world. Never again would the United States be powerless to defend itself at sea.

Ever since those early days, the U.S. Navy has been on station, ensuring America's right to use the sea for trade, for security, and for its growing role as a world power. As the nation grew stronger, the Navy also grew in size and capability. The early frigates that performed so well in battle with the French and British navies during the Quasi War and the War of 1812 gave way to the ironclad monitors of the Civil War, and these were superseded by the big-gun, armored battleships and high-speed cruisers that won the Spanish-American War in 1898.

In time, the United States emerged as a world power and the Navy's mission of preserving freedom of the seas became more vital than ever. New technology led to the development of new kinds of ships, such as destroyers and submarines, and the invention of the airplane and the aircraft carrier brought about the rise of naval aviation as a whole new component of the Navy. In the first half of the twentieth century, the U.S. Navy was called upon to fight the greatest sea war in history when Germany and Japan challenged America's freedom of the seas. Maintaining that freedom was a major factor in the victory over the Soviet Union in the Cold War. Today the Navy continues its role of preserving our free use of the global oceans, and *that is where your Sailor comes in.*

Against overwhelming odds, the fledgling U.S. Navy amazed the world by performing well against the powerful Royal Navy during the War of 1812. Here the Americans are victorious at the Battle of Lake Erie, 10 September 1813.

DETERRENCE

The most obvious reason for a maritime nation to have a navy is to ensure that no other nation attacks it by sea. Even when President Jefferson was trying to avoid having a navy in order to save money, he recognized this elemental need and tried to use his gunboat fleet as a deterrent to attack. One of the reasons for the United States building the Panama Canal in the early part of the twentieth century was to permit U.S. warships to move rapidly between Atlantic and Pacific and thereby bring greater sea power and deter many a potential enemy from attacking our shores.

Improvements in technology—such as the development of high-speed aircraft, powerful missiles, and long-range submarines—gradually increased our vulnerability to attack, and the Navy continued to play a vital role in protecting the nation by deterring our enemies, both real and potential. In 1962 the Soviet Union placed offensive nuclear missiles in Cuba. President John F. Kennedy, a former Sailor, imposed a naval "quarantine" around the island and threatened nuclear retaliation as deterrent measures to keep the Soviets from using these missiles against the United States and other nations in the Western Hemisphere. This ultimately forced the Soviets to take the missiles out of Cuba.

Throughout the Cold War, the U.S. Navy's fleet of ballistic-missile submarines patrolled the oceans of the world, armed with nuclear weapons ready to be launched on very short notice against an aggressor nation. This massive firepower, coupled with the striking power of U.S. aircraft carriers, land-based missiles, and the U.S. Air Force's long-range aircraft, effectively deterred the Soviet Union. Without this deterrence, the United States would have been very vulnerable to attack and would have struggled to stand up to the extremely powerful Soviet Union in moments of crisis.

Ballistic-missile submarines provided convincing deterrence during the Cold War. Here, USS *Henry M. Jackson* (SSBN 730) arrives home at Naval Base Kitsap-Bangor in Washington following a strategic deterrent patrol.

An example of America's ability to deal with Soviet intimidation occurred during the Middle East War of 1973. Although neither the Soviet Union nor the United States was directly involved in that war between Israel and most of the Arab nations, the United States supported Israel while the Soviet Union backed the Arab nations. When the Soviets began resupplying their clients by sending in massive quantities of weapons by airlift, the United States did the same for Israel. The U.S. 6th Fleet took up station in the Mediterranean to provide protection for its aircraft flying into the war zone. When the war began going badly for the Arabs, the Soviets threatened to intervene. The United States responded by putting its forces on increased alert worldwide and by moving naval units into striking position. Faced with this deterrent, the Soviets thought better of their intervention and the war was ultimately ended and settled on equitable terms.

Several times the Communist People's Republic of China has threatened to attack the Nationalist Chinese on the island of Taiwan, and each time the U.S. Navy has moved into position to successfully deter the Communists from attacking. Today, China is behaving more and more aggressively in the South China Sea, building bases and threatening to take control of islands and adjacent waters that are claimed by several of its Asian neighbors, such as Japan and the Philippines.

There are many such examples when the Navy has been called upon to deter others from taking actions that were seen as dangerous to the United States or were not in the nation's best interests. Just as an effective police patrol can deter criminals from committing crimes in a neighborhood, so the Navy preserves the peace and keeps our nation safe and prosperous by its mere existence and by its capabilities, forward presence, and ability to patrol the waters of the world.

FORWARD PRESENCE AND PARTNERSHIP

Another of the important missions of the Navy is based upon its ability to go virtually anywhere in the world. This capability allows the United States to be in a position to reassure our allies in a time of crisis, to intimidate potential enemies (a form of deterrence), to deliver humanitarian aid when disaster strikes, to rescue Americans or our allies from dangerous situations, or to be able to carry out offensive military action in a timely manner. This is called "forward presence" and explains why your Sailor may serve on a deployment to a far corner of the world.

Sometimes the presence of a single destroyer visiting a foreign port is all that is needed to carry out this vital mission. On other occasions, a carrier strike group or an entire fleet moving into a region is used to send a stronger message of warning or support. If hostilities become necessary, having units already at or near enemy territory can be a major advantage.

In 1854 Commodore Matthew Perry used forward presence as a means to open diplomatic relations and, ultimately, trade with Japan, a nation that, until Perry's visit, had shunned contact with the outside world. During the latter part of the nineteenth century, American naval ships patrolled the waters of the Far East to provide protection for our economic interests and the many American missionaries in that part of the world. When war broke out with Spain in 1898, the U.S. fleet already present in the Far East was able to strike a quick and decisive blow against the Spanish fleet in the Philippines. Throughout the Cold War, the U.S. Navy kept the 6th Fleet in the Mediterranean Sea and the 7th Fleet in the Far East to reassure our allies in those regions that we were nearby and ready to respond in the event of a crisis. Today the 5th Fleet makes our presence known in the Middle East and nearby regions.

Our modern American military forces have great striking power, and portions of those forces are maintained for quick response in Europe, the Middle East, and Asia. But that kind of forward presence can only exist at the invitation of other nations who are willing to give us bases on their territory. The Navy allows us to have a presence wherever there is water—almost everywhere. In times of increased tension, naval units can be moved to appropriate positions where American presence is needed, without having to negotiate any complicated diplomatic arrangements, without requiring much time.

Today, you often hear the term "globalization," which describes the increased interactivity of the world's nations. Used most often as an economic term, it explains how trade and financial activities are conducted among various countries, where raw materials might be grown

A tribute to Commodore Perry is carved out of snow for the annual International Snow Festival in Sapporo, Japan. Perry is famous throughout Japan for being the first American to officially open up the country to trade and relations with the United States during the nineteenth century.

or mined in one part of the world, converted into usable goods in another region, and purchased in still another, all relying on transportation systems (primarily ships) and world banking institutions to tie it all together.

This interconnectivity and dependence upon interwoven economic systems have led to a degree of globalization among the world's navies as well. Partnerships among nations with similar needs and interests are a natural offshoot of this global interconnectivity. The U.S. Navy maintains numerous partnerships with the navies of other nations through combined exercises, shared responsibilities, and special basing arrangements. These partnerships increase the effectiveness of the cooperating navies and contribute to the security of each nation.

POWER PROJECTION

Forward presence allows the Navy to be on station the world over, but just being there is not always enough. Sometimes, despite a nation's efforts to remain at peace, the use of force becomes necessary. When that occurs, the U.S. Navy has always been particularly effective in projecting American power where it is needed.

As early as the American Revolution, an American naval squadron sailed to the British-owned Bahamas to capture needed weapons, and John Paul Jones furthered the American cause by conducting a series of daring raids against the British Isles themselves.

In 1847, during the war with Mexico, the Navy transported a force of 12,000 Army troops to Vera Cruz and played a crucial role in the successful capture of that port city, ultimately leading to an American victory in that war.

Union ships not only carried out an effective blockade of Confederate ports during the Civil War, they also attacked key Southern ports and opened up the Mississippi River to Union use, effectively driving a wedge right into the heart of the Confederacy.

By escorting convoys, U.S. destroyers projected American power across the Atlantic to aid in an Allied victory during World War I. In World War II, American aircraft carriers, battleships, cruisers, destroyers, submarines, amphibious vessels, troop transports, oilers, ammunition ships, minesweepers, PT-boats, and a wide variety of other ships carried the fight to the far corners of the world, slugging it out with powerful Japanese fleets in the Pacific, dueling with German submarines in the Atlantic, safely transporting incredible amounts of supplies to the many theaters of war, and landing troops on distant islands and on the African, Asian, and European coasts.

During the Korean, Vietnam, and Gulf Wars, naval power guaranteed our ability to project our power ashore, and naval aircraft, guns, and missiles inflicted significant harm on our enemies.

When American embassies in Africa were bombed by terrorists in 1998, American cruisers, destroyers, and submarines retaliated, launching a Tomahawk-missile barrage at terrorist targets in Afghanistan and Sudan. In the following year, naval electronic warfare and strike aircraft were vital components of the air war in Kosovo, and in the opening years of the twenty-first century, the Navy has already played key roles in the wars in Afghanistan and Iraq. Not only did the Navy launch some of the earliest strikes against the Taliban and al Qaeda in Afghanistan, but tens of thousands of Navy personnel augmented Army and Marine ground units who were stretched thin over two operational theaters.

When power needs to be projected, American naval forces have always been ready, willing, and able to accomplish the mission.

MARITIME SECURITY

Threats other than those posed by hostile nations can emerge, such as piracy, terrorism, weapons proliferation, and drug trafficking. Countering these irregular threats and enforcing domestic and international law at sea protects our homeland, enhances global stability, and secures freedom of navigation for the benefit of all nations.

The Navy has many ways to project power into the far corners of the world when needed. Here an F/A-18 Hornet fires flares while conducting missions in support of Operation Enduring Freedom in Afghanistan.

In 1819 Congress declared the infamous slave trade to be piracy, and in response the Navy established an African Slave Trade Patrol to search for these dealers in human misery. In the decades leading up to the Civil War, USS *Constitution*, USS *Constellation*, and many other Navy ships relentlessly plied the waters off West Africa, South America, and the Cuban coast, capturing more than one hundred suspected slavers.

In more modern times, the "War Eagles" of Patrol Squadron 16, flying out of Jacksonville, Florida, played a vital role in the capture of forty-one tons of cocaine, and USS *Crommelin*, working with USS *Ticonderoga*, intercepted a drug shipment of seventy-two bales of cocaine with an estimated street value of $36 million.

These operations are not what first comes to mind when one thinks about a navy, but they are becoming more and more typical as economic globalization and asymmetric threats emerge from adversaries often known as "non-state actors" in the twenty-first century.

OTHER MISSIONS AND FEATS

Evacuating U.S. citizens from dangerous areas or situations has been a long-standing mission of the Navy, and helping people survive the ravages of natural disasters, such as earthquakes and hurricanes, is an unpredictable but vital task the Navy is often called upon to carry out.

Because of a potato blight in Ireland and western Scotland between 1846 and 1849, two million people either died or emigrated. In 1847 USS *Jamestown* and USS *Macedonian* carried food that had been donated by Americans to the relief of thousands. To show their gratitude for having been saved from starvation, some of the residents named their children after the two ships.

In 2005 Navy ships arrived off the United States' southern coast to assist Gulf Coast residents in the aftermath of a devastating hurricane named Katrina. USS *Bataan* and USS *Iwo Jima*, ships designed and trained to conduct amphibious assault operations, instead used their Sea Stallion and Seahawk helicopters to conduct search-and-rescue missions, while Navy hovercraft evacuated victims and SeaBees (Navy construction battalions) cleared debris and helped in many rebuilding efforts.

Figure 4. Poster produced by Navy Visual News Service depicting many of the contributions provided by the U.S. Navy in the days following Hurricanes Katrina and Rita

While combat operations are a well-known aspect of the Navy's history, there have been and will continue to be many occasions when the Navy is sent to save lives and help large numbers of people in distress. The Navy's expeditionary character and its great mobility make it uniquely positioned to provide assistance.

The U.S. Navy has also played an important role in other realms, such as exploration and scientific discovery. For example, a Navy exploration team led by Lieutenant Charles Wilkes took a squadron of ships around the world, exploring Antarctica and vast areas of the Pacific Ocean in the years 1838–42. His charts of the Pacific not only served mariners for many decades to come but were used in the invasion of Tarawa in the early part of World War II. Navy men Robert E. Peary and Richard E. Byrd were pioneers in polar exploration: Peary was the first man to reach the North Pole in 1909, and Byrd flew over the South Pole in 1929. When Captain Edward L. "Ned" Beach Jr. and his crew took their nuclear submarine USS *Triton* around the world in eighty-three days in 1960, it was not the first time anyone had circumnavigated the earth, but it was the first time anyone had done it submerged for the entire voyage of 41,500 miles. In that same year, Lieutenant Don Walsh went deeper than any human being has ever been when he and Jacques Picard took the bathyscaphe *Trieste* to the bottom of the Marianas Trench, 35,800 feet down (more than 6.5 miles beneath the surface). Astronaut Alan Shepard was in the Navy when he became the first American in space, and astronaut Neil Armstrong had been in the Navy before he became the first man to walk on the moon.

The Navy has often led the way or played a crucial role in many realms of scientific and technological development, such as electricity, radio communications, radar technology, computer science, and nuclear engineering. Among her many achievements in computer science, Rear Admiral Grace Hopper invented COBOL, one of the important computer languages that led the way in computer development. Today, a ship bears her name. The world of nuclear engineering has been forever affected by the work of Admiral Hyman Rickover, and Vice Admiral Charles Momsen, a Navy man known to his shipmates as "Swede," changed the deep-sea diving world by his inventions and his pioneering work.

Another Navy diver, Carl Brashear, worked his way up from cook to Master Diver, salvaging a nuclear weapon from the depths of the Atlantic and losing a leg in the process. His inspiring story was the basis for a major motion picture.

Another modern, multi-million-dollar movie included a reenactment of the feats of another Sailor who won the Navy Cross at Pearl Harbor. Dorie Miller was different from your Sailor only in circumstance, but how he responded to the Japanese attack on his ship USS *West Virginia*, manning guns and saving lives, later earned him the honor of having a ship named after him.

Boatswain's Mate James Elliott Williams left his southern rural home to join the Navy. In 1966 he was a petty officer first class in charge of a pair of patrol boats on narrow jungle waterways in Vietnam, when he found himself facing an entire enemy regiment trying to cross a canal. Without hesitation, Williams pressed the attack. Three hours later, more than a thousand enemy soldiers had been killed or captured and sixty-five enemy vessels had been destroyed. Williams was awarded the Medal of Honor and later retired from the Navy as its most decorated enlisted member, having earned the Navy Cross, two Silver Stars, the Navy and Marine Corps Medal, three Bronze Stars, the Navy and Marine Corps Commendation Medal, the Vietnamese Cross of Gallantry, and three Purple Hearts. In a second career, he won the continued respect of his fellow South Carolinians by serving as a federal marshal.

For more than two centuries, Sailors of the United States Navy have been recording an impressive history of courage, resourcefulness, sacrifice, innovation, humanitarianism, combat skill, and dedication to duty. Now it is your Sailor's turn to follow in their wakes and, circumstances permitting, leave her or his mark on the pages of this impressive record.

HERITAGE

Even in the best fiction, you will not likely find a better story than the one that makes up the true story of the U.S. Navy in action. It is full of excitement, adventure, and heroism.

While there are many good books, some magazines, and a few movies that will help you better understand the legacy your son or daughter has been entrusted with, there are other ways that you can learn about and grow to appreciate this proud heritage. When your Sailor reports to a ship, find out why the ship has the name she does. You may learn that the name once belonged to someone much like your child, a Sailor carrying out the missions of the Navy to the best of his or her ability. You may also be surprised to learn that there may well have been other ships that have had the same name and have passed it on to this latest bearer of the name. When a ship is lost in battle or dies of old age, her name is often given to a newly built ship to carry on the legacy of the name. This is similar to the ongoing process your Sailor is now participating in. As older Sailors move on to retirement, they pass the legacy on to younger Sailors who then are entrusted to carry out the

Navy's vital missions. This is obviously no small responsibility, but it is also a privilege that only a select group of Americans have had.

History can be uninspiring if it is merely a list of names and dates, but heritage is written in a special ink that is a blend of the blood of sacrifice, the sweat of hard work, and the tears of pride that go into this special kind of service. Make sure your Sailor knows how proud you are of the important role your child is playing in our nation's defense. And you too should feel a great deal of pride for having raised a citizen who is willing and able to take on this important responsibility.

5 NAVY ORGANIZATION

Article I, Section 8 of the Constitution of the United States of America states that "the Congress shall have Power . . . to provide and maintain a Navy." Article II, Section 1 further mandates that "the President shall be Commander in Chief of the Army and Navy of the United States." Beyond that, the Constitution offers no further guidance as to the organization of the Navy. What has emerged and evolved over the years is an organization that is unique and complex. Understanding it can be challenging.

Today the armed services frequently operate in concert, so it is not enough to merely understand how the Navy is organized; you must also have some idea of how it fits into the Department of Defense. This chapter will unravel some of the complexity and give you a better understanding of how the Navy is able to carry out its many assigned tasks.

COMPLICATIONS

Before trying to understand how the U.S. Navy is organized, you should be forewarned that it is complicated. One might think that setting up a navy organization would be a relatively simple thing; that ships would be organized into fleets to operate in certain waters of the world and that admirals would command those fleets; that a chain of command could be simply drawn from the commanding officers of ships to the commanders of fleets and ultimately to the senior-most admiral in charge of the whole navy. But this simplistic vision ignores a number of facts, and the reality is that there are actually a number of chains of command that must be understood if you are going to understand how the U.S. Navy is organized.

To begin with, the Navy consists of more than ships. There are also aircraft and submarines, SEALs, SeaBees, Marines, and more that make up what we can collectively describe as the "operating forces" of the Navy.

Further, these operating forces cannot function independently. There must be a logistics system to ensure that the operating forces have fuel, ammunition, and other supplies. Some means of repairing the ships, aircraft, and other kinds of equipment must be in place, and medical facilities must be available to keep the Navy's Sailors healthy and to care for battle casualties and the sick when needed. These and other considerations mean that there must be facilities ashore to support the forces operating on, over, and under the sea.

Another complication stems from the realization that navies rarely operate alone, that modern warfare and readiness for war require all of the armed forces to operate together—or jointly—in various ways.

One more complicating factor comes from the fact that our nation is a democracy, and one of our governing principles is civilian control of the military.

These essential factors—the operating forces needing support from ashore, the need for joint operations among the services, and the necessity for civilian control of the armed forces—all combine to make for a more complicated organization than we might wish for, but understanding that organization can be helped by keeping the following in mind:

- In the military, the term *chain of command* is roughly synonymous with "organization." The former is a path of actual legal authority, whereas the latter is a little less formal, but for most purposes the two terms can be considered the same.

- There are two separate (but sometimes overlapping) chains of command within the Navy:
  - › the operational chain of command, which is "task oriented," meaning that it is concerned with carrying out specific missions (combat operations, fleet exercises, humanitarian operations, etc.),
  - › the administrative chain of command, which takes care of matters such as personnel manning, education and training, repairs, and supply.
- The operating forces are permanently organized in an administrative chain of command, though they are frequently reassigned to different operational chains of command as needs arise.
- Even though the operational forces consist of more than just ships, they are often collectively referred to as simply "the Fleet."
- The Fleet is supported by a number of different commands and organizations known collectively as "the shore establishment."
- The Department of the Navy (DON) is an integral part of the Department of Defense (DOD), which also includes the Army and the Air Force, and the DON and the DOD are intertwined to a significant degree. To avoid any possible confusion you should know that according to Navy Regulations, there is a difference between the "Department of the Navy" (refers to the entire Navy organization—all operating forces including the Marine Corps) and the "Navy Department" (located at the seat of government in Washington, D.C., it comprises the Office of the Secretary of the Navy, the Office of the Chief of Naval Operations, and Headquarters, Marine Corps).
- There is a civilian head of the Navy, known as the Secretary of the Navy (SECNAV), and a military head, the Chief of Naval Operations (CNO). The CNO is subordinate to SECNAV.
- The U.S. Marine Corps is a part of the DON but is in many ways a separate service as well, having its own senior military commander (known as the Commandant of the Marine Corps) but answering to the same civilian official (SECNAV).

- There are also allied chains of command that sometimes must be considered. For example, because the United States is a key member of the North Atlantic Treaty Organization (NATO), a U.S. Navy admiral can be the NATO Supreme Allied Commander Europe and be responsible for forces belonging to member nations as well as those of the United States.

- Some individuals in this organizational structure may "wear two hats," an expression that means one person can actually have two jobs, and often those two (or more) jobs might be in different parts of the organizations described above. For example, the Commander of the Navy's 5th Fleet also currently holds the position of "Commander of U.S. Naval Forces, Central Command" (a joint command position within the DOD chain of command). The CNO "wears a number of hats" in that he or she is responsible for ensuring the readiness of the operating forces of the Navy but is also the head of the shore establishment, and though this admiral is the senior military officer in the Navy, he or she also works directly for the civilian SECNAV in many matters and serves as a member of the Joint Chiefs of Staff in matters that involve working with the other armed services.

Some final thoughts on dealing with the complicated nature of the Navy's organization. One is that you probably will not need to know every detail of that organization. The information provided below is there for an encompassing overview. Try to grasp the essentials—particularly those that apply directly to your Sailor's job—but do not worry if you cannot remember exactly how it all fits together. Few people can.

Something else to keep in mind is that this organization frequently changes. Commands are renamed, offices shift responsibilities. Also be wary of the Internet; though it is a wonderful information tool, it must be used with caution. Web sites are not always kept up-to-date, and older, out-of-date items will show up when using a general search engine.

Keeping the above explanations in mind, let us venture into the labyrinth of Navy organization, beginning first with a description of the larger Department of Defense to put the Navy into proper perspective.

DEPARTMENT OF DEFENSE

As discussed above, the Department of the Navy (DON) is part of the Department of Defense (DOD), and some of the Navy's organization is directly intertwined with the DOD joint command structure. In its simplest breakdown, there are four principal components to the DOD:

- the Secretary of Defense and his or her supporting staff
- the Joint Chiefs of Staff and the supporting staffs
- the individual military departments: Army, Air Force, and Navy
- the Unified Combatant Commands

Most people who watch even a little news are aware that there is a Secretary of Defense (SECDEF) heading up the DOD and that he or she is assisted by a senior military officer known as the Chairman of the Joint Chiefs of Staff (CJCS), who can come from any of the services and whose principal duties include advising the President, the National Security Council, and SECDEF. Those people who are more informed may also know that the senior military officers of each service (the CNO; the Commandant of the Marine Corps, the Chief of Staff of the Army; and the Chief of Staff of the Air Force) serve collectively as the Joint Chiefs of Staff (JCS) under the Chairman. Note that though the Marine Corps is a service within the DON, the Commandant is a member of the JCS.

The Coast Guard is another unique entity. It is, by law, the fifth military branch of the U.S. armed services, but it is assigned to the Department of Homeland Security, rather than the DOD. And though the Coast Guard frequently operates in support of the Navy and the DOD when it is called upon to perform national defense missions, the Commandant of the Coast Guard is not a formal member of the JCS. During wartime or national emergency, the President can have the Coast Guard assigned to the DON, but the last time this transfer occurred was just before and during World War II.

Both the Secretary of Defense and the Chairman of the Joint Chiefs of Staff have fairly large organizations working for them. Supporting SECDEF is a staff structure known collectively as the Office of the

Secretary of Defense (OSD), which includes a Deputy Secretary of Defense, a number of undersecretaries, assistant secretaries, and other officials in charge of specific aspects of running the DOD (see Figure 5).

Likewise, the Chairman of the Joint Chiefs of Staff also has a support organization called "The Joint Staff," part of which is shown in Figure 6. Note that specific areas of responsibility are assigned "J-codes," J-1 for Man-power and Personnel, J-2 for Intelligence, and so on. So if you hear someone say something like, "Smith over in J-4 needs to meet with us in the morning," you will know that the meeting will probably have something to do with logistics. The individual services mimic this system (with modifications) but use other letters. Intelligence on Army staffs is usually "G-2," and on Navy staffs it is "N-2," for example.

For operational matters—such as contingency planning, responding to an international crisis, going to war, or participating in a major joint operational exercise—the chain of command is a bit different. This operational chain of command is sometimes referred to as the "U.S. National Defense Command Structure" and begins with the President of the United States in his or her constitutional role as Commander in Chief of the Armed Forces. It then goes through SECDEF (with CJCS and the service chiefs serving as principal advisors) to those generals and admirals known as "unified combatant commanders" (sometimes referred to as just "unified commanders" and occasionally "combatant commanders") (see Figure 7). Each is responsible for a specific geographic region of the world (sometimes referred to as an Area of Responsibility or AOR) or has a worldwide functional AOR. It is through the unified commanders that the DOD and Navy operational organizations come together.

Some confusion sometimes arises as to the role of CJCS in the operational chain of command. The Chairman (with the assistance of the JCS) technically serves as the principal military advisor to the President, the National Security Council, the Homeland Security Council, and SECDEF, but he or she often issues directives to the unified commanders, which sometimes creates the illusion that CJCS is in the chain of command between SECDEF and the unified commanders; however, these directives are always issued with the understanding that they originate with SECDEF, not from CJCS.

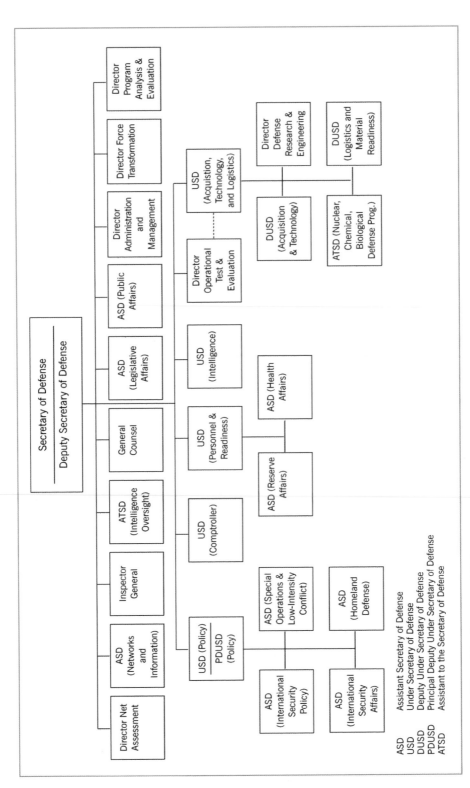

ASD   Assistant Secretary of Defense
USD   Under Secretary of Defense
DUSD   Deputy Under Secretary of Defense
PDUSD Principal Deputy Under Secretary of Defense
ATSD   Assistant to the Secretary of Defense

Figure 5. Office of the Secretary of Defense

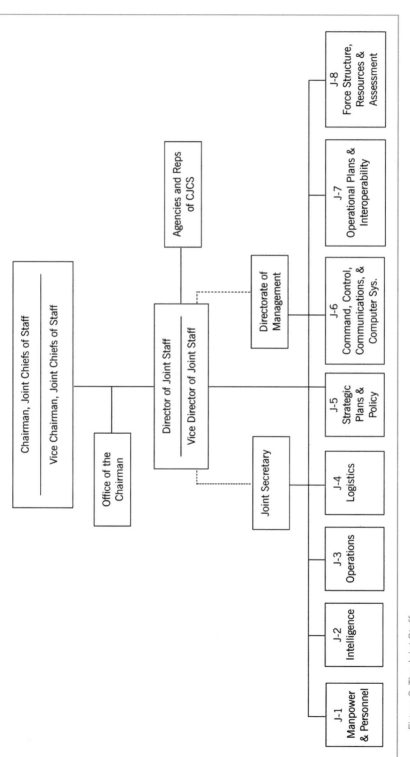

Figure 6. The Joint Staff

UNIFIED COMBATANT COMMANDS

There are currently nine unified commands. Six are responsible for specific geographic regions of the world (sometimes referred to as an Area of Responsibility or AOR): Northern Command, Southern Command, Pacific Command, European Command, Africa Command, and Central Command. The AORs are shown in Figure 8.

The other three commands have worldwide responsibilities that are functionally—rather than geographically—oriented: Strategic Command, Transportation Command, and Special Operations Command.

You should be aware that the formal titles of these commands include the prefix "United States," so "Northern Command (NORTH-COM)" is actually "United States Northern Command (USNORTH-COM)," but they are frequently referred to without the "US" prefix for brevity. We will use both in this discussion, but you should understand that they are one and the same.

All unified commanders answer directly to the Commander in Chief (the President of the United States) through SECDEF.

U.S. Northern Command (USNORTHCOM or NORTHCOM)

NORTHCOM was created as a result of the attacks on U.S. soil on 11 September 2001. Its primary purposes are to coordinate the homeland defense missions that are carried out by DOD activities and to provide military assistance to civil authorities as needed.

Headquarters: Peterson Air Force Base, Colorado Springs, Colorado

Geographic responsibility: Continental United States, Alaska, Canada, Mexico, Puerto Rico, U.S. Virgin Islands, and surrounding waters out to five hundred nautical miles. The command includes the Gulf of Mexico and some of the Caribbean, although most of the latter is under Southern Command (see below). Hawaii, Guam, and other U.S. territories and possessions in the Pacific are the responsibility of the Pacific Command.

Naval component: No permanent naval forces are assigned, but components from the Atlantic Fleet are frequently assigned for training and advisory functions as needed.

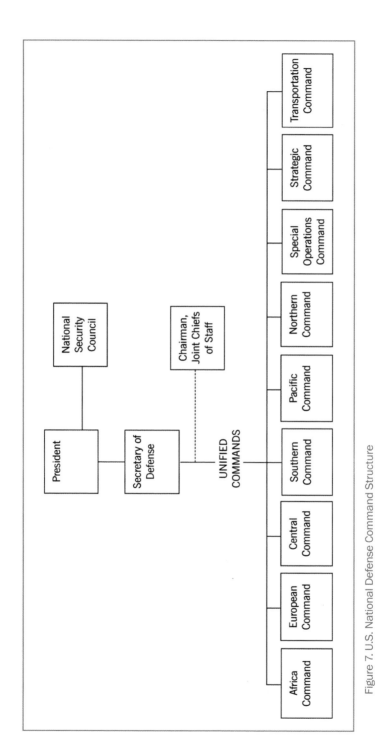

Figure 7. U.S. National Defense Command Structure

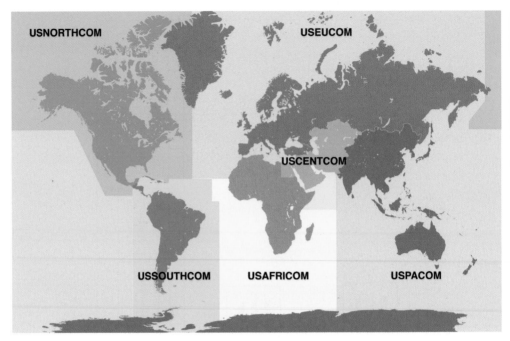

Figure 8. Geographic Areas of Responsibility for Unified Commands

U.S. Southern Command (USSOUTHCOM or SOUTHCOM)

The other unified command covering the Western Hemisphere is SOUTHCOM. It encompasses thirty-two nations (nineteen in Central and South America with the other thirteen in the Caribbean) and covers nearly 15 million square miles.

Headquarters: Miami, Florida

Geographic responsibility: The land mass of Latin America south of Mexico, the waters adjacent to Central and South America, and the Caribbean.

Naval component: U.S. Naval Forces Southern Command (USNAVSO)/4th Fleet. Serves as the primary link between the U.S. Navy and other navies of the region for combined exercises, counter-drug operations, humanitarian missions, and so on. No permanent fleet assets are assigned, but units are periodically provided and assigned to the 4th Fleet for specific purposes, such as the annual "UNITAS" multinational exercises aimed at building hemispheric cooperation and mutual defense.

U.S. Pacific Command (USPACOM or PACOM)

Encompassing the largest geographic area of all the regional unified combatant commanders, PACOM includes the Indian Ocean as well as the Pacific.

Headquarters: Camp H. M. Smith, Oahu, Hawaii

Geographic responsibility: Pacific and Indian oceans (less the Arabian Sea, which is the responsibility of CENTCOM), much of the Asian landmass (less Russia and some portions of Southwest Asia), Australia, New Zealand, and Antarctica.

Naval component: The Pacific Fleet (which includes the 3rd Fleet and 7th Fleet).

U.S. Central Command (USCENTCOM or CENTCOM)

A direct descendant of what was once called the "rapid deployment force," which had been primarily a contingency force, CENTCOM has become one of the most active combatant commands, having responsibility for combat operations in Afghanistan and Iraq.

Headquarters: MacDill Air Force Base, Tampa, Florida

Geographic responsibility: CENTCOM is responsible for operations in twenty countries that fall in the "central" area of the globe: Afghanistan, Bahrain, Egypt, Iran, Iraq, Jordan, Kazakhstan, Kuwait, Kyrgyzstan, Lebanon, Oman, Pakistan, Qatar, Saudi Arabia, Syria, Tajikistan, Turkmenistan, United Arab Emirates, Uzbekistan, and Yemen.

Naval component: U.S. Naval Forces Central Command (which includes the 5th Fleet).

U.S. European Command (USEUCOM or EUCOM)

Those areas not covered by the previous regional unified combatant commanders are covered by EUCOM. The commander also has allied responsibilities through NATO.

Headquarters: Stuttgart-Vaihingen, Germany

Geographic responsibility: Besides the continent of Europe, EUCOM includes Russia and several of the nations previously included in the now defunct Soviet Union (Ukraine, Belarus, Georgia, Moldova, Armenia, and Azerbaijan), and Israel.

Naval component: Naval Forces Europe, which includes the 6th Fleet.

U.S. Africa Command (USAFRICOM or AFRICOM)

The newest of the Unified Combatant Commands, AFRICOM was officially activated on 1 October 2007 to enable the Department of Defense to work with other elements of the U.S. government and international partners toward a stable and secure environment in support of U.S. foreign policy in that strategically important region of the world. AFRICOM conducts a wide range of programs and activities that help African states and regional organizations to meet their goals of building capable and professional militaries that are subordinate to civilian authority, respect human rights, and adhere to the rule of law. AFRICOM's forward operating task force located at Camp Lemonnier in Djibouti is known as the Combined Joint Task Force–Horn of Africa (CJTF-HOA) with many of its personnel "embedded" in partner nations performing a range of activities—building partner security capability, capacity, and infrastructure through regional cooperation; military-to-military programs; civil-military affairs projects; and professional military education programs.

Headquarters: Stuttgart, Germany

Geographic responsibility: All of the nations of Africa except Egypt, which is covered by CENTCOM.

Naval component: U.S. Naval Forces Africa. No permanent fleet assets are assigned, but Navy units are periodically assigned as needed.

U.S. Strategic Command (USSTRATCOM or STRATCOM)

As the command and control organization for all U.S. strategic forces (missile submarines, long-range bombers, ICBM systems, etc.), military space systems and operations, computer network systems, information operations, early warning systems, and strategic planning, STRATCOM is tasked with meeting both deterrent and decisive national security objectives. It includes the U.S. Cyber Command (USCYBERCOM) as well as components of the old Space Command (SPACECOM), the Air Force's Strategic Air Command (SAC), and the Navy's fleet ballistic-missile submarine forces, among others.

Headquarters: Offutt Air Force Base, Nebraska

Geographic responsibility: Worldwide

Naval component: Submarines in Navy Task Forces 134 (Pacific) and 144 (Atlantic).

U.S. Transportation Command (USTRANSCOM or TRANSCOM)
The mission of this unified command is to provide air, land, and sea transportation for the DOD, in both peace and war. TRANSCOM directly controls nearly ninety ships, more than a thousand aircraft, and more than two thousand railcars, and indirectly, through commercial partners, has access to many more transport assets. Component commands include the Air Force's Air Mobility Command (AMC), the Army's Surface Deployment and Distribution Command (SDDC), and the Navy's Military Sealift Command (MSC). Together, these commands meet the transport needs of the DOD (including air refueling, aeromedical evacuation, land transport, ocean terminal management, commercial shipping interface, replenishment at sea, and a variety of other services that accom-plish strategic and tactical airlift as well as move DOD personnel, their families, and their household goods worldwide).
  Headquarters: Scott Air Force Base, Illinois
  Geographic responsibility: Worldwide
  Naval component: Military Sealift Command (MSC).

U.S. Special Operations Command (USSOCOM or SOCOM)
Operations conducted by Special Forces (SEALs, "Green Berets," etc.) are coordinated by SOCOM through the subordinate commanders of the geographic unified commanders (PACOM, CENTCOM, etc.).
  Headquarters: MacDill Air Force Base, Tampa, Florida
  Geographic responsibility: Worldwide
  Naval component: Naval Special Warfare Command

THE NAVY

As described above, the Navy is organized in two different (but related) ways at the same time: the *operational* chain of command and the *administrative* chain of command. Depending upon where your Sailor is assigned, she or he may be part of one or both of these organizations.

The operational chain of command controls forces that are assigned to combat operations, operational readiness exercises, humanitarian relief missions, and evacuations, or are on station carrying out missions like sea control and deterrence. The administrative chain of command is what keeps the Navy functioning on a day-to-day basis so that the ships, aircraft, and so on are able to carry out operational tasks when assigned. This is the chain of command that takes care of the less colorful but essential elements of preparedness, such as training, repair, supply, personnel assignment, intelligence support, communications facilities, weather prediction, medical treatment, and so on.

Both of these chains of command have the President of the United States at the top as Commander in Chief. Below the President is the Secretary of Defense, with the Joint Chiefs of Staff as his or her principal advisors. Below SECDEF, the chains are different. For operational matters, SECDEF issues tasking orders directly to the unified commanders, and for administrative matters, SECDEF relies upon the Secretary of the Navy to keep the Navy and Marine Corps ready. The rest of these chains of command are explained below.

THE OPERATIONAL CHAIN OF COMMAND

In centuries past, naval warfare could be effectively waged more or less independently, but in the modern age the importance of joint warfare cannot be overemphasized. In the vast majority of modern operations, whether they are combat, humanitarian, readiness, deterrent, or specialized, several or all of the U.S. Armed Forces must cooperate, coordinate, and combine their forces and plans to maximize their effectiveness and ensure mission accomplishment.

The Navy's operational chain of command is headed by the appropriate unified combatant commands (COCOMs) described above. As previously mentioned, the officers commanding these COCOMs may be from any of the armed services (except the Coast Guard). The chain becomes purely naval below the COCOM with "naval component commanders" exercising operational control over one or more of the "numbered fleet commanders."

Naval Component Commanders

COCOMs have component commanders assigned to them. Once a unified commander has determined what assets (such as troops, ships, and aircraft) he or she will need to carry out a specific mission, that commander will rely upon the component commanders to provide those forces and coordinate their actions.

As already stated, this is the first level of command in the joint forces structure that is purely naval. There are a number of these naval component commands to meet the needs of the various COCOMs.

United States Pacific Fleet (USPACFLT or simply PACFLT)
This naval component commander primarily serves the naval needs of the PACOM unified commander, and the primary AOR is the same as that of PACOM (Pacific and Indian Oceans), but PACFLT also provides assets to CENTCOM, SOUTHCOM, EUCOM, and STRATCOM when required. PACFLT is headquartered at Pearl Harbor, Hawaii, and exercises control of both the 3rd and 7th Fleets.

United States Naval Forces Europe (USNAVEUR or simply NAVEUR)
From headquarters in Naples, Italy, COMUSNAVEUR plans, conducts, and supports naval operations in the European AOR during peacetime, crises, or war, answering directly to the EUCOM unified commander. He or she is supported by the Commander of the 6th Fleet and by the Commander, Navy Region Europe, also headquartered in Naples, Italy.

United States Naval Forces Central Command
(USNAVCENT or simply NAVCENT)
Serving as naval component commander for the U.S. Central Command, NAVCENT, headquartered in Bahrain, is responsible for naval activities in the Arabian Sea, Persian Gulf, Red Sea, and part of the Indian Ocean. The vice admiral in command of this component also wears a second hat as Commander of the 5th Fleet.

United States Fleet Forces Command (USFLTFORCOM
or simply FLTFORCOM)
Headquartered in Norfolk, Virginia, FLTFORCOM supports both STRATCOM and NORTHCOM as well as providing some naval support to EUCOM and CENTCOM.

United States Naval Forces Southern Command
(USNAVSO or simply NAVSO)
Headquartered at Naval Station Mayport, Florida, NAVSO's areas of operation are in South America, Central America, the Caribbean, and surrounding waters.

United States Naval Special Warfare Command
(NAVSPECWARCOM or simply NAVSOC)
Headquartered at the Naval Amphibious Base Coronado in San Diego, California, this is the naval component of the United States Special Operations Command.

United States Fleet Cyber Command/U.S. Tenth Fleet (FCC-C10F)
Headquartered at Fort Meade, Maryland, this naval component command is an operational component of the U.S. Navy Information Warfare Community and serves as the central operational authority for networks, cryptologic/signals intelligence, information operations, electronic warfare, and space capabilities in support of forces afloat and ashore.

Numbered Fleet Commanders
Commanding the ships, submarines, and aircraft that operate in direct support of the naval component commanders are vice admirals in charge of the numbered fleets. Like the component commanders, these commanders have support staffs and facilities ashore, but the numbered fleet commanders also have a flagship from which to conduct operations at sea as missions require. Individual ships, submarines, and aircraft squadrons are assigned to different fleets at different times during their operational schedules. For example, a destroyer assigned to 2nd Fleet while operating out of its homeport of Norfolk might later deploy to the 6th Fleet in the Mediterranean for several months. There are currently six numbered fleets in the U.S. Navy.

Fleet	Primary Operational Area
3rd	Eastern Pacific Ocean
4th	Caribbean, Central and South America, and surrounding waters
5th	Middle Eastern waters
6th	Mediterranean Sea
7th	Western Pacific/Indian Oceans
10th	Cyber Domain

The apparent gaps (no 1st or 2nd Fleets, for example) are a result of historical evolution rather than oversight. Numbered fleets come and go according to the current needs.

3rd Fleet

With shore headquarters in San Diego, California, 3rd Fleet operates primarily in the Eastern Pacific and supplies units on a rotational basis to 7th Fleet in the Western Pacific and Indian Oceans and to 5th Fleet in the Middle East.

4th Fleet

With shore headquarters in Mayport, Florida, 4th Fleet has operational control of those units operating in the SOUTHCOM AOR.

5th Fleet

With shore headquarters in Bahrain on the Persian Gulf, 5th Fleet has operational control of those units operating in the CENTCOM AOR.

6th Fleet

Operating in the Mediterranean Sea, 6th Fleet has both U.S. and NATO responsibilities (the latter as components of the NATO Strike and Support Forces, Southern Europe).

7th Fleet

With shore headquarters in Yokosuka, Japan, 7th Fleet is responsible for the Western Pacific and Indian Ocean. The majority of units come from 3rd Fleet on a rotational basis, but there are some permanently assigned assets in the 7th Fleet that are homeported in Japan.

10th Fleet

Fleet Cyber Command. Described above in Naval Component Commanders.

Task Organization

An entire fleet is too large to be used for most specific operations, but a particular task may require more than one ship. To better organize ships into useful groups, the Navy developed an organizational system that has been in use since World War II. Using this system, a fleet can be divided into task forces, and they can be further subdivided into task groups. If these task groups still need to be further divided, task units can be created, and they can be further subdivided into task elements.

A numbering system is used to make it clear what each of these divisions is. The 7th Fleet, for example, might be divided into two task forces numbered TF 71 and TF 72. If TF 72 needed to be divided into three separate divisions, they would be task groups numbered TG 72.1, TG 72.2, and TG 72.3. If TG 72.3 needed to be subdivided, it could be broken into task units numbered TU 72.3.1 and TU 72.3.2 (this "decimal" system might not sit well with your high school math teacher, but it works for the Navy). Further divisions of TU 72.3.1 would be elements numbered TE 72.3.1.1 and TE 72.3.1.2. This system can be used to create virtually any number of task forces, groups, units, and elements, limited only by the number of ships available.

Using the operational chain of command shown in Figure 9 we can imagine an example of how this system might work from one ship up through a COCOM. Keep in mind that this shows only one path up the chain—there would also be other ships assigned to the various task elements and units, and there might be other task components (such as a Task Element 76.1.1.2 and Task Groups 76.2 and 76.3, etc.).

In this example, USS *Fort McHenry* (LSD 43) has been tasked with delivering Marines to one of several key locations in the Pacific as part of a larger operation that is responding to a crisis. Task Force 76 shown in the figure is responsible for carrying out amphibious operations in the Pacific operating area, and the commander (CTF 76) has divided her task force into two task groups, one to cover the eastern part of her area of responsibility (TG 76.1) and the other (TG 76.2) to cover the western part. CTG 76.1 has further divided his assigned forces into two task units (TU 76.1.1 and TU 76.1.2), the first tasked with transporting Marines to a troubled area and the other made up of destroyers to protect the transport unit. There are two LSDs assigned to TU 76.1.1, and the task unit commander has designated each of them as task elements with each given a specific landing beach. The commanding officer of USS *Fort McHenry* has been designated CTE76.1.1.1 to coordinate landing the Marines in her ship onto the northern beach, and the CO of the other LSD will do the same for the southern beach.

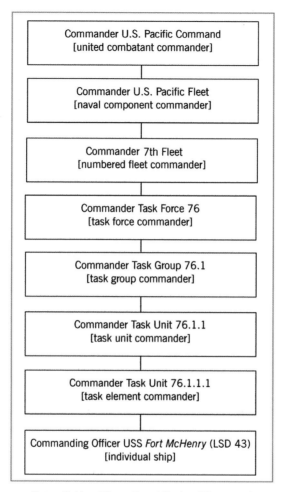

Figure 9. Naval Operational Chain of Command

THE ADMINISTRATIVE CHAIN OF COMMAND

As mentioned above, there is a chain of command within the Navy that is parallel to the operational one; this one involves many (but not all) of the same people who "wear more than one hat" in order to carry out functions within each chain. The administrative chain is concerned with readiness more than execution, focusing on such vital matters as manning, training, and supply, so that the operating forces are prepared to carry out those missions assigned by the operational chain of command.

Secretary of the Navy

SECNAV has an Undersecretary of the Navy as his or her direct assistant and, as can be seen in Figure 10, there are several Assistant Secretaries of the Navy to handle specific administrative areas of the Navy.

In addition to these civilian assistants, SECNAV also has a number of military assistants, such as the Navy's Judge Advocate General, the Naval Inspector General, and the Chief of Information. Other military officers answer directly to SECNAV's civilian assistants, such as the Chief of Naval Research who reports to the Assistant Secretary of the Navy for Research, Development, and Acquisition, and the Auditor General who reports to the Undersecretary of the Navy.

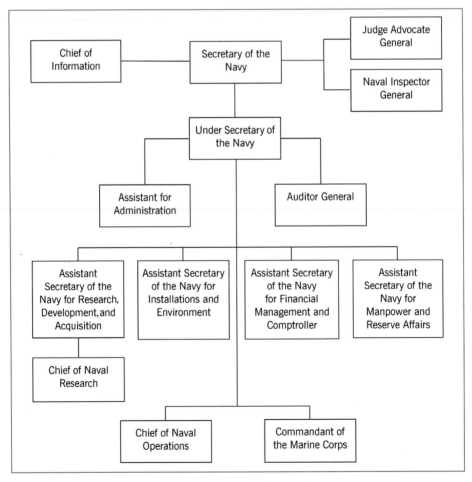

Figure 10. The Secretary of the Navy and his or her assistants

Chief of Naval Operations

Reporting directly to SECNAV is the Chief of Naval Operations. The CNO is the senior military officer in the Navy and as such, he or she is a member of the JCS (discussed above) and is also the principal advisor to the President and to SECDEF for naval matters. The CNO is a four-star admiral and is responsible to SECNAV for the manning, training, maintaining, and equipping of the Navy, as well as its operating efficiency. Despite the name, he or she is not in the operational chain of command.

Office of the Chief of Naval Operations (OPNAV)

Collectively, the CNO's staff is commonly referred to as "the Navy Staff" or "OPNAV" (derived from "operations of the Navy," but is better thought of as simply the "Office of the Chief of Naval Operations"). OPNAV also assists SECNAV, the undersecretary, and the assistant secretaries of the Navy.

These admirals have staffs and subordinate commanders working for them, with many of these officers identified by subordinate "N-codes" as well. For example, the vice admiral who is assigned as DCNO for Integration of Capabilities and Resources has a number of rear admirals working for him or her as N85 (Expeditionary Warfare), N86 (Surface Warfare), N87 (Submarine Warfare), N88 (Air Warfare), and so on.

There are numerous other assistants to the CNO on the OPNAV staff, such as the Special Assistant for Legislative Support (N09L), the Director of Naval Education and Training (N00T), the Surgeon General of the Navy (N093) who oversees all medical activities within the Department of the Navy, the Chief of Chaplains (N097), and the Director of Navy Reserve (N095).

The Director, Navy Staff directs OPNAV Staff Principal Officials in support of CNO executive decision-making, delivers management support to the OPNAV staff, and serves as sponsor for thirty of the Navy's most important naval commands.

Shore Establishment

In addition to the OPNAV staff, there are a number of shore commands directly under the CNO that support the Fleet, including the Office

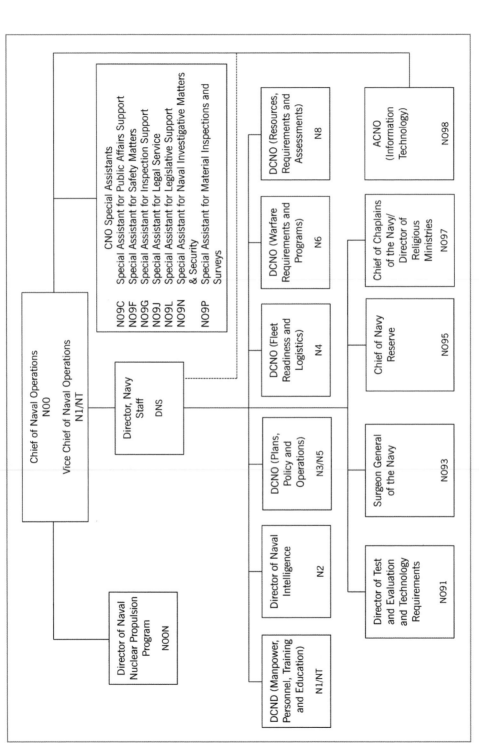

Figure 11. Office of the Chief of Naval Operations (OPNAV)

of Naval Intelligence, the Naval Security Group Command, the Naval Safety Center, the Naval Meteorology and Oceanography Command, the Naval Strike and Air Warfare Center, the Naval Legal Service Command, the Bureau of Naval Personnel, the Naval Education and Training Command, and the Bureau of Medicine and Surgery. A number of these commands are dual-hatted: for example, the head of the Bureau of Naval Personnel (known officially as the "Chief of Naval Personnel") is also the Deputy CNO for Manpower and Personnel (N1), and the Commander Naval Education and Training Command serves as a member of the OPNAV staff, advising the CNO as the Director of Naval Education and Training (N00T).

Systems Commands

There are also five systems commands that oversee many of the technical requirements of the Navy and report to the CNO and SECNAV.

Naval Sea Systems Command (NAVSEA) is the largest and serves as the central activity for the building of ships, their maintenance and repair, and the procurement of those systems and equipments necessary to keep them operational. Among its many functions and responsibilities, NAVSEA also oversees explosive ordnance safety as well as salvage and diving operations within the Navy.

Naval Air Systems Command (NAVAIR) researches, acquires, develops, and supports technical systems and components for the aviation requirements of the Navy, Marine Corps, and Coast Guard.

Space and Naval Warfare Systems Command (SPAWAR) is responsible for the Navy's command, control, communications, computer, intelligence, and surveillance systems. These systems are used in combat operations, weather and oceanographic forecasting, navigation, and space operations.

Naval Supply Systems Command (NAVSUP) provides logistic support to the Navy, ensuring that adequate supplies of ammunition, fuel, food, repair parts, and so on are acquired and distributed worldwide to naval forces.

Naval Facilities Engineering Command (NAVFAC) is responsible for the planning, design, and construction of public works, housing,

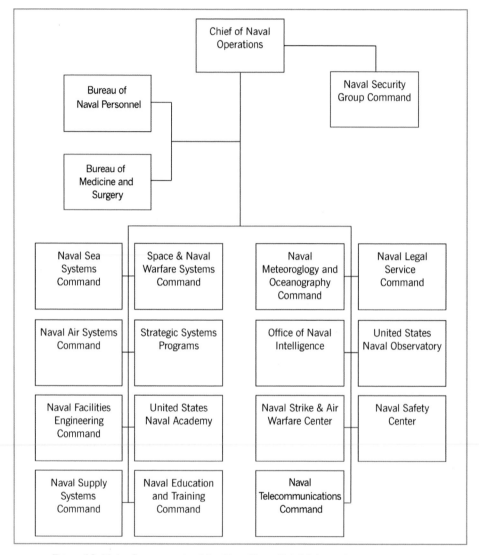

Figure 12. Major Components of the Navy Shore Establishment

and public utilities for the Navy around the world. NAVFAC manages the Navy's real estate and oversees environmental projects while keeping its bases running efficiently.

Type Commands

For administrative purposes (personnel manning, training, scheduled repairs, etc.), the Pacific and Atlantic fleets have ships and aircraft classified and organized into commands related directly to their type. These groupings are called, appropriately enough, "type commands," and there are six as follows:

- *Naval Surface Force, U.S. Atlantic Fleet (SURFLANT)* administers to the needs and ensures the readiness of all surface ships (cruisers and destroyers, as well as amphibious, service, and mine-warfare ships) assigned to the Atlantic. This type commander is known as COMNAVSURFLANT, and his or her headquarters are in Norfolk, Virginia.
- *Naval Surface Force, U.S. Pacific Fleet (SURFPAC)* administers to the needs and ensures the readiness of all surface ships assigned to the Commander of the U.S. Pacific Fleet. This type commander is known as COMNAVSURFPAC, and his or her headquarters are in San Diego, California.
- *Naval Submarine Force, U.S. Atlantic Fleet (SUBLANT)* administers to the needs and ensures the readiness of all submarines assigned to the U.S. Atlantic Fleet. This type commander is known as COMNAVSUBLANT, and his or her headquarters are in Norfolk, Virginia.
- *Naval Submarine Force, U.S. Pacific Fleet (SUBPAC)* administers to the needs and ensures the readiness of all submarines assigned to the Commander of the U.S. Pacific Fleet. This type commander is known as COMNAVSUBPAC, and his or her headquarters are in Pearl Harbor, Hawaii.
- *Naval Air Force, U.S. Atlantic Fleet (AIRLANT)* administers to the needs and ensures the readiness of all aircraft assigned to the U.S. Atlantic Fleet. This type commander is known as COMNAVAIRLANT, and his or her headquarters are in Norfolk, Virginia.
- *Naval Air Force, U.S. Pacific Fleet (AIRPAC)* administers to the needs and ensures the readiness of all aircraft assigned to the Commander of the U.S. Pacific Fleet. This type commander is known as COMNAVAIRPAC, and his or her headquarters are in North Island, California.

Even though there are separate type commanders on the different coasts, for coordination purposes, one is senior to the other and ensures compatibility of resources and procedures. For example, COMNAV-SURFLANT is a three-star admiral and COMNAVSURFPAC is a two-star, the latter in charge of surface activities in the Pacific, yet deferring to her or his counterpart on the Atlantic to ensure that the two are synchronized.

Other Components to the Administrative Chain of Command

Beneath the type commanders are group commanders, and below them are ship squadron commanders or air wing commanders. For example, below COMNAVSURFLANT is Commander Naval Surface Group 2 with Destroyer Squadrons (DESRON) 6 and 14. Do not look for any regular pattern in these numbering systems—except that components on the East Coast are generally even-numbered and components on the West Coast are odd-numbered—that is, just because Surface Group 2 has DESRONs 6 and 14 does not mean it will also have those numbers in between.

SHIP AND SQUADRON ORGANIZATION

Because the missions and number of people assigned differ for each type of ship or aircraft squadron, each one is organized differently. An aircraft carrier, for example, has more departments and divisions than a destroyer, which is much smaller and has fewer Sailors assigned. An aircraft carrier has need of an air department, but a submarine does not.

Despite these differences, all ships and squadrons have certain things in common. All commissioned ships and aircraft squadrons have a commanding officer who has overall responsibility and an executive officer who is second in command. All are divided into departments, and these are in turn subdivided into divisions.

SHIPS

Every Navy ship operates under the authority of an officer assigned by BUPERS as that ship's *commanding officer*. The CO, as she or he is sometimes known, may be a lieutenant if the vessel is small, or a captain if the ship is very large. But no matter what the rank, the commanding officer is always called "Captain."

In case of absence or death, the CO's duties are assumed by the line officer next in command, whose official title is *executive officer*. The XO, as he or she is often called, is responsible for all matters relating to personnel, ship routine, and discipline. All orders issued by the XO have the same force and effect as though they were issued by the CO.

Executive Assistants

Depending on the size of the ship, certain officers and enlisted personnel are detailed as executive assistants. All answer to the XO, but some, such as the ship's secretary, will work directly for the captain in some matters. These jobs may be full-time assignments or may be assigned to individuals as collateral, or secondary, duties, depending upon the size of the ship's crew. Some are always filled by officers, others are always by enlisted personnel, but many can be either. Even those with "officer" in the title are sometimes filled by qualified enlisted personnel. A lot depends upon the size of the command and the relative qualifications of the individuals concerned. Some examples of executive assistants are Chaplains, Career Counselors, Educational Service Officer, Legal Officer, and Safety Officer.

Departments and Divisions

Different ships have different departments, depending upon their size and mission. Commonly seen departments include engineering, operations, and supply. Ships whose primary mission is combat may have a weapons department, or it may be called combat systems on more sophisticated ships. Ships whose primary mission is logistical—involving replenishment of fuel, ammunition, or other supplies at sea—will often have a deck department.

Departments are subdivided into divisions, and divisions are often further subdivided into work centers, watches, and/or sections.

Each ship's department has a department head, an officer who is responsible for its organization, training, and performance. The larger the ship, the more senior the department head will be. In a destroyer the department head is often a senior lieutenant, while in aircraft carriers department heads are usually commanders or lieutenant commanders.

Departments are often divided into divisions and have a division officer responsible for them. The division is the basic working unit of the Navy. It may consist of twenty specialists on small ships or as many as several hundred persons in an aircraft carrier. The division officer is the boss; he or she reports to the department head and is frequently a junior officer but can be a chief petty officer or a more senior petty officer if the situation calls for it. The division officer is the one officer with whom division personnel come into contact every day. The division chief and the leading petty officer are the division officer's principal assistants. Larger divisions may have more than one chief assigned and may even have other junior officers assigned as assistants.

AIRCRAFT SQUADRONS

Operating squadrons, like ships, have a CO, an XO, department heads, and division officers.

The CO, also known as the squadron commander and, less formally, as "the Skipper," has the usual duties and responsibilities of any captain insofar as they are applicable to an aircraft squadron. These include issuing operational orders to the squadron as well as looking after morale, discipline, readiness, and efficiency.

The executive officer (XO), the second senior naval aviator in the squadron, is the direct representative of the CO. The XO sees that the squadron is administered properly and that the CO's orders are carried out. The executive officer, as second in command, will take over command of the squadron whenever the CO is not present.

Operational squadrons are organized into several departments, each with its own department head who is responsible for organization, training, personnel assignments, departmental planning and operations, security, safety, cleanliness of assigned areas, and maintenance of records and reports. Just as in ships, the number and functions of departments vary somewhat according to the squadron's mission. Most squadrons have at least four departments: operations, administration, maintenance, and safety. Many have a training department as well.

COMPLICATED BUT FUNCTIONAL

As you can see from the above, the Navy's organization is indeed complicated, but considering all that must be done to keep the world's most powerful Navy ready and able to carry out a very wide variety of missions, that organization is capable of meeting the many needs of the Fleet as it serves the much larger defense establishment that guards the nation's vital interests and keeps America safe.

N-codes and task unit designations with multiple decimal points may seem intimidating at first, but those who operate within them are soon comfortable with it all. Once your Sailor is assigned to a specific command somewhere in that vast organization, you can rather quickly learn those parts of the chains of command that are important to him or her, and you will soon be using the Navy's alphabet soup of terminology with the best of them.

6 NAVY TITLES

This chapter will help you understand the many titles that Navy people have and how to recognize these titles in the various alphanumeric designations that are often used to identify them. You will learn the rank structures, what the differences are in such things as ranks and billets, what are warfare specialties, and, more practically, how to properly address Navy people, both in person and in writing.

SAILOR

Arleigh Burke, one of the Navy's most famous and revered admirals, sent a powerful message to his Navy when, despite his *many* titles and qualifications, he had "Sailor" prominently placed after his name on his granite tombstone in the U.S. Naval Academy cemetery.

As explained in Chapter 1, everyone in uniform in the U.S. Navy is a Sailor, no matter what his or her rank, gender, or occupational or warfare specialty. Although you may see it in lower case outside the Navy (and sometimes, mistakenly, within) the term is properly capitalized within the Navy. This is a result of decree (by the Secretary of the Navy) and by practice, and is meant to distinguish this term from more common uses in other contexts. A person enjoying an outing on a sailboat is a "sailor"; your son or daughter who is serving in the U.S. Navy is a "Sailor."

BILLETS, RANKS, AND PAYGRADES

Among the things most alien to newcomers to the Navy are the many titles that people have. These titles fall into a number of categories, and understanding the distinctions among them can go a long way toward understanding the Navy (and the other services for that matter). Most people understand the concept of military "rank." One encounters its use in movies or television for example, where *generals* or *admirals* advise the president on how best to deal with a crisis, or *sergeants* and *lieutenants* share a quiet moment in a foxhole to talk of home just before the big battle begins.

While the military services share the term and the usage of ranks, they do not all use the same titles for each. A *major* in the Army, Air Force, and Marine Corps is a *lieutenant commander* in the Navy and Coast Guard. And, even more confusing, all the services use the title of *captain* but in very different ways.

Generally less understood than ranks are the terms "billet" and "paygrade," as well as a number of other related ones, such as "warfare specialty," "rate," and "rating."

BILLETS

To begin with, it is important to distinguish between a "billet" and a rank. A billet in the Navy is a current assignment and is much like a job title elsewhere in the world. Just as the head of a corporation might be called a "chief executive officer," so a military person might be called a "chief" (as in "Chief of Naval Operations") or a "commander" (as in "Commander 7th Fleet"). Some examples of other billet titles (among thousands) in the Navy are "Work Center Supervisor," "Combat Systems Officer," "Leading Seaman," "Executive Officer," "Deck Division Chief," "Ship's Secretary," and "G Division Officer."

One thing that distinguishes the military services from corporate America is that military people also have ranks in addition to their billets. Those who have worked in the federal government as civilians will find the idea of ranks a little less alien because of the "GS" (General

Schedule) system that gives a government employee a GS rating, establishing what that person will be paid and placing him or her within a hierarchy of relative authority and responsibility. Ranks in the military are similar but with some notable differences. For one thing, people in the government have to ask to learn of another's GS rating, whereas military personnel wear their ranks on their sleeves, collars, or shoulders. But like GS ratings, ranks denote a person's ability to take on responsibility and authority, and they also determine paygrades (as explained below).

All of this is to say that a newcomer to the Navy should be aware that billets and ranks are related. A person might need the *rank* of lieutenant in order to be eligible to fill a specific *billet*, such as being the weapons officer on a particular kind of ship, but the two are also separate in their own ways.

There are thousands and thousands of billets in the Navy just as there are many job titles in any large company. But there are a much smaller number of ranks, and you will go a long way toward understanding what the Navy is all about by learning a bit about the Navy's (and the other services') ranks.

Before moving on to rank titles, one word of clarification about billets in the Navy. The heads of many units (such as ships, aircraft squadrons, etc.) are known by the generic billet title of "commanding officer." This is true of all the armed services. But, with a nod to tradition, the Navy *also* uses the term "captain" for many of these billets (as in, "He is the captain of that destroyer," or, "She is the captain of that cruiser"). But you will soon see that "captain" is also the name of a rank in the Navy (and in the other armed services as well—though at a different level). This means that the commanding officer of a destroyer might hold the rank of commander but still be called the "captain" of that ship. And the captain of an aircraft carrier usually holds the *rank* of captain as well

RANKS AND PAYGRADES

The best way to begin to understand the rank structure of the Navy is to look at Table 2. To begin with, let's look at the column marked "Paygrades." While each service has the same structure (E-1 through O-10), titles vary.

A man enlisting in the Air Force and a woman enlisting in the Navy will both have a paygrade of "E-1" even though he will have the rank of "Airman Basic" and she will be a "Seaman Recruit," but addressed as a Seaman. Paygrades are common to all the armed forces and are what determine the basic pay of a person in the military. There are E-1s through O-10s in all the armed services, though they will be called different things as we shall soon see.

Note that in the Navy there are some alternatives in title that depend upon what occupational part of the Navy the young person is slated (by desire and qualifications) to serve in. For example, a young woman who enters the Navy with a follow-on assignment after Boot Camp to attend a school in shipboard engineering and then to serve in a ship as a Gas Turbine Systems Technician will become a "Fireman Recruit" (instead of Seaman Recruit) upon entry, and her first promotion will be to Fireman Apprentice, followed by "Fireman." Those who will be working in aviation occupational specialties will be "Airman Recruits"; those who are slated to work in construction-related occupations (known popularly as "SeaBees," or "CBs," short for Construction Battalion) will be "Constructionman Recruits"; and those who will be working in medical or dental occupations will be "Hospitalman Recruits."

Note also that the term "Petty Officer" can be replaced with the individual's rating title (see Enlisted Rates and Ratings later in this chapter).

Although you will occasionally hear someone say something like, "oh, she may be an E-3 but she deserves to be an E-4," such references to paygrade are rare and are more appropriate when discussing money matters than those of relative authority and responsibility. In those cases, ranks are the appropriate terms.

Each paygrade comes with an accompanying title that is the individual's rank. In the U.S. Navy, Sailors in paygrades E1 through E3 are addressed as "Seaman," E4 through E6 are called "Petty Officer Third/Second/First Class" as appropriate, and Senior enlisted in paygrades E7 through E9 are "Chief," "Senior Chief," or "Master Chief" Petty Officer depending on their paygrades.

Table 2. Navy Paygrades and Ranks

PAYGRADE	RANKS
O-10	Admiral
O-9	Vice Admiral
O-8	Rear Admiral (Upper Half)
O-7	Rear Admiral (Lower Half)
O-6	Captain
O-5	Commander
O-4	Lieutenant Commander
O-3	Lieutenant
O-2	Lieutenant (Junior Grade)
O-1	Ensign
W-5	Chief Warrant Officer
W-4	Chief Warrant Officer
W-3	Chief Warrant Officer
W-2	Chief Warrant Officer
W-1	Warrant Officer (Not currently in use.)
E-9	Master Chief Petty Officer
E-8	Senior Chief Petty Officer
E-7	Chief Petty Officer
E-6	Petty Officer First Class
E-5	Petty Officer Second Class
E-4	Petty Officer Third Class
E-3	Seaman
E-2	Seaman Apprentice
E-1	Seaman Recruit

Officers and Enlisted

Looking at Table 2, it might at first seem obvious that Sailors would start at the bottom (E-1) upon entering the Navy and move up through the various levels until they either reach the top or leave the Navy for another career or retire. But it is not that simple! Note that the table does not go from E-1 at the bottom to E-something at the top. Instead, it shifts from "E" to "W" and "O" scales along the way. This is because the Navy (like all the services) has enlisted Sailors and officer Sailors (with warrant officers in between in all but one of the services).

As explained in Chapter 1, in earlier times—before the United States of America changed the world with its successful democracy—the militaries of Europe differentiated between officers and enlisted based upon social class. Even though our Army and Navy were modeled after the armies and navies of Europe, this class system was obviously not going to work in a democratic America. Instead of relying on social class as the major criterion for distinguishing between officers and enlisted personnel, education became the standard.

With the above in mind, a young man fresh out of high school who decides that he wants to serve in the Navy would enter the service (enlist is the proper term) with the paygrade of E-1. After completing Boot Camp, he would be promoted to E-2 and subsequently move up through the enlisted paygrades (E-3, E-4, and so on). A young woman fresh out of college on the other hand might want to enter the Navy as an officer because of her advanced education, beginning her service as an Ensign with a paygrade of O-1. She could then move up through the officer ranks as a Lieutenant (Junior Grade) (O-2), then a Lieutenant (O-3), and upward. In a "normal" career, the young man who enlisted in the Navy could aspire to make Master Chief Petty Officer (E-9) in a very successful career. The young woman could reasonably hope to become an Admiral in her very successful career.

Keep in mind that there are many exceptions to this simple pattern I have described. One exception is that a person may enter the service with a college degree but may prefer to be enlisted rather than become an officer. Another exception is that some young men and women who have demonstrated the appropriate potential may receive appointments to the U.S. Naval Academy, in which case they will enter the service without a college degree but will earn one at the Academy and become O-1 upon graduation. There are also many ways that enlisted Sailors can become officers part way through their careers. One example is the Seaman to Admiral Program (explained in Chapter 2), which selects enlisted Sailors (with the right qualifications and desire) to earn a college degree at the Navy's expense and then become officers upon graduation.

People who join the Navy as enlisted personnel are said to have "enlisted" in the Navy, but those who join the Navy as officers are said to be "commissioned." For example, "Seaman Knott enlisted in the Navy fresh out of a Baltimore high school and Lieutenant Shipp was commissioned after receiving her degree from Norwich University."

Warrant Officers

Enlisted Sailors who are recognized as exceptionally proficient in their Navy occupations may be promoted to "Warrant Officer." These are indicated as W-1 through W-5 paygrades in Table 2. For complicated reasons the Navy no longer uses the W-1 paygrade; Sailors selected to be warrant officers go directly to W-2 (Chief Warrant Officer) and then move up to W-3, and so on.

SPECIALTIES

The complexities of modern warfare and advancements in technology often dictate that Navy personnel have specialties in addition to their ranks. Many billets require these specialties in addition to designated levels of rank. These can be occupational specialties, such as electronics or gunnery, or they can be warfare specialties, such as aviators and submariners. In virtually all cases, additional training is required to acquire these specialties, ranging from specialized skill training (such as for pilots and medical technicians) to advanced degrees for lawyers and chaplains.

ENLISTED RATES AND RATINGS

Though the Navy uses ranks like the other armed services, it also uses the additional terms "rate" and "rating" in distinctive ways. *Rates* are similar to ranks and are the titles used to describe the various levels of paygrade for enlisted Sailors, while *ratings* are used to describe Sailors' occupational specialties. Where this becomes a bit confusing is that *rate* actually combines paygrade with ratings.

Ratings have specific names—like "Gunner's Mate" or "Gas Turbine Systems Technician" or "Equipment Operator"—and each has a specific symbol that is worn on the uniform as part of the rating badge. See Appendix E for more information.

As technology changed over the years, ratings likewise changed, and the number of ratings varied as occupational needs changed; for example, there once was a "Sailmaker" rating, but that was discontinued once Navy ships gave up their sails for more modern propulsion systems. Many ratings are obvious by their titles, such as "Intelligence Specialist," "Air Traffic Controller," and "Musician." But others—like "Quartermaster" (navigation specialist)—are less so. Some can be misleading, such as "Fire Control Technician," which one might surmise refers to a firefighter but is actually a person who controls the firing of guns or missiles. Firefighting specialists in the Navy are "Damage Controlmen."

When a person's rating is combined with his paygrade, the result is his "rate." For example, when a Sailor is promoted to E-4 (Petty Officer Third Class) and her rating is "Gunner's Mate," her *rate* is Gunner's Mate Third Class. When promoted to E-5, she becomes a Gunner's Mate Second Class.

Once a Sailor has achieved his occupational specialty (rating), he is said to be "rated"; those Sailors who have not are described as "nonrated." A Sailor cannot be a petty officer without also having a rating, so we can deduce that all petty officers are rated.

WARFARE SPECIALTIES

Another "title" common to many Sailors is their warfare specialty, obtained through an additional qualification process involving schooling, practical experience, or a combination of both. Both officers and enlisted Sailors may have one or more of these specialties. These are in addition to, and independent of, their paygrade and rank. Some—but not all—of these specialties are surface warfare, air warfare, submarine warfare, and special warfare. Enlisted Sailors append identifying letters in parentheses after their ranks; for example, "PO3 (SW) John P. Jones USN." Some examples of identifying letters are "SW" for surface warfare, "AW" for air warfare, and "SS" for submarine warfare. Both officers and enlisted personnel wear metal pins on the breasts of their uniforms that identify these specialties.

ADDITIONAL OFFICER SPECIALTIES

Officers can be roughly divided into two groups: *line* and *staff*. Line officers are those who are eligible for command at sea; they command or may someday command ships, submarines, or aircraft squadrons. Staff officers fill important support functions as doctors, lawyers, chaplains, supply corps officers, and more.

The term "line officer" stems from the days of sail when groups of ships would form lines of battle to face each other in combat. The officers who commanded—or aspired to command—these ships were referred to as line officers. Staff officers were those who were less likely to be on the line of battle but would instead support the Fleet in other important ways.

Line officers do not append their warfare specialties to their names, but *staff* officers do (such as "SC" for Supply Corps, "CHC" for Chaplain Corps, and "JAG" for Judge Advocate General [lawyer], etc.). For example, a lawyer would be "LT Clarence Darrow, JAG, USN."

ADDRESSING SAILORS

There are "rules" for addressing Sailors in the Navy. Let's begin by expanding Table 2 a bit and call it Table 3. Keeping this table handy and referring to it for a while will eventually lead to your using these forms of address as second nature. As with Table 2, we see the pay-grades (E-1 through E-9, W-1 through W-5, and O-1 through O-10) and the names of the ranks and rates. But this table has some additional useful features.

The "Abbreviations" column lists the proper abbreviations of the ranks *as they are used by the Navy*. Be aware that you will see other abbreviations used elsewhere; for example, civilian book publishers do not like to use all capital letters because they feel it is distracting on a printed page, and though the Navy's abbreviations have a certain military logic to them, they are not always clear to people not familiar with the Navy. As a result, you will often see such things as "Lt. Cmdr." (instead of LCDR), or "Vice Adm." (instead of VADM), or "Smn." (instead of SN). But when dealing with or within the Navy, you will

Table 3. Navy Paygrades, Ranks/Ratings, Abbreviations, Salutations, and Forms of Address

PAYGRADE	RANKS/RATINGS	ABBREVIATIONS[a]	DEAR—[b]	DIRECT ADDRESS[c]
O-11	Fleet Admiral	FADM	Not currently in use.	
O-10	Admiral	ADM	Admiral	Admiral
O-9	Vice Admiral	VADM	Admiral	Admiral
O-8	Rear Admiral (Upper Half)	RADM	Admiral	Admiral
O-7	Rear Admiral (Lower Half)	RDML	Admiral	Admiral
O-6	Captain	CAPT	Captain	Captain
O-5	Commander	CDR	Commander	Commander
O-4	Lieutenant Commander	LCDR	Commander	Commander
O-3	Lieutenant	LT	Lieutenant	Lieutenant
O-2	Lieutenant (Junior Grade)	LTJG	Lieutenant	Lieutenant
O-1	Ensign	ENS	Ensign	Ensign
W-5	Chief Warrant Officer	CWO5	Chief Warrant Officer	Warrants are usually addressed by their specialty; as in "Boatswain," "Gunner," etc.
W-4	Chief Warrant Officer	CWO4	Chief Warrant Officer	
W-3	Chief Warrant Officer	CWO3	Chief Warrant Officer	
W-2	Chief Warrant Officer	CWO2	Chief Warrant Officer	
W-1	Warrant Officer	Not currently in use.		
E-9	Master Chief Petty Officer of the Navy	MCPON	MCPON	MCPON (pronounced "mick-pon")
"	Fleet Master Chief Petty Officer	FLTCM	Fleet Master Chief	Fleet
"	Force Master Chief Petty Officer	FORCM	Force Master Chief	Force

Table 3. (*continued*)

PAYGRADE	RANKS/RATINGS	ABBREVIATIONS[a]	DEAR—[b]	DIRECT ADDRESS[c]
"	Command Master Chief Petty Officer	CMDCM	Command Master Chief	Master Chief
"	Master Chief Petty Officer	MCPO	Master Chief	Master Chief
E-8	Senior Chief Petty Officer	SCPO	Senior Chief	Senior
E-7	Chief Petty Officer	CPO	Chief	Chief
E-6	Petty Officer First Class	PO1	Petty Officer	Petty Officer
E-5	Petty Officer Second Class	PO2	Petty Officer	Petty Officer
E-4	Petty Officer Third Class	PO3	Petty Officer	Petty Officer
E-3	Seaman	SN	Seaman[d]	Seaman[d]
E-2	Seaman Apprentice	SA	Seaman[d]	Seaman[d]
E-1	Seaman Recruit	SA	Seaman[d]	Seaman[d]

a Use the "Abbreviation" column for addressees on letters and envelopes (e.g., "LCDR Stephen Decatur USN").

b Use the "Dear" column (followed by person's surname) for salutations and introductions (e.g., "Dear Commander Decatur").

c Use the "Address" column when addressing someone directly (e.g., "Good morning, Commander," or, "Force, the admiral wants to see you on the flag bridge").

d Note that, depending upon the occupational specialty, "Seaman" is replaced with "Fireman," "Airman," "Constructionman," or "Hospitalman."

have more credibility if you use the Navy's versions of abbreviations as shown in Table 3. These abbreviations are used fairly often in the Navy on official forms or in documents. They are also used on the outside envelope when addressing letters to people in the Navy.

If you were going to send a letter to Seaman Grace Smith, you would write her name on the outside of the envelope as "SN Grace Smith, USN." Inside the letter, you should again use the Navy abbreviation in the address part of the letter, but in the salutation, you should use the spelled-out form provided in Table 3's column labeled "Dear—." See the example below:

30 August 2016

SN Grace Smith, USN
USS Ronald Reagan (CVN 76)
FPO AP 96616-2876

Dear Seaman Smith:

Your copy of *The Bluejacket's Manual* was found in this
office and is enclosed.

Sincerely,

J. Q. Adams

John Q. Adams

The last column in Table 3 ("Direct Address") tells you how you
should address a Sailor in polite conversation, as in, "Good morning,
Captain Halsey," or, "Chief Williams, would you please explain why
you have all those stripes on your lower left sleeve?"

When introducing a Sailor to someone else, you should use his
or her full title the first time but then use the "direct address" form
from then on. For example: "Doctor Thomas Dooley, this is Lieutenant
Commander Stephen Decatur. Commander Decatur is headed for the
Mediterranean next month."

Note that these addresses are mostly logical and simple, but there
are a few quirks. In most cases, brevity rules. Lieutenant Commander
becomes simply "Commander," for example. Note, however, that you
should not address a Senior Chief Petty Officer as "Chief" and that
"Master Chief Petty Officer" does not become "Master."

Keep in mind that chief petty officers are always referred to in that
order, never "Petty Officer Chief." But you may (particularly when in
less formal circumstances) drop the "petty officer" part. For example,
the following is correct: "This is Chief Petty Officer Jane Jones. Chief
Jones and Senior Chief Smith were shipmates together in USS *Independence* back before they were promoted to chief."

Another complicating factor is that, as we have seen, enlisted Sailors have rates as well as paygrades so that a Sailor can, for example, be a Petty Officer Third Class and a Gunner's Mate Third Class at the same time.

To make this clearer, let's focus on a young petty officer third class and call him "Christopher Garrett." We know from Tables 2 and 3 that a Sailor who has attained the paygrade of E-4 is a Petty Officer Third Class. And we know that to be a petty officer, he also must have a specialty occupation known as a rating. Let's assume that he is a sharp Sailor and has already attained his warfare qualification in surface warfare. All of that means that he would sign an official log book or appear on a formal document as

GM3 (SW) Christopher Garrett USN

But in addressing him, you can look at all that alphabet soup and know that simply calling him "Petty Officer Garrett" is all you need to do.

The warfare qualification "SW" always appears in parentheses after the name and can be ignored for all intents and purposes. Though it is important to young Garrett and something he is rightfully proud of, it has no bearing on how you communicate with him.

The "USN" after his name simply indicates that he is in the Navy as opposed to one of the other services, all of which are logical and easily deciphered: USA for Army; USMC for Marine Corps; USCG for Coast Guard; and USAF for Air Force.

The tricky part is the "GM3" before his name. And if you understand that the "GM" signifies his rating, all you need focus on is the "3" to know that he is a Petty Officer Third Class. That is all you really need to know to be able to properly address him. The fact that "GM" stands for "Gunner's Mate" is nice to know—and certainly important to him—but it is not necessary knowledge for you to be able to answer a letter from him or to greet him properly in person.

What does all this mean? Simply that *the "3" is really the only clue you need.*

If he sent you a letter a year later and identified himself as "GM2 (SW, AW) Christopher Garrett USN," you would repeat all the alphabet soup on the outside of the envelope and in the address part of your response to him, but you still need only focus on the "2" to know that he still should be addressed as "Dear Petty Officer Garrett" in the salutation.

And if a young woman sends you a letter and signs it "AE1 (SW) Rachel Alexander USN," all you would need to focus on is the numeral "1" to know that you should answer her letter "Dear Petty Officer Alexander."

Bottom line: if you see a 1, 2, or 3 in a person's alphabet soup, you may address him or her simply as "Petty Officer" followed by his or her last name.

It may help to know that *almost* all ratings are signified by two letters, so you would expect to see two letters before the numeral in a person's name. Unfortunately, there are a few ratings that are signified by three letters, rather than merely two, so don't let it throw you if you see something like "ABF3 Reuben James USN." You do not need to know that he is an "Aviation Boatswain's Mate (Fuels)," only that he is a petty officer.

Having mastered E-4 through E-6 in Table 3, we can move up to E-7 through E-9. As a few more years pass and Christopher Garrett continues to be promoted, he reaches E-7; referring to Table 3, we see that he is now a "Chief Petty Officer" and his official name now becomes

GMC (SW, AW) Christopher Garrett USN

As before, his rating ("GM") is virtually irrelevant for our purposes, and the pertinent clue is found following those initial letters. But now we see that he has traded his numbers for a "C" to symbolize his new position and title. Now we must be sure to recognize his achievement by calling him "Chief Petty Officer Garrett," or simply "Chief Garrett." Bottom line, if you see a "C" at the end, he or she should be addressed as "Chief."

Once Chief Garrett is promoted to E-8, we know from Table 3 that he is now a Senior Chief Petty Officer. If you think that the logical thing to do would be to add an "S," you would be correct, *but beware*: the "S" is appended *after* the "C," not before. Now, Garrett becomes

GMCS (SW, AW) Christopher Garrett USN

The bottom line here is that if you see the letters "CS" at the end of the initial portion, you know that individual is an E-8 and is properly addressed as "Senior Chief Garrett."

Promotion to E-9 makes a person a "Master Chief Petty Officer." The "logic" applied to senior chiefs is continued to master chiefs. Senior Chief Garrett becomes

GMCM (SW, AW) Christopher Garrett USN

The "M" indicates master and follows the "C." So when you see the letters "CM" at the end of the initial portion, you know that individual is an E-9 and is properly addressed as "Master Chief Garrett."

Now one last bit of potential confusion, and then some simplification. Nonrated Sailors (E-1 through E-3) who achieve certain milestones—such as successful completion of a school in their chosen rating—are known as "strikers." In Navy parlance, they are "striking for" a certain rating. If they are formally designated as strikers, they combine the appropriate letters (of the rating) to the ones that describe their paygrades. For example, let's say that young Garrett graduates from Boot Camp and is promoted to E-2 (Seaman Apprentice). At that point, he would be "SA Christopher Garrett USN." After Boot Camp, he goes to what the Navy calls a Class "A" School to learn the skills of a Gunner's Mate. Upon successful completion of the school, he is formally designated a Gunner's Mate striker. At that point he becomes "GMSA Christopher Garrett USN." When next promoted, he will become "GMSN Christopher Garrett USN." He still will be considered "nonrated" but will also be recognized as a striker.

Just as with the petty officers and chief petty officers, all you really need to look for are some key letters. If you see an "SA" or an "SN," either standing alone or after some other letters, you know that Sailor should be addressed as "Seaman." Someone with an "FA" or "FN" should be addressed as "Fireman." The appropriate address for "AA" and "AN" is "Airman." "CA" and "CN" are called "Constructionman," and "HA" and "HN" are "Hospitalman." So if you encountered "AEAN Rachel Alexander USN," you would know that you should call her "Airman Alexander," because of the letters "AN" (you may ignore the letters "AE," which signify that she is striking for Aviation Electrician's Mate). Once she is promoted to E-4, she will become an Aviation Electrician's Mate Third Class (AE3 Rachel Alexander USN), and remembering the clues explained earlier, you would now call her simply "Petty Officer Alexander."

There are a few other "quirks" you should be aware of. There is only one Master Chief Petty Officer of the Navy, and he or she is the most senior enlisted Sailor in the Navy. He or she is referred to as "the MCPON" and is often addressed as "MCPON." As indicated in the table, this is pronounced "mick-pon" ("pon" rhyming with "John," not "loan").

Note that there are also multiple forms of E-9 and that their addresses require a little extra attention. This is a case where billets and ranks overlap a bit. A master chief petty officer who is assigned as the principal enlisted advisor to the commanding officer of a ship or some other unit would take on the title of "Command Master Chief Petty Officer"— more frequently referred to as simply "the Command Master Chief." A master chief who has been assigned as the principal enlisted advisor to a fleet commander would be the "Fleet Master Chief."

I have included the rank of "Fleet Admiral" in Table 3 because it technically exists and was once used. In World War II, Admirals Leahy, King, Nimitz, and Halsey were promoted to Fleet Admiral (also known as "five-star Admiral"), but no one has been given that rank since.

Note that a newly promoted admiral becomes a "Rear Admiral (Lower Half)" and if later promoted would become a "Rear Admiral (Upper Half)." These odd titles are compromises reached after years of trying different titles. An O-7 was a "Commodore" during World

War II; at one time, O-7s and O-8s both had the title of "Rear Admiral" with no distinctions in title; and for a while an O-7 was called a "Commodore Admiral." The titles in Table 3 are the correct ones at this time. A good-natured rear admiral (lower half) who had just received word that he had been promoted to rear admiral (upper half) quipped, "That's great news. Now I can wear my shoulder boards on my shoulders instead of my hips!"

One last clarification. As noted above, "Commodore" was a rank in the Navy for a time. Though that has changed, you may still encounter the term; but if you do, be aware that it is probably associated with a billet rather than a rank. This comes about when an officer who is not an admiral is given command of a group of ships, such as a destroyer squadron. Each ship has its own commanding officer (also known as "Captain" as explained earlier), so to avoid confusion (and to grant a degree of honor), the officer in charge of the group of ships is called the "Commodore." She or he may hold the rank of "captain" but is referred to as "Commodore" by virtue of commanding more than one ship.

SUMMARY

Navy titles can be confusing, to be sure. They are a blend of military and nautical tradition that has evolved—and is still evolving—as technology and culture change. Below are some basic things to remember that will help you remain conversant with your Sailor.

- "Sailor" is a generic term that applies to *all* Navy uniformed personnel (officer and enlisted).
- Military personnel have both *billets* (current jobs) and *ranks* (qualified levels that grant pay, authority, and responsibility).
- All military personnel have *paygrades,* and although the pay at each level is the same for all services, different services use different names (ranks) to identify each paygrade.
- There are *enlisted* (E-1 through E-9) and *officer* (O-1 through O-10) paygrades in all the services. Warrant officers (W-1 through W-5) come between the officer and enlisted ranks.

- In the Navy enlisted personnel have ratings and rates. Although they are confusingly similar, ratings are occupational specialties (such as "Gunner's Mate") and rates are combinations of pay-grades and ratings (as in "Gunner's Mate Second Class").
- Both officers and enlisted personnel can have warfare specialties that identify them as qualified in such specialties as air, surface, and submarine warfare.
- Officers are either *line* (eligible for command at sea) or *staff* (providing important support services as doctors, lawyers, chaplains, and the like).

7 READING UNIFORMS

Uniforms—defined as the clothes worn by military personnel and the various accoutrements that go on them—serve a variety of purposes: identification (as someone in the armed services), standardization (as belonging to a specific service), differentiation (as a means of establishing where one fits in the hierarchy of the service), and recognition (of individual achievements). In civilian life, we often make reasonable assumptions about people based upon their attire—what they are wearing and where they are wearing it. Though this is not a foolproof system, noting that a person is wearing a three-piece suit or sweat pants or cowboy boots can often lead us to some reasonable conclusions about that individual. The same is true with military uniforms, even though the reasons are a bit different. Being able to "read" military uniforms can be most helpful when you are surrounded by them.

Once you become familiar with some of the characteristics and the variations in uniforms, you will be able to tell a great deal about individuals simply by observing what they are wearing. This makes for smoother professional relations and can serve as a good vehicle to social conversation: "I see you are an aviator; what kind of aircraft do you fly?"

One difference you will be able to see is whether a person is an officer or enlisted. A closer look may tell you such things as what the person's rank is, how many years he or she has served in the Navy, what her or his occupational specialty is, and whether or not he or she has had any special assignments in the Navy or has achieved any special qualifications. If you are really good at reading uniforms, you will be able to tell some of the places in which a person has served and whether or not he or she has received special recognition while serving in one or more billets.

After you have absorbed the material in this chapter, you will be able to meet a woman in uniform and, without a spoken word between you, tell that she is a petty officer second class with at least four years of service, that she has been on sea duty, and that she has been to the Middle East at least once. Even the great detective Sherlock Holmes might be impressed by that kind of deduction!

There are a great many variations of uniform worn by all service members, depending upon where they are, what they are doing, and what time of year it is. There are uniforms designed for heavy-duty working aboard ship, others more appropriate for working ashore in an office, still others for ceremonial occasions, some for very formal evening wear, and nearly all have variations depending upon seasonal conditions.

OFFICERS

Though there is no quick, absolute way to tell officers by their uniforms, there are clues.

RANK DEVICES

The most reliable way to tell if an individual is an officer is by the actual device worn somewhere on the uniform that tells you his or her specific rank.

Keep in mind that rank indications can appear in different places on the uniform, depending upon which uniform is being worn.

Among the various rank indicators worn by officers, collar devices are the ones common to all (though not worn on every uniform). When worn, these are the same for all officers of all services, although they do actually appear slightly different in some instances (for example, Army collar devices are noticeably larger than those worn by the other services). Whether the lowest ranking officers are called "ensigns" in the Navy and Coast Guard or "second lieutenants" in the other services, they will wear gold bars on their collars (if the particular uniform they are wearing requires a collar device). If you see a person wearing a gold bar anywhere on his or her uniform, you can be sure he or she is an officer with the paygrade of O-1.

Strangely, the military puts silver above gold in its rank devices. So even though an O-2 (lieutenant junior grade or first lieutenant, depending upon the service) outranks an O-1, the collar device of the O-2 is silver, whereas that of the O-1 is gold. This occurs again at the O-4 (lieutenant commander or major) and O-5 levels, where the commander or lieutenant colonel wears a silver oak leaf and the more junior O-4 wears a gold one.

Although I have been referring to these as collar devices for simplicity, they are also worn on the shoulders at various times and on some caps or hats. The size of these devices will vary accordingly.

NAVY AND COAST GUARD SLEEVES AND SHOULDER BOARDS

Navy and Coast Guard officers have some additional ways of wearing their ranks. Gold stripes are often worn by officers of these two services, either on their lower sleeves or on "shoulder boards." The various combinations of stripes determine their actual ranks. An ensign (O-1) wears a single half-inch stripe, a lieutenant junior grade (O-2) wears a half-inch plus a quarter-inch stripe, a lieutenant (O-3) wears two half-inch stripes, and so on. When these officers reach flag rank (become admirals), they keep going with the stripes on their sleeves, using combinations of one-inch and half-inch stripes, but on their shoulder boards (now gold instead of black) they wear one or more silver stars along with an anchor to show their ranks—a vice admiral having three stars, for example. You will note that there is some logic in that the number of stars on their shoulder boards matches the number of stars they wear when using collar devices.

Fleet Admiral
General of the Army/Air Force
O-10

Admiral
General
O-10

Vice Admiral
Lieutenant General
O-9

Rear Admiral (Upper Half)
Major General
O-8

Rear Admiral (Lower Half)
Brigadier General
O-7

Captain
Colonel
O-6

Commander
Lieutenant Colonel
O-5

Lieutenant Commander
Major
O-4

Lieutenant
Captain
O-3

Lieutenant Junior Grade
First Lieutenant
O-2

Ensign
Second Lieutenant
O-1

Figure 13. Officer collar devices depicting ranks

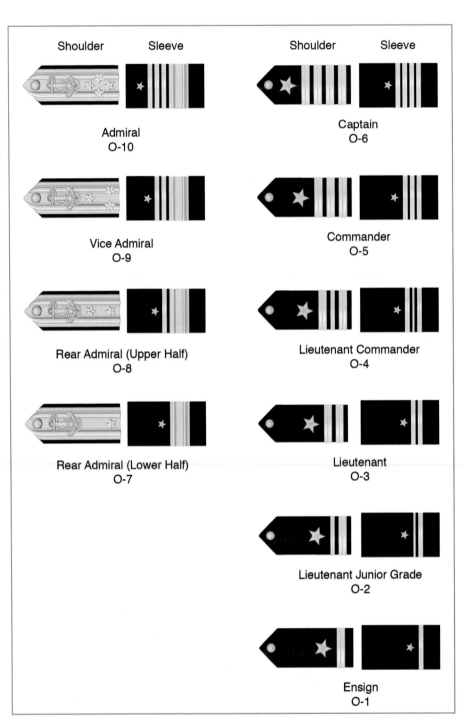

Figure 14. Officer sleeve markings and shoulder boards

STAFF VERSUS LINE OFFICERS IN THE NAVY

The majority of naval officers are *line* officers, whereas others are *staff* officers (see Chapter 6). Line officers all look alike in that, depending upon the uniform they are wearing, they all wear their rank devices on both collars or they all wear a gold star with the stripes on their lower sleeves or on their shoulder boards. Staff officers, on the other hand, have distinguishing devices that they wear on their uniforms to tell you what their specialties are. If they are wearing collar devices, these devices are worn on their left collars whereas their rank devices are on their right collars (memory aid: "Rank on Right"). If they are wearing shoulder boards or stripes on their lower sleeves, the star worn by line officers is replaced by this same specialty device.

These devices vary according to the specialty. As you become familiar with them, you will be able to tell something about these individuals without a word spoken between you. For example, if you encounter an officer with a cross on her left collar point, you can be sure she is a Christian chaplain. There are other appropriate symbols for other religions, such as tablets with a Star of David for Jewish chaplains and a crescent for Muslim chaplains.

An officer wearing a gold oak leaf with a silver acorn centered on it is a doctor; one wearing a gold oak leaf but no acorn is a nurse; one wearing a gold oak leaf and two silver acorns at the bottom is a dentist; and one wearing a gold oak leaf sprouting from a gold twig is a medical service officer. Be aware that these oak leaves are a different design from those worn as rank devices at the O-4 and O-5 levels.

Supply Corps officers wear yet another differently shaped oak leaf with three gold acorns that is traditionally called a "pork chop." Civil engineers wear a cluster of overlapping, elongated oak leaves. Lawyers wear a strange-looking device that consists of two curved gold oak leaves bracketing a silver "mill rinde" (an object that once kept stone-grinding wheels an equal distance apart and was used by sixteenth-century English lawyers to symbolize the "wheels of justice grinding exceedingly fine and even").

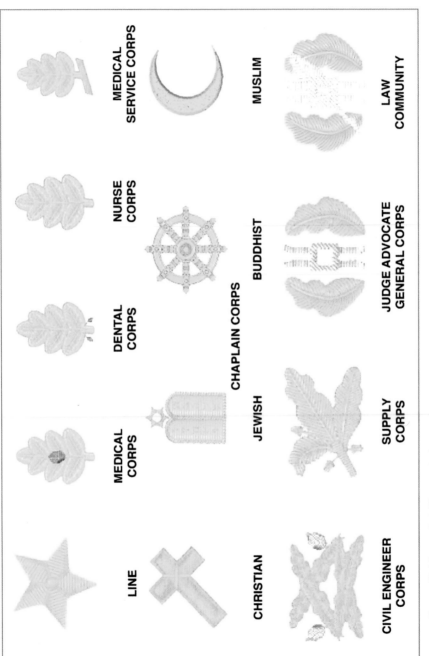

LINE

MEDICAL CORPS

DENTAL CORPS

NURSE CORPS

MEDICAL SERVICE CORPS

CHRISTIAN

JEWISH

CHAPLAIN CORPS

BUDDHIST

MUSLIM

CIVIL ENGINEER CORPS

SUPPLY CORPS

JUDGE ADVOCATE GENERAL CORPS

LAW COMMUNITY

Figure 15. Line and staff corps devices

WARRANT OFFICERS

Warrant officers in the Navy, Coast Guard, Marine Corps, and Army have their own rank devices that vary with the different services. The Navy and Coast Guard have sleeve markings, shoulder boards, and collar devices to identify their ranks, while the Marine Corps and Army have only collar devices (which, as noted above, are also sometimes worn on the shoulders in larger versions).

Warrant officers also have their own devices reflecting their specialties, such as crossed quills for "Ship's Clerk" and an L-square for a "Repair Technician" (as seen in Figure 16). In the Navy and Coast Guard, these specialty devices are worn on the shoulder boards, sleeves, and left collars.

There are no warrant officers in the Air Force.

ENLISTED PERSONNEL

Just as with officers, the most reliable way to tell enlisted personnel is by their rank devices. Familiarizing yourself with the various indications of enlisted rank is virtually foolproof but not easily done, because there are so many (there is much less commonality among the enlisted rank devices of the various services than among the officers).

If someone is wearing an indication of rank on his or her *upper* arm, that person is enlisted. This is true of all services: though enlisted personnel may wear collar devices with some uniforms, you will never see officers wearing any indication of rank on their upper arms. In the other services these upper-arm markings are worn on both arms, but in the Navy and Coast Guard, they are worn only on the left arm.

Referring to Figure 17, you can see that Navy enlisted personnel above E-3 currently wear a patch on their arms that is a combination of an eagle (more traditionally called a "crow") and one or more chevrons—a chevron looks like a flattened "V," and there is one for a petty officer third class, two for a second class, and three for a first class. Once promoted to E-7, an arch is added to the top chevron, and E-8s and E-9s use stars.

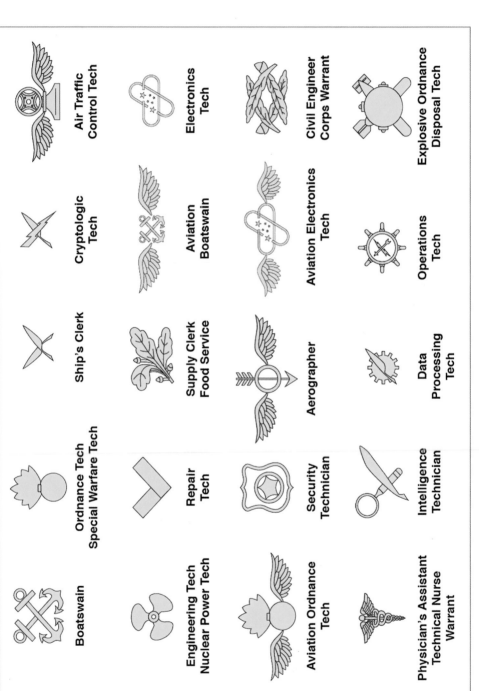

Figure 16. Some of the specialty devices worn by warrant officers in the Navy

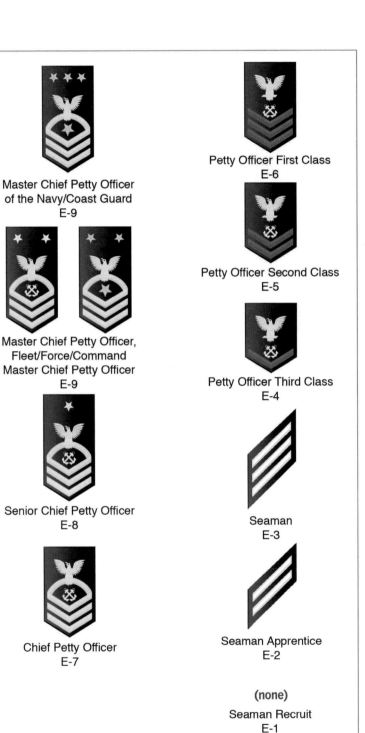

Master Chief Petty Officer
of the Navy/Coast Guard
E-9

Master Chief Petty Officer,
Fleet/Force/Command
Master Chief Petty Officer
E-9

Senior Chief Petty Officer
E-8

Chief Petty Officer
E-7

Petty Officer First Class
E-6

Petty Officer Second Class
E-5

Petty Officer Third Class
E-4

Seaman
E-3

Seaman Apprentice
E-2

(none)
Seaman Recruit
E-1

Figure 17. Navy enlisted ranks

In the Navy and Coast Guard, enlisted personnel may wear one or more long, diagonal stripes on the *lower* left forearm of some of their uniforms. Do not confuse these with the smaller diagonal stripes worn on the *upper* arm by junior enlisted personnel in both services to indicate paygrade. These longer stripes indicate years of service: one stripe for every four years of completed service. A person wearing three of these stripes has *at least* twelve years of service—but he might have as much as fifteen years, eleven months, and thirty days of service because he does not rate another stripe until another four years of service have been *completed*. In the Navy, these stripes will be dark blue on white uniforms, but they can be either red or gold on blue uniforms—the difference is these stripes go from red to gold after twelve continuous years of service with good conduct. Officers do not wear these service stripes.

OTHER SERVICE RANKS

Coast Guard ranks are similar to those of the Navy, except that they also wear a federal shield to distinguish themselves from the Navy. The Marine Corps, Army, and Air Force have their own versions of enlisted ranks as illustrated in Figures 18, 19, and 20.

RATING SYMBOLS

The Navy and Coast Guard currently are unique among the services in that enlisted personnel wear indications of their occupational specialties (called "ratings" in the Navy) on their uniforms. As explained in Chapter 6, the Navy is transitioning from using ratings when addressing each other to calling Sailors by their ranks, such as Seaman, Petty Officer Second Class, or Chief. But as of this writing, rating symbols remain a part of the enlisted ranks worn on the upper left arm. This may well change, but until it does, we must be aware of these symbols and what they mean.

In Figure 17, you see a pair of crossed anchors between the chevrons and the "crow." These are not the same for every petty officer. The crossed anchor symbol in this example represents the occupational specialty known as "boatswain's mate," one who is a specialist at seamanship, working with boats, anchoring equipment, mooring lines, and so on. If an individual has a different rating, he or she wears some other symbol in place of the crossed anchors. For example, a Gunner's Mate wears a pair of crossed cannons, and a Musician is represented by a lyre.

There are too many of these to memorize, but some familiarity with them provides some insight to an individual's occupational specialty in the Navy. Until the current system of including ratings is changed, your Sailor may proudly show you his or her rating symbol and explain it in detail.

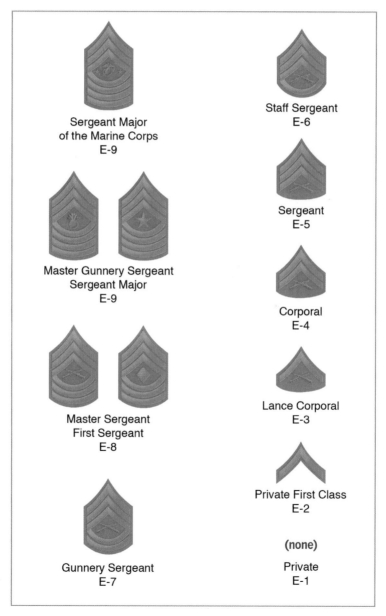

Figure 18. Marine Corps enlisted ranks

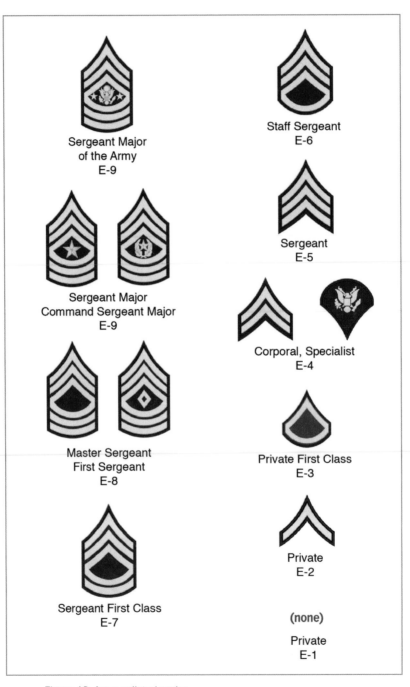

Figure 19. Army enlisted ranks

Chief Master Sergeant
of the Air Force
E-9

Technical Sergeant
E-6

Chief Master Sergeant
First Sergeant
Command Chief Master Sergeant
E-9

Staff Sergeant
E-5

Senior Master Sergeant
First Sergeant
E-8

Senior Airman
E-4

Airman First Class
E-3

Master Sergeant
First Sergeant
E-7

Airman
E-2

(none)

Airman Basic
E-1

Figure 20. Air Force enlisted ranks

RIBBONS AND MEDALS

In the military, special achievements are recognized by the awarding of ribbons and medals. You are probably familiar with the Medal of Honor, the highest honor that is awarded for combat valor, and you may well have heard of the Purple Heart, the medal that is awarded to those who have been wounded in combat.

Medals and ribbons have long been the military's way of recognizing special achievements. Here Senior Chief Edward C. Byers Jr. stands at attention wearing his many ribbons on his chest and a newly awarded Medal of Honor around his neck during his Hall of Heroes induction ceremony at the Pentagon Auditorium. Byers was awarded the medal for his actions during a hostage rescue operation in Afghanistan in December 2012.

When a person is awarded one of these medals, or one of the many others that have been authorized, she or he only wears the actual medal on special occasions, such as for a formal change of command or a visit by a dignitary. More frequently, an abbreviated version is worn on dress uniforms (not working ones). That version is called a "ribbon" and is created by taking just the top portion of the cloth from which the medal is suspended.

Be aware that every medal has an abbreviated ribbon, but there are a number of ribbons that have been created that do not have an associated medal; for example, the Combat Action Ribbon and the Presidential Unit Citation.

Most of the medals and ribbons are awarded to individuals, but some are awarded to whole units at a time. For example, a ship that excels during a battle or a major operation might be awarded the Presidential Unit Citation, the Navy Unit Citation, or the Meritorious Unit

Medals are worn only on full-dress uniforms for formal occasions, such as a change of command.

Figure 21. One example of a Navy ribbon is the Navy Honor Graduate Ribbon, awarded to Recruits for superb performance during basic training, in academics, in physical fitness, in leadership, and in commitment to the Navy core values of honor, courage, and commitment.

Commendation. Virtually any unit (aircraft squadrons, SEAL teams, construction battalions, schools, systems commands, etc.) can be given a unit award for outstanding service. In the sea services (Navy, Marine Corps, Coast Guard), when a unit award is received, all personnel assigned to that unit at the time of the special service are authorized to wear that unit award. These individuals then wear that ribbon for the rest of their careers. The Army does this very differently. Individual Soldiers wear unit awards only when they are serving in a unit that received the award sometime in its past (regardless of whether the individual was in the unit at the time); they then remove the ribbon from their uniforms when they are transferred out of that unit. One other distinction is that they wear these unit awards on the right side of their chests, separate from the other ribbons, which are worn on the left. Sea service personnel integrate their unit ribbons among their others.

When the unit receiving an award includes civilians, a special lapel pin version of the ribbon is awarded to them. Civilians are eligible for some other awards as well—such as the Navy Distinguished Civilian Service Award and the Navy Distinguished Achievement Science Award.

There are too many ribbons to memorize. Charts showing most or all of the medals or ribbons worn by Sailors are available online. **The Navy maintains an official one at www.public.navy.mil/bupers-npc/support /uniforms/uniformregulations/Pages/NavyAwardsPrecedenceChart .aspx, but there are actually better ones available at commercial websites that sell ribbons and medals.**

Recognizing some of these allows you to know certain things about an individual just by looking at these patterns of color. For example, the Combat Action Ribbon tells you that a person was in some kind of combat, and if you recognize a Purple Heart among an individual's ribbons, you know that he or she was wounded in combat. The Navy Cross is second only to the Medal of Honor for heroism in combat, and the Navy and Marine Corps Medal is given for heroism not involving combat, such as rescuing someone from a fire.

Ribbons are arranged in a specific order of precedence. For example, the Medal of Honor is always given the highest precedence and the Purple Heart is higher than the Good Conduct Medal. When wearing them on a uniform, a Sailor who has been awarded more than one award will arrange them in rows of three in the proper order. Higher precedence awards go above and to the right of lower ones (appearing to the left to an observer).

As more awards are earned, they are inserted in the proper order, adding rows of one, two, or three on top. Soldiers, Airmen, and Marines who have a lot of ribbons wear them in rows of four, but Navy awards are always in rows of three, no matter how many a Sailor has been awarded.

To simplify things, individuals have the option of wearing only the top three ribbons in a single row; so if you see someone wearing only three ribbons and one of them is a high precedence award like the Silver Star or the Legion of Merit, chances are that individual has more ribbons sitting on the dresser at home.

You will see various attachments on some of the ribbons. Some of these (like the "E" on the Navy E Ribbon for "excellence") are a part of the ribbon and are always there. Other devices are added to ribbons to represent such things as multiple campaigns in the same theater of operations or the number of sorties flown. A "V" (for "valor") indicates the award was received for service under combat conditions. When individuals earn an award more than once, they do not wear the same ribbon twice; gold stars are added to the ribbon instead. If you see someone wearing a Bronze Star ribbon with a gold star on it, you know she or he has received it on two separate occasions.

PINS AND BADGES

Another thing common to uniforms are the various pins and badges that indicate special qualifications or assignments.

WARFARE QUALIFICATIONS

Most of us are familiar with aviator wings. There is a certain logic that goes with a person who can fly aircraft wearing a set of wings on her or his chest. We have seen airline pilots wearing them and aviators in the movies doing the same.

When submarines appeared, it seemed similarly logical to recognize the submariner in the same manner. Like the aviators who had taken to the sky like birds, these pioneers of a new realm, descending to the depths like fish, also deserved to proudly proclaim their special abilities to the world by wearing a pair of stylized dolphins on their chests. There was probably some thought given to the idea that if we were going to ask people to do such dangerous things, it might help to let them "boast" a bit by wearing their daring for all the world to see.

This seemed to work for a while, until one day, someone realized that this practice was not quite fair. Surface Sailors had been venturing into the hostile realm of the sea for thousands of years, taking risks and using specially acquired skills in a manner that is comparable to those of their fellow aviators and submariners. But because they had been doing it for so long, it was taken for granted, and they were not permitted to "boast" about it on their chests. So the "surface warrior" was born. This new (actually quite old) breed of Sailor was at last given due recognition by being permitted to add a special pin to his or her chest that shows the bow of a ship, a stylized series of waves, and a pair of crossed swords for officers or cutlasses for enlisted surface warriors. You might hear this pin called (unofficially, of course) "water wings."

The inevitable then occurred, and soon pins were designed for SEALs, SeaBees, Sailors assigned to Marine Corps units (Fleet Marine Force Enlisted Warfare Specialists), and others with special warfare qualifications.

Figure 22. Some of the pins and badges that may be earned and worn by Sailors

Aviation Variations

At first, only pilots wore wings. But over time, others making special contributions to aviation were given their own wings. Officers who controlled weapons, navigation, and other systems were distinguished from pilots (officially called "Naval Aviators") by a new designation called "Naval Flight Officer" (or more commonly, "NFO"). Pilots wear wings with a single vertically oriented anchor behind a federal shield; NFOs wear wings with a pair of crossed anchors behind the shield.

Astronauts, Aircrew, Flight Surgeons, and others also wear specialized wings. Enlisted personnel who complete a rigorous qualification program, similar to those in submarines and surface ships, are awarded the silver wings of an "Enlisted Aviation Warfare Specialist."

Combinations

"Flight Surgeons" are doctors with special qualifications for handling the specialized medical needs of aviators. Others with special combinations of knowledge and skills are also recognized by specialized pins. Supply officers on surface ships, engineers on submarines, nurses on surface ships, and a host of other combinations all have specially designed pins proclaiming their special contributions to naval service. These look much like their parent warfare pins but have different features, like the "Naval Aviation Supply Corps" officer's pin, which has a supply oak leaf ("pork chop") in place of the shield and anchors of the pilots and NFOs.

OTHER CHEST HARDWARE

Besides those pins that proclaim a warfare specialty, there are other pins and badges that recognize additional qualifications or special assignments.

Special Qualifications

Individuals who jump out of a perfectly good aircraft wear "jump wings" if they (a) wear a parachute and (b) do it as part of their Navy duties or training. Those who complete jump school training wear the silver version of jump wings, whereas those individuals who have completed ten or more authorized jumps earn the gold "Naval Parachutist" wings.

There are other pins that also recognize other special qualifications. There are a number of pins for divers and several for those who disarm bombs and the like ("Explosive Ordnance Disposal").

Command Pins

An officer who has been given command of a ship, submarine, or an aviation unit such as a squadron wears the "Command-at-Sea" pin, a circular pin with a star as its most prominent feature. An officer who commands a unit ashore, such as a naval base, or heads a large, important project like the development of a major new weapons system, wears a similar pin that has a trident as its predominant feature.

Where these pins are worn gives you an additional clue to "read." If you see one of these pins worn on the right side of the chest, that individual is currently in command. If the pin is on the left side, that individual was once in command but is not currently. Once an individual is promoted to flag rank, he or she no longer wears command pins.

Command Pin Equivalents

During the Vietnam War, when junior officer and senior enlisted Sailors were in charge of coastal and riverine craft, engaging the enemy "up close and personal"—something approximating the responsibility of command of ships at sea—the decision was made that they too should have a pin. The "Small Craft" pin was adopted in a gold version for officers and a silver version for enlisted. For those in charge of small craft such as tugs, there is a "Craftmaster" badge.

Command Master Chiefs and the Like

Recognizing the value of the experience and accumulated wisdom of senior enlisted personnel, the Navy appoints one individual at nearly every command to serve at the right hand of the commanding officer, providing advice on matters affecting the enlisted personnel in the command and sharing in some of the decisions that affect the command as a whole. At most commands these individuals are known as the "Command Master Chief." Aboard submarines they are known as the "Chief of the Boat."

Those who are performing similar functions, serving admirals rather than less-senior commanding officers, are known by titles reflecting their particular assignments. An individual serving as the principal enlisted advisor to a fleet commander is known as the "Fleet Master Chief." One serving a force commander or a flag officer of a major command (like the Naval Education and Training Command) is known as a "Force Master Chief."

Key Personnel Billets

Because people are the Navy's most important resource, there are several assignments that are recognized by special identifying badges. Individuals serving as recruiters for the Navy, Recruit Division Commanders (training Recruits at Boot Camp—equivalent to Marine Drill Instructors), or Career Counselors (specially trained to assist Sailors in making important career decisions, such as reenlisting) all wear specially designed emblems on their uniforms (left side, below the ribbons). These badges are worn only while actually serving in the billet.

Security and Law Enforcement

Just as police officers wear special badges in civilian life, naval personnel who are providing security or law enforcement functions wear special badges on their uniforms. Examples of such personnel are those providing base patrol or serving as brig (jail) and gate guards. Aboard ship, individuals who perform these functions are often called "Master-at-Arms." These badges are only worn by personnel actually performing one of these functions.

SILVER VERSUS GOLD

Be careful *not* to apply logic to the meaning of silver versus gold in these various uniform accoutrements. We have seen that silver outranks gold among officer's collar devices, yet some (not all) of the warfare pins come in both silver and gold varieties—and it is the officers who wear the gold and the enlisted get the silver! But command master chief pins (recognizing senior enlisted personnel) are predominantly gold (although they contain both silver and gold). Some of the pins (like basic jump wings and explosive ordnance disposal pins) come in silver only and are worn by both officers and enlisted.

AIGUILLETTES

You may on occasion see someone wearing a colored ropelike loop (or loops) over his or her shoulder. Sometimes these are rather elaborate, with multiple loops and some metal hardware on the tips (unofficially called "pencils"). Some are less elaborate, having only a single loop or a few loops perched on the end of the shoulder and going under the arm.

These are called "aiguillettes" and have special meanings. They are worn by various aides to high-ranking officers (admirals and generals) and officials (such as the President, Vice President, and Secretary of Defense). They are also worn by naval attachés at diplomatic missions. (Note: Only aides to the President wear their aiguillettes on their right shoulder.)

Special aiguillettes are sometimes worn by members of drill teams and by various ranking individuals in special training commands, such as Recruit Division Commanders at Recruit Training Command (Boot Camp).

BRASSARDS

Brassards are bands of cloth, suitably marked with symbols, letters, or words, indicating a *temporary* duty to which the wearer is assigned, such as Officer of the Day (OOD), Junior Officer of the Day (JOOD), Master-at-Arms (MAA), or Shore Patrol (SP). They are worn on the right arm, midway between the shoulder and the elbow, on outermost garments.

Another variation is the mourning badge, made of black crepe, which may be worn on the sleeve of the outermost garment, halfway between shoulder and elbow for funerals, memorial services, and similar occasions. Officers wear it on their left sleeve and enlisted personnel wear it on the right.

COVERS

Caps or hats in the Navy are generically called *covers* and sometimes *headgear*. You will also sometimes hear them described as "caps" and as "hats" when referring to specific types (as in "white hats"). A Sailor wearing some kind of headgear is said to be *covered* and one who is not is *uncovered*.

One way to sometimes tell an officer from an enlisted person is by his or her cover, although this can get a bit complicated.

All officers of all services wear (at some time or another) what we call a "combination cover." These are the caps that have a visor on the front and are similar to what airline pilots, bus drivers, and police officers often wear. All enlisted personnel in the Army, Air Force, Marines, and Coast Guard also sometimes wear combination covers, and in the Navy, paygrades E-7 through E-9 also wear them.

One component of these combination covers is the *chin strap*, a narrow strap that is just above the visor (called a "chin strap" because it can be extended to hook under the chin in windy conditions, though it rarely is). If that chin strap is gold, the person wearing it is an officer. In the Army, Navy, and Coast Guard, these chin straps are always gold for officers and always black for enlisted personnel. In the Air Force, they are black for both officers and enlisted. In the Marine Corps, they are gold (with a thin red stripe) for officers and black for enlisted when they are wearing a white cover, but are black for both officers and enlisted when wearing the green combination cover.

If the visor of a combination cover has "stuff" on it—what we usually refer to informally as "scrambled eggs"—the person is definitely an officer—a more senior one. In all the services except the Air Force, these added decorations are gold combinations of oak leaves and acorns; in the Air Force, they are silver clouds and lightning bolts. In the Army, Air Force, and Marines, an officer gets to wear "scrambled eggs" on his or her cover at the O-4 level and above; in the Navy and Coast Guard, they are worn by O-5 and above!

Keep in mind that officers do not always wear combination covers. In the Navy you will also see officers wearing garrison caps, baseball-type caps, or eight-point covers. Sometimes these will have an indication of rank on them, sometimes not.

Enlisted Sailors sometimes also wear garrison caps, and they also wear the iconic Sailor cap that you will often hear described as a "White Hat Dixie Cup."

There are also eight-point covers for wear with the Navy Working Uniform and various other covers for special uniforms and situations.

A petty officer first class with her rank device on her cover as well as her collar points. Note her ten ribbons and her Air Warfare insignia worn above.

TELLING THE SERVICES APART

There are many variations and combinations that sometimes make discernment difficult. A few general characteristics can narrow the possibilities and help you identify which service you are encountering. Be aware that military people use some odd terminology at times (for example, the equivalent of a suit or sport jacket is called a "blouse"), but I will use more familiar terminology here to avoid confusion. Also, be aware that "navy blue" is virtually *black*.

One uniform worn by Navy enlisted Sailors (E-1 through E-6) is known officially as "Service Dress Blue" but is affectionately called the "Crackerjack" uniform (white Sailor hat, top shirt with a flap on the back, neckerchief, and bell-bottom trousers). It is very distinctive and not likely to cause much confusion. That's the good news; the bad news is that it is worn only by enlisted personnel in the bottom six paygrades and not as often as some of the other Navy uniforms.

When dressed formally, Marines are very distinctive. The "choker" (high collar with no necktie) collars on their blue uniforms are unique. Marine trousers with those choker blues will usually be lighter blue (many, but not all, with red stripes down the outer pant leg); an exception is that in summer, officers may wear white trousers with this uniform. Marine officers also occasionally wear choker collar uniforms that are all white, a color that is also worn by Coast Guard and Navy officers and chief petty officers. No other services have choker collars (except at service academies).

If a person is wearing white, navy blue (black), or khaki from head to toe, he or she is probably Navy. There are a few other all-white uniforms in the armed services (such as Marines in "choker" whites and Air Force medical personnel), but these are infrequently encountered. You are more likely to encounter Navy personnel dressed in all white.

Navy uniforms for E-6 and below incorporate both khaki and black (khaki shirts with black trousers or skirts).

Army, Air Force, and Coast Guard personnel also wear blue, but they are noticeably different shades. The Army's blue is darker than the

Air Force's and Coast Guard's. Air Force blue has more gray in it, and the Coast Guard blue is more of a royal blue. Air Force suit jackets have silver buttons while the Army and Coast Guard suit jackets have gold.

Light blue shirts usually mean Air Force unless there are Coast Guard personnel around—they also wear light blue shirts.

Naval officers and chief petty officers wear white shirts with some uniforms, with or without suit jackets or sweaters.

Marines also wear green suit jackets at times with matching trousers or skirts, and their jacket buttons are black.

If a service member is wearing a multitude of colors all at the same time (khaki shirt, blue trousers, and a white cap), he or she is a Marine.

A khaki necktie means Marine; blue neckties (in slightly different shades) are worn by the Air Force and Coast Guard; black neckties are worn by both Army and Navy.

Bottom line: If in doubt, *ask individuals what service they are in*— they are used to it and much prefer that you ask, rather than make assumptions such as "commercial airline pilot" or "doorman"!

CAMOUFLAGE UNIFORMS

One example of uniforms that are difficult to identify are camouflaged fatigues. There are variations of these depending upon the location and purpose (for example, jungle or woodland camouflage is predominantly green, whereas desert camouflage is predominantly brown or tan, and urban camouflage is made up of blacks and grays). The Navy is transitioning from Navy Working Uniform (NWU) Type I, the blue and gray ones, to NWU Type III, which are the woodland green ones. You may see both versions of this uniform until 2019, when the transition period ends and NWU III becomes the standard.

All the services wear these various camouflage uniforms at different times. The bad news is that they are often hard to tell apart from any distance; the good news is that if you get up close, they usually have their service name embroidered or stenciled over one of the pockets.

FINAL THOUGHTS

Reading uniforms is not the easiest thing in the world. Trying to memorize all of the variations is probably not worth your time. A better approach is to be generally familiar with what these things mean, commit a few of the more prominent features to memory, and keep this guide handy for reference so that you can identify specific variations as you encounter them. Also, you can equip yourself for that awkward moment when you meet someone for the first time and wonder, "What do I talk about?" Trust me, you will score a lot more points with someone in uniform if you say, "I see you served in Afghanistan," rather than, "I hear it's supposed to rain later today."

8 SHIPS

The oldest element of sea power is the ship. From the rowed galleys of ancient Greece, to the sailed frigates of the Napoleonic era, to the nuclear-powered aircraft carriers of today, ships have always been the backbone of any navy.

Having some basic knowledge of the ships that give the Navy much of its formidable capability goes a long way toward understanding what the Navy is all about.

Countless volumes would be required to cover all the myriad details of Navy ships, but here we will provide the basics to get you started and allow you to function with a measure of understanding and credibility in the complex, technical world of the Navy.

This chapter deals with ships from an *external* view, explaining how to describe them and providing a basic understanding of their naval uses. For those who actually go aboard ships, Chapter 3 and Appendix C describe ships with a more detailed *interior* view.

WHAT TO CALL SHIPS

One of the quickest ways to establish yourself as a naval novice is to refer to a ship as a boat. Unfortunately, there is no absolute way to define the difference, but the following guidance will work most of the time. In general, a boat is a watercraft that is small enough to be carried

The oldest element of sea power is the ship. Here we see a guided-missile cruiser followed by a guided-missile destroyer. Integrated with other elements—such as the airpower represented by the naval aircraft overhead—the Navy has come a long way since the days of sail and cannons.

aboard a larger vessel, and that "larger vessel" is a ship. This is sometimes expressed this way: "A ship can carry a boat, but a boat can never carry a ship." Also, it is helpful to remember that if a vessel has a permanent crew with a commanding officer assigned, it is more than likely a ship. If a vessel is only manned part of the time (when it is in use), it is probably a boat. Another distinction sometimes made is that a ship is designed to "navigate in deep waters," but there are some pitfalls with this, too. The best rule that works most of the time is that *if it is big, it is a ship*. Don't call a frigate or a destroyer or a cruiser a "boat."

Now for some confusion. Using the above guidance, submarines are technically ships. Yet they are traditionally referred to as boats. The original submarines were very small and manned only when in use, so "boat" was appropriate. But as they developed into larger vessels, and should rightfully have been called "ships," the original term stuck. There was an attempt by some submariners to change them over to "ships" when the large nuclear subs began to appear, but as with many things in the Navy, tradition trumped logic, and today, all submarines—even the giant "boomers" (fleet ballistic-missile submarines)—are called boats.

Another exception is that sometimes personnel who are assigned to air wings embarked in aircraft carriers will refer to the carrier as "the boat." There is no official sanction for this, but it seems to be a kind of affectionate irreverence that they use to set themselves apart from their fellow Sailors who are assigned to the carrier as a part of its permanent crew. Make no mistake: an aircraft carrier is a ship—let others call it a boat if they must.

One term that causes some consternation in naval circles is the word "vessel." There are some cantankerous would-be purists who insist that a vessel is "something used to carry water, not to go to sea in." But the *Dictionary of Naval Terms* defines "vessel" as "every description of craft, ship, or other contrivance used as a means of transportation on water." Other dictionaries (including *Webster's*: "a watercraft bigger than a rowboat") confirm the acceptability of this term, and "The Official Inventory of U.S. Naval Ships and Service Craft" is officially known as the "Naval Vessel Register." So, the bottom line is that "vessel" is an acceptable term in most naval circles, but if you happen to work for one of the aforementioned "purists," I would not advise arguing with him or her.

One last comment regarding ship references. Tradition has long mandated the use of feminine pronouns when referring to ships (as in, "She has a new sonar, making her a good ASW ship"). This practice may be a dying one (Lloyds of London, the long-standing maritime British insurance company, no longer uses the feminine), and you will no longer be "keelhauled" for not using it, but you will still frequently encounter the practice, so you should be aware of it. Being a traditionalist, I use feminine ship references in this book. Whether to use them yourself or not is largely a function of the old adage, "Know your audience."

HOW SHIPS ARE EMPLOYED

The U.S. Navy operates hundreds of ships. Some of these are *active* ships, which means they have a full complement of active duty personnel (crew) and, unless they are temporarily undergoing heavy maintenance or repair, are fully capable of carrying out an assigned mission on short notice.

The Navy also keeps a number of vessels in *reserve* status, which means that they are fully functional ships but are only partially manned with active duty personnel. The rest of the crew is made up of reserve personnel, who only man the ships periodically for training and when called upon in national emergencies. For this reason, these ships are mission-capable and are an essential part of the Fleet but are usually less readily available than are ships in active status.

The Navy also operates a number of vessels for the Department of Defense under the "Military Sealift Command" (MSC). These ships usually have only a very small contingent of Navy personnel on board, and the majority of the crews are civilians. MSC ships have a support role and are not used as front-line combatants. They are considered to be "in service" rather than "in commission." Many of these ships, such as vehicle cargo ships and transport oilers, serve the Army and Air Force as well as the Navy. Other MSC ships perform special-duty projects, such as surveying, oceanographic research, and laying and repairing of cables on the ocean floor for various purposes.

Of special interest is a group of various MSC ships that make up the Naval Fleet Auxiliary Force (NFAF). These ships are the lifeline to U.S. Navy ships at sea, providing fuel, food, ammunition, spare parts, and other supplies to the operating forces, alleviating the need for them

USNS *Rappahannock* (T-AO 204) is one of the Military
Sealift Command's fleet replenishment oilers.

to constantly return to port for supplies. As with other MSC ships, they
have civilian officers and crews, but they operate under Navy orders
and have a contingent of Navy personnel aboard, performing visual
and radio communications and otherwise assisting the ship's civilian
master and crew in coordinating operations with other naval units.

WAYS TO DESCRIBE SHIPS

You don't have to see very many Navy ships before you realize that
there are many different types. There are a number of ways to describe
them, some generic and some more specific, dealing with such things as
size and capabilities.

DIMENSIONS

A ship's length is called just that ("length"), but her width is called *beam*.
Her *displacement* is for all intents and purposes her weight. *Draft* is
how deep into the water a ship's hull reaches and is generally expressed
in feet; obviously it would not be a good idea for a ship with a draft of
twenty-five feet to venture into waters with a depth of twenty feet.

SPEED

Ships have different speed capabilities, depending upon their mission. When describing a ship's speed, it is given in knots, which are slightly more than miles-per-hour: one knot = 1.152 miles per hour (or 1.85 kilometers per hour).

PROPULSION

Various kinds of propulsion are used in today's ships, including steam, nuclear, gas turbine, and diesel.

Steam

The primary method of marine propulsion for more than a century, early steam plants burned wood or coal in boiler furnaces to heat water until it became steam. Most modern steam plants use oil as the heat source. The steam is then converted into usable energy by turbines that drive the propeller shafts.

With near-infinite quantities of water surrounding ships at sea, it would seem that a water supply for steam plants is not a problem. But saltwater does not work well in steam systems, so ships must use freshwater and obviously cannot carry unlimited amounts. To preserve the precious freshwater, shipboard steam plants operate as a closed cycle—meaning that the water and steam are theoretically contained in the system and not allowed to escape. Steam is retrieved from the turbines and returned to condensers that convert the spent steam back into freshwater, which is then returned to the boilers to be reheated into energy-filled steam again. This "steam cycle," as it is called, is repeated over and over to propel a ship through the water. Even though this is a closed cycle, a certain amount of the freshwater is used up, so that a continuous supply of feedwater is required for sustained operations. Shipboard distilling plants create the feedwater by converting sea(salt)-water into freshwater.

The fuel needed is carried in fuel tanks on board—much as an automobile has a gas tank—and must be periodically replenished either in port or from oilers at sea.

Nuclear Power

Although using very sophisticated technology, shipboard nuclear power plants are actually just a variation of steam propulsion. Instead of using oil-fired boilers, nuclear-powered ships have reactors that produce the heat to convert freshwater to steam.

Nuclear power gives a ship the advantage of great endurance at high speed. Instead of refueling every few thousand miles like an oil-burning ship, a nuclear-powered ship can operate for years on one reactor core, so it can steam almost indefinitely, limited only by its need to replenish food, spare parts, and ammunition.

Another favorable feature of nuclear power is that, unlike conventional oil-fired systems, the generation of nuclear power does not require oxygen. This makes it particularly useful as a means of submarine propulsion. Nuclear-powered submarines can operate completely submerged for extended periods of time.

Gas Turbines

This modern form of propulsion uses jet engines that are very much like the ones used in aircraft but have been adapted for use on ships. The burning fuel spins turbines in the engines that convert the energy created into usable power that turns the ship's propellers.

Although some of the principles are the same, some of the primary differences between these propulsion plants and those that use steam are that the gas turbines combine the functions of the boiler and the turbines into one element, and gas turbines have no need of feedwater. This means that they are smaller, more efficient, and easier to maintain. They are also much more quickly "brought on the line" (turned on). A steam-powered vessel requires hours to prepare to get under way, whereas gas turbine–powered ships can be ready in minutes.

The obvious advantages of gas-turbine technology have caused the U.S. Navy to build more and more of these ships. Whereas steam was once the main means of naval propulsion, today there are more gas-turbine ships in the Navy than any other kind of propulsion.

Diesel Engines

Frequently used in ships that need less horsepower, diesels are lighter, take up less space, and are more efficient than steam turbines. Marine diesels are basically larger versions of the engines used in trucks, buses, and some automobiles, except that their power is put to propellers rather than wheels. The diesel engine can be coupled directly to the propeller shaft through reduction gears and perhaps a clutch; or it can drive a generator that produces electrical current for the main drive.

Diesel engines are preferred over gasoline engines because they are more efficient and because diesel fuel is not as dangerous and volatile as gasoline.

Sails

Utilizing wind to propel ships through the water, sails were once the primary means of propulsion for ships. Although naval vessels no longer use them, with a nod toward tradition, Navy ships are often said to "sail" from one place to another (as in, "The fleet sailed for the Middle East").

Another generic term that is still often used in the same context (despite the proliferation of gas turbine ships) is "steam" (as in, "The destroyer steamed into the Persian Gulf").

So far, no one has used "turbined" in this context (and probably never will).

MISSIONS

Ships' primary missions are often described by acronyms. If a ship is capable of engaging aircraft or incoming missiles, she is said to be an AAW (antiair warfare) ship. Her ability to engage other ships is described as ASUW (anti-surface warfare) and opposing enemy submarines is known as ASW (antisubmarine warfare). The term USW (undersea warfare) is a more recent term that includes mine warfare (MIW) as well as ASW. Strike warfare refers to the ability to attack land targets.

A number of things determine a ship's mission capabilities, including the weapons she is armed with and the sensors (radar, sonar, etc.) she carries.

HOW THE NAVY IDENTIFIES SHIPS

You will often see U.S. Navy ships identified by a combination of letters and numbers such as

USS *Enterprise* (CVN 65)

Most Navy ships have both a name (such as "*Enterprise*") and what we call a "ship's designation" (such as "CVN 65") to identify them. Though the name is a convenient and traditional means of identification, there have been many Navy ships bearing the same names throughout history, so the ship's designation—which is unique to each individual ship—is the only way to positively identify a specific naval vessel. The ship's designation tells what *type* it is (in this case, "CVN" identifies her as a nuclear-powered aircraft carrier) and assigns a specific *hull number* (in this case, "65") to the vessel. Ships are also grouped into *classes* to identify those with identical, or nearly identical, characteristics. The name of the first ship in a class is used to identify the class. For example, USS *Arleigh Burke* was the first of a class of guided-missile destroyers; even though the next ship built has her own name (USS *Barry*), she is considered to be an *Arleigh Burke*-class destroyer.

NAME

The name is unique to a ship in that there can only be one Navy ship in commission at one time with a given name. But as already mentioned, there may have been other ships with the same name in the past—in fact, it is fairly common practice in the Navy for ships to carry the name of an earlier ship that served with honor. For example, there have been eight U.S. Navy ships named *Enterprise*. This count of course does not include the starship *Enterprise* of *Star Trek* fame, but the creator of the hit television and movie series, Gene Roddenberry, recognized the long tradition of passing on ship names and carried it on in his futuristic vision.

The name of a Navy ship in commission (active or reserve) is preceded by the letters "USS," which stands for "United States Ship." By convention, the name (but not the "USS") is usually written in *italics*, or both are written in all capital letters (such as USS ENTERPRISE). The "USS" designation also applies to submarines, even though, as earlier noted, they are most often referred to as "boats."

MSC ships are somewhat different. Because they are considered to be "in service" rather than "in commission," names of MSC ships are preceded by the letters "USNS" (for United States Naval Ship) instead of "USS."

The U.S. Coast Guard operates ships carrying the prefix USCGC, for "United States Coast Guard Cutter."

Other navies of the world use similar systems. In the Royal Navy, vessels carry the prefix "HMS," which stands for "Her Majesty's Ship" (or "His Majesty's Ship" if there is a reigning king instead of a queen). The navies of many other nations are similarly identified, using their own unique system.

The Secretary of the Navy is the person responsible for naming U.S. Navy ships, although he or she gets plenty of help from politicians, historians, admirals, families of famous people, and so on, who all have their own ideas of what the next ship should be named. There are some "rules" (actually conventions) to ship naming, although these conventions are sometimes broken and have changed over the years. At one time, battleships were named for states and cruisers for cities, but today submarines are mostly named for states with some named for cities (*Henry M. Jackson*, *Jimmy Carter*, *John W. Warner*, and *Seawolf* being notable exceptions). Aircraft carriers are now mostly named for presidents, though there are one admiral (*Nimitz*) and two congressmen (*John C. Stennis* and *Carl Vinson*). Cruisers are named for important battles in U.S. history. Destroyers are named for people—Sailors or Marines who have served or sacrificed exceptionally (*Winston S. Churchill* being an exception). Amphibious ships are a mix of battles (*Tarawa*, *Saipan*, etc.), cities (*Anchorage*, *Nashville*, etc.), famous American landmarks (*Rushmore*, *Hermitage*, etc.), and former famous ships (*Kearsarge*, *Bon Homme Richard*, etc.).

Sailors traditionally often add nicknames to their seagoing homes. Among aircraft carriers, for instance, USS *Theodore Roosevelt* is "TR," and *Dwight D. Eisenhower* is "Ike." Some nicknames are more "colorful" and it is probably better not to record them here.

The crew members of the aircraft carrier USS *Eisenhower* (CVN 69) often refer to their ship informally as "Ike" just as the former president and five-star general was known in his day.

DESIGNATIONS

Though a ship's name gives her some identity, her *designation*—which consists of a combination of letters and numbers—is a unique identification that tells you two additional things about the ship: her type and her place in the construction sequence. The USS *Theodore Roosevelt*, for instance, has the designation CVN 71. CVN is her type classification, "CV" standing for aircraft carrier and "N" meaning nuclear propulsion. The number 71 indicates that she is the seventy-first aircraft carrier authorized for construction. The term "hull number" actually refers only to the number part of the ship's designation, but you will commonly hear it used instead of "ship's designation," referring to the letter and number combination (as in, "USS *Barry*'s hull number is DDG 52"). Ships' hull numbers (numerals only) are frequently painted on their bows and near the stern. Aircraft carriers have their hull numbers painted on the forward part of the flight deck and on the "island" (superstructure).

Since 1920 the Navy has used letter symbols to identify the types of ships, boats, and service craft. This is called "type classification" and is used as part of the ship's designation. Some of the more common type classifications are listed below. Keep in mind that some of these type classifications may not be currently in use, but they are listed because you may come across them historically, or they may be reactivated at some later date.

AD	destroyer tender
AE	ammunition ship
AFS	combat store ship
AGF	miscellaneous command ship
AH	hospital ship
AKA	attack cargo ship
AO	oiler
AOE	fast combat-support ship
AOG	gasoline tanker
AOR	replenishment oiler
APA	attack transport ship
APB	self-propelled barracks ship
APL	barracks craft (non-self-propelled)
AR	repair ship
ARS	salvage ship
AS	submarine tender
ASR	submarine rescue ship
ATF	fleet ocean tug
AVT	auxiliary aircraft landing training ship
BB	battleship
CA	heavy cruiser
CAG	guided-missile heavy cruiser
CC	command cruiser
CG	guided-missile cruiser
CGN	guided-missile cruiser (nuclear propulsion)
CL	light cruiser

CLAA	antiaircraft cruiser
CLGN	guided-missile light cruiser (nuclear propulsion)
CV	multipurpose aircraft carrier
CVA	attack aircraft carrier
CVL	light aircraft carrier
CVN	multipurpose aircraft carrier (nuclear propulsion)
CVS	antisubmarine warfare aircraft carrier
DD	destroyer
DDG	guided-missile destroyer
DDR	radar picket destroyer
DD(X)	prototype destroyer
DE	destroyer escort (also ocean escort)
DEG	Guided-missile ocean escort
DER	radar picket destroyer escort
DL	destroyer leader (once also called "frigate")
DLG	Guided-missile destroyer leader (once also called "guided-missile frigate")
DLGN	nuclear-powered guided-missile destroyer leader (also "frigate")
DM	destroyer minelayer
DSRV	deep-submergence rescue vehicle
FF	frigate
FFG	guided-missile frigate
HSV	high-speed vessel
IX	unclassified miscellaneous
LCAC	landing craft, air cushioned
LCC	amphibious command ship
LCH	landing craft, heavy
LCIL	landing craft, infantry, large
LCM	landing craft, mechanized
LCPL	landing craft, personnel, large
LCS	littoral combat ship
LCU	landing craft, utility
LCVP	landing craft, vehicle and personnel

LHA	amphibious assault ship (general purpose)
LHD	amphibious assault ship (multipurpose)
LKA	amphibious cargo ship
LPD	amphibious transport dock
LPH	amphibious assault ship (helicopter)
LSD	dock landing ship
LSIL	landing ship, infantry, large
LSM	landing ship, medium
LSSC	light SEAL support craft
LSSL	landing ship, support, large
LST	tank-landing ship
MCM	mine-countermeasures ship
MCS	mine-countermeasures support ship
MHC	coastal minehunter
MSC	coastal minesweeper
MSO	ocean-going minesweeper
PB	patrol boat
PBR	river patrol boat
PC	coastal patrol craft
PCF	fast patrol craft ("swift boat")
PG	patrol gunboat
PHM	patrol hydrofoil missile
PT	patrol torpedo boat
SS	submarine
SSG	guided-missile submarine
SSBN	fleet ballistic-missile submarine (nuclear powered)
SSGN	guided-missile submarine (nuclear powered)
SSN	submarine, attack (nuclear powered)
YD	floating crane
YP	yard patrol
YTB	large harbor tug
YTL	small harbor tug
YTM	medium harbor tug

Ships of the Military Sealift Command (MSC) are distinguished from other Navy ships by having a "T" before their letter designations. Below are some examples of MSC ship types:

T-ACS	crane ship
T-AE	ammunition ship
T-AFS	combat stores ship
T-AGM	missile range instrumentation ship
T-AGOS	ocean surveillance ship
T-AGS	oceanographic survey
T-AH	hospital ship
T-AK	maritime pre-positioning ship
T-AKR	vehicle cargo ship
T-AO	oiler
T-AOT	tanker
T-AP	troop ship
T-ARC	cable repair
T-ATF	fleet ocean tug
T-AVB	aviation logistic ship

Coast Guard cutters also use this type of classification and are distinguished by having "W" as the first letter in their designation. Examples of Coast Guard ship types are:

WHEC	high endurance cutter
WMEC	medium endurance cutter
WAGB	ice breaker
WLB	seagoing buoy tender
WLM	coastal buoy tender
WPB	patrol boat

CLASS

Within a type classification of vessels there are classes. Ships belonging to a particular class are built from the same plans and are very much alike, essentially identical except for the different hull number painted on their bows and a different assigned name. In reality, one can always find some minor differences, and occasionally individual ships within a class may be significantly altered.

The first ship built to a specific design determines the name of the class. For example, after World War II the United States redesigned its aircraft carriers to accommodate the newly invented jet aircraft then entering the Fleet. The first of these new aircraft carriers to be built was commissioned as USS *Forrestal* (CV 59). She was the fifty-ninth aircraft carrier, but the first of this new class. Satisfied with this new ship, the Navy built three more—USS *Saratoga* (CV 60), USS *Ranger* (CV 61), and USS *Independence* (CV 62)—all of which are referred to as *Forrestal*-class carriers.

Later, some major improvements were deemed necessary, so the Navy redesigned its aircraft carriers significantly enough that they were considered a new class of carrier. The first of these new and different carriers was named USS *Kitty Hawk* (CV 63), so the next ship built after her, USS *Constellation* (CV 64), was considered a *Kitty Hawk*–class aircraft carrier. And so the process goes.

Sometimes you will hear a class identified by the hull number of the first ship. For example, the *Arleigh Burke* class of guided-missile destroyers is sometimes referred to as the "DDG 51-class," and the *Los Angeles* class of nuclear attack submarines are often called "the 688s."

SHIP TYPES AND THEIR MISSIONS

The many different types of vessels in the Navy have specific functions or missions. Some exist primarily to engage in combat with enemy forces (other vessels, aircraft, or land targets) and are generally referred to as *combatants*. Others, known as *auxiliaries*, exist to deliver the supplies (fuel, ammunition, food, and repair parts) needed by the operating forces, to provide maintenance and repair services, to conduct salvage operations, and to provide a host of other support functions. Still others, known as *amphibious* vessels, are designed to take troops where they are needed and get them ashore, and *mine-warfare* vessels locate and destroy underwater mines.

The major combatants can be divided into three groups: *aircraft carriers*, *submarines*, and *surface combatants*.

Aircraft Carriers

These gigantic ships have been described as the world's largest combatant ships and the world's smallest airfields. Their displacement is between 80,000 and 100,000 tons (depending upon the class), they are more than 1,000 feet long, and they have beams exceeding 250 feet. They carry about 85 aircraft, and the number of personnel required to operate the ship and its aircraft is more than 5,000.

Aircraft carriers carry an assortment of aircraft capable of performing a wide variety of missions, including air support to troops ashore, bombardment missions, antisubmarine operations, rescue missions, reconnaissance, and antiair warfare. They are capable of staying at sea for long periods of time, making them potent weapons in a wide variety of scenarios.

You may hear the term "aircraft carrier" used to describe the Navy's large amphibious ships—designated LHA and LHD—that carry and operate helicopters and special aircraft that are designed for very short or even vertical take-offs and landings. While this is not entirely incorrect, that term is more commonly reserved for the larger predominantly jet-carrying ships—the CVNs.

Aircraft carriers are frequently referred to as just "carriers," sometimes by the nicknames "flattop," and "bird farm."

Submarines

Though in many ways submarines are ships, they are different enough to warrant a separate treatment. As explained earlier, despite their size and complex capabilities, they are traditionally called "boats."

The U.S. Navy has three major types of submarine—SSN, SSBN, and SSGN—all of which are nuclear powered. The *attack submarines*, designated SSN, have the primary mission of other submarines and surface ships, but they are also assigned secondary missions, which may include surveillance and reconnaissance, direct task-force support, landing-force support, land attack, mine laying, and rescue. The SSN's principal weapons are high-speed, wire-guided torpedoes and cruise missiles for use against surface and land targets.

USS *Hartford* (SSN 768) is an example of an attack submarine.

The *fleet ballistic-missile submarines* (SSBN) have a strategic mission, in that they are meant to deter or to participate in a nuclear-missile exchange. They are the "sea leg" of the U.S. nuclear strike triad—the other two components being Air Force strategic bombers and land-based intercontinental ballistic missile (ICBM) systems. SSBNs carry submarine-launched ballistic missiles (SLBMs) that are highly sophisticated, specially adapted for use at sea ICBMs that have multiple nuclear warheads and are capable of hitting targets many thousands of miles away and causing tremendous destruction. You may hear them referred to by the nickname "boomer boat" or just "boomer."

SSBNs must remain submerged—"invisible"—for long periods of time, virtually out of contact with the rest of the world, serving primarily as a deterrent but essentially waiting to carry out a mission that

Fleet ballistic-missile submarines, such as USS *Nevada* (SSBN 733) seen here, carry missiles armed with nuclear warheads that can be launched from under the sea and travel thousands of miles to their designated targets.

could be devastating to much of the world. This is a stressful environment for the crews, and to alleviate some of that stress, SSBNs are operated during alternate periods by two separate crews. One is called the blue crew and the other the gold crew. On return from an extended patrol, one crew relieves the other, and the ship returns to patrol following a brief period in port. The relieved crew enters a month-long period of rest, recreation, and leave, followed by two months of training. This system allows each crew time ashore, while keeping these important ships cruising on deep patrol except for very brief periods.

The third major type of submarine currently in the U.S. arsenal is the *guided-missile submarine* (SSGN). Converted *Ohio*-class SSBNs, these submarines are armed with Tomahawk tactical missiles for land attack missions and are designed for a variety of specialized missions, including the ability to transport, insert, and support SEALs or other special operations forces for prolonged periods. Secondary missions are the traditional attack submarine missions of intelligence, surveillance, and reconnaissance (ISR), battle space preparation, and sea control.

Surface Combatants

The largest surface combatants ever built were the *battleships*. They played significant roles in naval combat for much of the twentieth century but have not survived into the twenty-first (except as museum ships). There is a tendency among the uninformed (television reporters, for example) to refer to any combatant as a "battleship"; such references make the informed cringe, so it is to be avoided.

Today, U.S. Navy surface combatants include *cruisers*, *destroyers*, *frigates*, and *littoral combat ships* (LCS).

Cruisers

These powerful ships are extremely capable in AAW, ASW, and ASUW missions. They are equipped with missiles that can knock out incoming raids from enemy aircraft or missile attacks. With other specially designed missiles, they are able to hit land or sea targets at substantial distances.

Currently, the Navy's cruisers are all *Ticonderoga*-class ships and are designated CG. They are powered by four gas turbines driving twin screws at speeds greater than thirty knots and are equipped with the very sophisticated Aegis combat system. This integrated combat system is highly automated, exceptionally fast, and capable of conducting anti-air, anti-surface, and antisubmarine warfare simultaneously. These ships fire a variety of missiles (Tomahawk and Standard) as well as torpedoes and ASROCs (antisubmarine rockets) and have two MK 45 5-inch guns. They also are equipped with two Phalanx close-in weapons systems (a rapid-firing gun that is used to knock down an incoming missile if other systems have failed to bring it down).

USS *Port Royal* (CG 73) is one of the Navy's guided-missile cruisers.

Destroyers

Destroyers have always performed a wide range of missions. They can serve as part of a screen unit in a carrier task group, protecting it from various forms of attack. They can detect and engage enemy submarines, aircraft, missiles, and surface ships. In an amphibious assault, a destroyer's weapons help protect against enemy forces at sea and deliver needed firepower ashore. In short, destroyers have a well-deserved reputation of being the "workhorses of the Fleet."

Earlier classes of destroyer were rather small—some displacing as little as four hundred tons—but today's *Arleigh Burke*–class destroyers displace as much as ninety-two hundred tons. They are a little more than five hundred feet in length with a beam of nearly sixty feet. These powerful ships are powered by four gas turbine engines that drive two screws and make the ship capable of speeds greater than thirty knots. Like the *Ticonderoga*-class cruisers, they are equipped with the Aegis combat system, making them the most potent class of destroyer ever built. At one time, the differences between cruisers and destroyers were significant. Today, the differences are not so obvious.

Earlier versions of the *Arleigh Burke* class have a flight deck for helicopters and drones but no hangar, whereas the newer versions do have a hangar. They are capable of firing a variety of missiles (Harpoon, Tomahawk, Standard, and Evolved Sea Sparrow) against ships, land targets, aircraft, and enemy missiles. They can also fire torpedoes and the ASROC to destroy enemy submarines, and they have the powerful Mk 45 gun system. They also are equipped with the Phalanx close-in weapons system.

A new type of destroyer named the *Zumwalt* class is a highly capable platform that includes sophisticated "stealth" (low susceptibility to

A line of *Arleigh Burke*–class guided-missile destroyers

radar detection) technology, efficient electric drive systems, low manning requirements, a very long-range gun system, and other impressive innovations.

Destroyers are sometimes called "tin-cans," a traditional nickname that was much more appropriate to earlier classes than to the highly sophisticated marvels of today. They have also long been affectionately known as "greyhounds of the Sea."

Littoral Combat Ships

Described by the Secretary of the Navy as "fast and capable ships [that] . . . provide us with an ability to operate in the littoral areas of the world where the enemies of freedom seek to operate and hide," the basic idea behind this new type of ship is to allow the U.S. Navy to operate closer to shore than it has traditionally. Although there are times in the Navy's past when it has operated in these areas (Civil War, Vietnam, etc.), the U.S. Navy has been primarily a "blue-water" (meaning "deep ocean") fleet for the majority of its existence. With the rise of terrorism, the need for projecting power ashore as part of joint operations, and the current lack of a blue-water competitor, the Navy now focuses more attention on the coastal regions of the world. "Littoral" is used rather than "coastal" because it is meant to convey a broader area. "Coastal" more precisely defines the *edge* where land and sea meet, whereas "littoral" is meant to include more of the adjacent waters and the land area where power must be projected in the accomplishment of various missions in the modern environment. The older term "brown-water operations" (generally describing coastal and riverine operations) comes close but is too "wet," not embracing the adjacent land areas as an integral component.

The littoral combat ship (LCS) is therefore a new breed of vessel. Designed to be fast and maneuverable as well as being stealthy (difficult to detect on radar) with a shallow draft, these vessels also incorporate modularity to make them flexible. This simply means that they can be rigged with different "packages" of electronics, weapons, and so on to tailor them to specific missions and that these packages can be changed

The littoral combat ship USS *Independence* (LCS 2)

relatively easily as different missions need to be carried out. These packages include deployable manned and unmanned vehicles (boats and aircraft) that extend the reach of these vessels in the littoral. Among the different missions these vessels are able to carry out are reconnaissance, Special Forces insertion and support, maritime interdiction (search and seizure of other vessels), mine countermeasures, and antiterrorism force protection. These capabilities permit the Navy to penetrate areas that have long been off limits or very high risk for the larger and very expensive combatants, such as cruisers and destroyers.

You may encounter some LCS-type ships being called "frigates," using a term that harkens back to the days of sail.

Auxiliaries

Besides the combatants, the Navy has a large number of auxiliaries that provide support services to the Fleet.

Underway replenishment (UNREP) ships allow combatants to remain at sea for long periods of time without having to return to port by bringing fuel, provisions, repair parts, and ammunition to the ships and transferring them at sea. The U.S. Navy is highly proficient at underway replenishment techniques, using special cargo-handling gear to make transfers from one ship to another while the two are steaming abreast or, in some rare cases, astern. Vertical replenishment (VERTREP) is a form of UNREP in which cargo-carrying helicopters are used to transfer goods from one ship to another. In the past, underway replenishment ships were part of the operating fleet, but today most of the UNREP delivery capability of the Navy is carried out by MSC ships.

Submarine tenders (AS) have maintenance and repair shops and are manned by technicians with a wide variety of skills so that vessels coming alongside can receive extensive repairs or have major maintenance performed on them.

Somewhere in the Philippine Sea, the forward-deployed *Arleigh Burke*–class guided-missile destroyer USS *Barry* (DDG 52) conducts an evening underway replenishment with the Military Sealift Command (MSC) dry cargo and ammunition ship USNS *Cesar Chavez* (T-AKE 14).

Salvage vessels and rescue vessels provide rapid firefighting, dewatering, battle-damage repair, and towing assistance to save ships that have been in battle or victims of some other disaster from further loss or damage. Some have specialized equipment and are manned by salvage divers so that they can also perform submarine rescue and salvage operations underwater.

Also among the Navy's waterborne resources is a large and varied group of service craft. Some are huge vessels like the large auxiliary floating drydocks that can take very large vessels aboard and raise them out of the water for repairs. Barracks craft accommodate crews when their ships are being overhauled or repaired. Lighters are barges used to store and transport materials and to house pier-side repair shops. Some gasoline barges, fuel-oil barges, and water barges are self-propelled and do not depend on tugs. Floating cranes and wrecking derricks are towed

USS *Peleliu* (LHA 5), a multipurpose assault ship that is one example of an amphibious warfare ship, whose primary mission is to support the insertion of Marines ashore

from place to place as needed. Diving tenders support diving operations. Ferryboats or launches—which carry people, automobiles, and equipment—are usually located at Navy bases where facilities are spread out over large distances. Best known of the service craft are the harbor tugs, large and small, that aid ships in docking and undocking, provide firefighting services when needed, perform rescues, and haul lighters from place to place.

Amphibious Warfare Ships

Often referred to as "amphibs" or "gators," these ships work mainly where sea and land meet, where assault landings are carried out by Navy–Marine Corps teams. Such operations call for a variety of ship types. Many are transports of varied designs, used to sealift Marines and their equipment from bases to landing beaches. The differences lie

Mine-countermeasure ships, such as USS *Avenger* (MCM 1), specialize in locating and destroying enemy mines.

in ship design and the way troops and their gear are moved from ship to shore, relying upon different combinations of landing craft, helicopters, or tracked amphibious vehicles.

They include dock landing ships (LSD) and amphibious transport docks (LPD) that deliver troops and equipment primarily by landing craft, as well as general purpose assault ships (LHA) and multipurpose assault ships (LHD) that have large flight decks for massive helicopter operations and can also accommodate vertical/short takeoff and landing (V/STOL) jet aircraft to provide significant strike and support capability.

Mine-Warfare Ships

The *Avenger*-class mine-countermeasures ships with the designation MCM specialize in detecting and locating today's highly sophisticated mines and are tasked with removing or destroying them. Specially configured helicopters also play a very large role in mine-warfare operations in the U.S. Navy. Specially designed ships used to be used to lay mines in enemy waters, but this function, if employed today, would be carried out primarily by aircraft or submarines.

9 AIRCRAFT

In chapter 3 we discussed some basic aircraft terminology. In this chapter, we will explore naval aviation, an essential element of sea power, in more detail.

The U.S. Navy has thousands of aircraft in its inventory, performing a wide variety of missions, many from the decks of ships and others from naval air stations all over the world. The many kinds of aircraft flown by the Navy include fighter, attack, combined fighter-attack, antisubmarine, patrol, early warning, general utility, in-flight refueling, transport, trainers, and unmanned "drone."

Naval aircraft are organized into squadrons, and these are further grouped into air wings.

TYPES OF NAVAL AIRCRAFT

There are many different types of aircraft in the U.S. Navy's inventory. Some of these were designed specifically for naval use, but many are used by the other armed forces as well. Some are fixed-wing, whereas others are rotary-wing (helicopters).

Fighters are used to destroy other aircraft and incoming missiles. They are the aircraft you would normally see involved in a "dogfight." Fighters are very fast and highly maneuverable. They patrol above friendly forces in what are called "combat air patrols" (CAP) and intercept and engage incoming enemy aircraft or missiles. They also penetrate

The U.S. Navy has many different types of aircraft in its inventory. Here a propeller-driven Hawkeye joins a formation of jet-powered Hornets assigned to Carrier Air Wing 9 during an airpower demonstration in the South China Sea.

enemy air space to engage the enemy's aircraft and escort other kinds of aircraft when they are carrying out their missions in hostile areas. All fighters are fixed-wing.

Attack aircraft are designed to destroy enemy targets, at sea and ashore, such as ships, vehicles, transportation systems, airfields, enemy troops, and so on. To accomplish these missions, attack aircraft are armed with various configurations of rockets, guided missiles, gun systems, torpedoes, mines, and bombs. Attack aircraft can be either fixed-wing or helicopters. Some aircraft are designed to carry out both fighter and attack missions.

Patrol aircraft are tasked primarily with finding enemy forces. They are designed more for long range and time on station than for speed. Although they may be armed, sensors (such as radar, infrared, acoustic, and magnetic-detection devices) are their most important components.

The F/A-18E Super Hornet functions as
both a fighter and an attack aircraft.

The Navy's P-8 Poseidon is a long-range
patrol aircraft that is based ashore.

Antisubmarine aircraft search out submarines visually, by radar and magnetic detection, or by signals sent from floating sonobuoys, and then destroy them with rockets, depth charges, or homing torpedoes. Both helicopters and fixed-wing aircraft are used for antisubmarine warfare.

Mine-warfare aircraft lay mines in enemy waters or sweep enemy mines from friendly waters or objective areas. Both rotary- and fixed-wing aircraft can be used in mine warfare.

Command and control aircraft coordinate various operations within the battle space using sophisticated sensors, communications, and computer equipment.

Electronic-warfare aircraft are designed and built specifically for tactical electronic warfare operations, such as jamming enemy radars for a significant tactical advantage.

The E-2D Hawkeye is a carrier-based command and control aircraft. By flying high above the carrier, the Hawkeye's highly sophisticated radar can "see" well beyond the ship's horizon.

Transport aircraft are used to carry cargo and personnel. As with any of the types of aircraft in the Navy's inventory, some are land-based and others can be operated from aircraft carriers. Both helicopters and fixed-wing aircraft are used for transport missions.

Trainer aircraft are generally two-seat fixed-wing or rotary-wing aircraft that allow instructors and students to go aloft together to learn or perfect the techniques of flying.

IDENTIFYING AIRCRAFT

There are thousands of aircraft in the Navy, and they have names and official letter and number designations to distinguish one from the other. This designation system is explained in some detail below, followed by a simpler version for those who do not need or want quite so much precision.

One thing to keep in mind is that the current aircraft designation system has been in effect only since 1962, so if you are reading about aircraft in World War II, for example, the aircraft designations will not be the same.

AIRCRAFT NAMES

Many types, designs, and modifications of aircraft form the naval air arm of the Navy. Like ships, aircraft have names, usually chosen by the designers or developers and approved by the Navy. The names are colorful—there have been some great ones, like Phantom, Corsair, Hellcat, and Banshee—but they are the least revealing when it comes to type, mission, and so on. Unlike ships, individual aircraft do not have specific names but are identified by a system of "tail numbers" instead. More comparable to "class" in ships, all aircraft of a certain type bear the same name. For example, there are more Hornets in the Navy than you would care to count.

AIRCRAFT DESIGNATIONS

More revealing than the names is a system of letters and numbers (sometimes referred to as the MDS [Mission Design Series] system) that is used to distinguish among the many types and variations of naval aircraft in service. The aircraft designation is a letter and number combination that tells you certain basic facts about the aircraft. The bad news is that this system is a little intimidating at first—when you first encounter "F/A-18E/F," representing the Super Hornet, you can't help but think this is something only for cryptanalysts—but the good news is that it *is* mostly logical and definitely decipherable. Some more good news is that this system of identification is the same for all the armed forces.

Probably the simplest way to begin deciphering these designations is to remember this: *one thing common to all aircraft designations is the dash*. Whether the aircraft is a P-8A, or an EA-18G, or an F/A-18E/F, there is always a dash in the designation. If you use that as your starting point, you will have a consistent reference from which to begin cracking this code. Think of the dash in this system as being much like the decimal point in a number system. In mathematics, where numbers appear in relation to the decimal point indicates their value (tens, hundreds, positive, negative, etc.); in the aircraft designation system, where letters or numbers appear relative to the dash helps you understand their meaning.

In the forthcoming explanation, let's take a few examples from the real world by "decoding" the following aircraft designations: T-45C, SH-60B, EA-6B, NKC-135A, and F/A-18C/D. All these aircraft are in the Navy's inventory as of this writing, except NKC-135A Stratotanker, which is an Air Force plane. It is included because it is an example of an aircraft identified by three letters to the left of the dash. Currently, no Navy aircraft are so designated, but one could be in the future.

TYPE OR MISSION

Let's begin with the first letter to the left of the dash. It tells you one of two things: either the *type* or the basic *mission* of the aircraft.

By "type," we mean whether it is a regular airplane—with fixed wings, engine(s), etc.—or some special kind of aircraft, like a helicopter. There is no letter for a regular airplane type (it is assumed by omission), but the following letters are used to tell you that the aircraft is a special type, as indicated:

G	glider
H	helicopter
Q	UAV (unmanned aerial vehicle)
S	spaceplane
V	V/STOL (vertical/short take off and landing)
Z	lighter than air (dirigible, etc.)

By "mission," we mean the primary purpose of the aircraft. The following letters describe aircraft missions as indicated:

A	attack
B	bomber
C	transport
E	special electronic installation
F	fighter
L	laser
O	observation
P	patrol
R	reconnaissance
S	antisubmarine
T	trainer
U	utility
X	research

If the aircraft is a special *type*, such as a glider or a helicopter, the first letter to the left of the dash will be one of those from the type list previously shown: G, H, Q, S, V, or Z. If it is *not* one of these special types (in other words, it's just a regular fixed-wing airplane), then there is *no letter* indicating type. It will be understood that no type letter indicates a regular fixed-wing airplane type. If that is the case, then the first letter to the left of the dash will be one from the *mission* list above: A, B, C, E, and so on.

Because the first letter to the left of the dash will indicate *either* the type or the mission of the aircraft, and the two lists do not overlap (except in one instance), you can combine the two lists into one and translate them appropriately. One minor problem is that this system uses the letter "S" for both type (spaceplane) and mission (antisubmarine). You are not likely to find this a problem—spaceplanes are rare and usually obvious.

In our examples from above, we know that the T-45C is a regular fixed-wing airplane with a primary mission of *training*; the SH-60B is a *helicopter*; the EA-6B is a regular airplane with a primary mission of *attack*; and the NKC-135A is a regular airplane with *transport* as its primary mission. The F/A-18C/D is a a special case: the slash between the F and the A indicates that this is a regular airplane that has two primary missions: it is both a *fighter* and an *attack* aircraft.

MODIFIED MISSION

Now, let's look to the second letter to the left of the dash. This letter (if there is one) is called the mission modifier. The following letters, when appearing in this position, have the meanings indicated:

The T-45C Goshawk—here seen landing on the flight deck of the carrier USS *George Washington* (CVN 73)—is a fixed-wing airplane with a primary mission of training.

A	attack
C	transport
D	director
E	special electronic installation
F	fighter
H	search and rescue/MEDEVAC (medical evacuation)
K	tanker
L	cold weather
M	multi-mission
O	observation
P	patrol
Q	drone (unmanned)
R	reconnaissance
S	antisubmarine
T	trainer
U	utility
V	staff
W	weather

These letters can be combined with *either* a type or a mission indicator in the first position to the left of the dash to tell you more about what an aircraft is used for. In our examples, the T-45C has no mission modifier, so it remains simply a trainer aircraft; the "S" of the SH-60B helicopter tells us that it is used for antisubmarine warfare; the EA-6B original attack mission has been modified by adding special electronics; and the NKC-135A is used as a tanker (for refueling other aircraft in the air). Because the two letters ("F" and "A") are separated by a slash in the F/A-18C/D, the F is not a mission modifier but is considered coequal with the A, so this is an aircraft that is capable of carrying out both fighter and attack missions with equal capability.

To better understand this process, consider that the H-60 helicopter has been modified into several different versions in today's Navy. The SH-60 version is used for antisubmarine warfare; the HH-60 is a helicopter of the same basic design, but this version is used for search and rescue purposes; and there are other versions as well, such as the MH-60, which is considered a "multi-mission" aircraft.

The MH-60R Sea Hawk is a "multi-mission" aircraft as designated by the "M" mission modifier.

Sometimes a mission modifier results in a change of the name as well. An example of this is the EA-6B. Originally, there was (no longer in service) an A-6 Intruder. It was (as indicated by the "A" to the left of the dash) an attack aircraft. This original design was later significantly modified (by adding some seats and a whole lot of complex electronic equipment) so that it could perform electronic warfare missions. It was redesignated the EA-6 and renamed Prowler.

STATUS PREFIX

One more place (the third) to the left of the dash is sometimes occupied by a letter called the status prefix. These letters are used for aircraft that are in a special status as follows:

G	grounded
J	special test (temporary)
N	special test (permanent)
X	experimental
Y	prototype
Z	planning

The only one of our selected examples that has a letter in this position is the NKC-135A, and we can see from the list above that it is being used for a special test (permanently). You will not often see these letters used, but it is good to be aware of them should you encounter them.

LEFT-OF-THE-DASH SUMMARY

Before moving to the right side of the dash, review Table 4 for a summary of all items that *may* appear to the left of the dash in an aircraft designation.

DESIGN

Now it is time to consider what is on the *right* side of the dash. This side is a bit easier because it does not require any memorization.

You will recall that earlier we established that aircraft designations are sometimes referred to as the MDS (Mission Design Series) system. The letters to the left of the dash make up the "mission" part of that, and the letters and numbers to the right comprise the "design" and "series" parts.

Immediately to the right of the dash is the design number. All this number means is that this aircraft is a specific design of the particular type or mission. The first design of a patrol aircraft was designated "P-1," and when a whole new design of an aircraft for patrolling was accepted by the Defense Department, it was designated "P-2," and so on.

In our chosen examples, the T-45C is the forty-fifth design of a trainer aircraft that has been accepted by DOD; the SH-60B is the sixtieth helicopter design; the EA-6B is the sixth attack aircraft design; and the NKC-135A is the 135th transport design. The F/A-18C/D is the eighteenth fighter design accepted by DOD.

Table 4. Left-of-the-Dash Summary

STATUS PREFIX	MODIFIED MISSION	BASIC MISSION	VEHICLE TYPE
G permanently grounded	A attack	A attack	G glider
J special test (temporary)	C transport	B bomber	H helicopter
N special test (permanent)	D director	C transport	Q unmanned
X experimental	E special electronics	E special electronics	S spaceplane
Y prototype	F fighter	F fighter	V V/STOL
Z planning	H search and rescue	L laser	Z lighter than air
	K tanker	O observation	(If none of the above letters appear, it is a "regular" fixed-wing aircraft.)
	L cold weather	P patrol	
	M multi-mission	R reconnaissance	
	O observation	S antisubmarine	
	P patrol	T trainer	
	Q drone (unmanned)	U utility	
	R reconnaissance	X research	
	S antisubmarine		
	T trainer		
	U utility		
	V staff		
	W weather		

SERIES

Many times the basic design of an aircraft is modified in some way, so that it is no longer the same aircraft as originally designed, but it has not been changed enough to warrant calling it a whole new design. To indicate this significant modification (version), a series letter is appended to the design number. The aircraft in its original design is considered to be "A" in the series. The first modification would be "B," the next would be "C," and so on. "I" and "O" are not used because they might be confused with one and zero.

So we now know that the NKC-135A is an original design (as indicated by the "A" series indicator) and that the SH-60B and the EA-6B have each been modified once. The F/A-18C/D is, once again, a special case. There are actually two different versions of the Hornet in service; one has only one seat and is designated the "C" version, whereas the "D" version has two seats. Because both are in service you will often see them listed as "C/D" when referring to them generically.

THE SIMPLER WAY

All the above information is provided for those who want to know precisely what the aircraft designation system is telling them. But below I have compiled all the codes covering type, mission, and status into one list. In truth, if you use this list to decipher the information to the left of the dash without concerning yourself where these particular letters fall, you will know the essentials about the aircraft and only rarely get confused.

Most of the time, the letters will be clear in context. For example, if you are given a picture of an aircraft that has the designation ZSH-7A and it has rotating blades on it, the chances are the "Z" indicates that it is in "planning" rather than being a "lighter-than-air" craft, and the "S" more than likely indicates "antisubmarine" rather than "spaceplane." So, use the letters below without worrying about where they fall to the left of the dash and you will, *in most cases*, know all you need to about an aircraft:

A	attack
B	bomber
C	transport
D	director
E	special electronic installation
F	fighter
G	glider *or* grounded
H	helicopter or search and rescue
J	special test (temporary)

K	tanker
L	laser *or* cold weather
M	multi-mission
N	special test (permanent)
O	observation
P	patrol
Q	drone (unmanned)
R	reconnaissance
S	antisubmarine *or* spaceplane
T	trainer
U	utility
V	V/STOL *or* staff
W	weather
X	research *or* experimental
Y	prototype
Z	lighter than air *or* planning

The MQ-8B Fire Scout is the second version of
a multi-mission, unmanned (drone) aircraft.

AIRCRAFT ORGANIZATION

The basic organizational element for naval aircraft is the *squadron*. Some squadrons are carrier-based, spending part of their time on board aircraft carriers; others are land-based, and if their mission requires it, they may periodically deploy to other locations. Some squadrons are subdivided into detachments and are scattered to various ships or bases.

Though squadrons often have informal names that have more to do with morale than identification ("Black Knights," "Diamondbacks," etc.), they are officially identified by letter-number designations that, like ship hull numbers, tell something about their mission while giving them a unique identity. The first letter in a squadron designation is either a "V" or an "H." The V indicates fixed-wing aircraft and H is used for squadrons made up entirely of helicopters. If a squadron has *both* helicopters and fixed-wing aircraft, it is designated by a V. In the days when there was a third type of aircraft, the lighter-than-air (or dirigible) types, squadrons of those aircraft were designated by a Z.

The letter or letters following the V or H indicate the squadron's mission or missions. For example, a squadron whose primary purpose is training pilots to fly fixed-wing aircraft would be designated "VT." By adding a number, an individual squadron takes on a unique identity; for example, "VT-3." The numbers, in most cases, have some logic to them—such as even numbers indicating Atlantic Fleet squadrons and odd numbers designating Pacific Fleet—but movement and the periodic establishment and disestablishment of various squadrons has clouded some of the original intended logic.

Some of the squadron designations you might encounter are:

HM	helicopter mine countermeasures
HT	helicopter training
VA	attack
VAQ	tactical electronic warfare
VAW	carrier airborne early warning
VC	fleet composite
VF	fighter

VFA	strike fighter
VFC	fighter composite
VP	patrol
VQ	reconnaissance/strategic communications
VR	fleet logistics support
VRC	carrier logistics support
VS	sea control (antisubmarine warfare, etc.)
VT	training
VX	test and evaluation

Aircraft squadrons are typically grouped into larger organizational units called "air wings." A carrier air wing (CVW) is usually made up of about eight squadrons, each serving different but integrated purposes. With these various squadrons on board, an aircraft carrier can carry out a wide variety of missions.

APPENDIX A
GLOSSARY OF NAVY TERMS AND ABBREVIATIONS

Abaft—Farther aft, as in "abaft the beam"

Abeam—Abreast; on a relative bearing of 090 or 270 degrees

Aboard—On or in a ship or naval station

Accommodation ladder—A ladder resembling stairs that is suspended over the side of a ship to facilitate boarding from boats

Adrift—Loose from moorings and out of control (applied to anything lost, out of hand, or left lying about)

AFRICOM—African Command

Aft—Toward the stern (not as specific as abaft)

After—That which is farthest aft

Afternoon watch—The 1200 to 1600 watch

Ahoy—A hail or call for attention, as in "Boat ahoy"

Alee—Downwind

All hands—The entire ship's company

Aloft—Generally speaking, any area above the highest deck

Alongside—By the side of the ship or pier

Amidships—An indefinite area midway between the bow and the stern; "rudder amidships" means that the rudder is in line with the ship's centerline

ARG—Amphibious ready group

Armament—The weapons of a ship

Ashore—On the beach or shore

ASROC—Antisubmarine rocket

Astern—Behind a ship

ASVAB—Armed Services Vocational Aptitude Battery

Athwart—Across; at right angles to

Auxiliary—Extra, or secondary, as in "auxiliary engine"; a vessel whose mission is to supply or support combatant forces

Avast—Stop, as in "avast heaving"

Aweigh—An anchoring term used to describe the anchor clear of the bottom (the weight of the anchor is on the cable)

Aye, aye—Reply to a command or order, meaning "I understand and will obey"

Batten down—The closing of any watertight fixture

Battle lantern—A battery-powered lantern for emergency use

BCD—Bad conduct discharge

Beam—The extreme width (breadth) of a vessel, as in "a CV has a greater beam [is wider] than a destroyer"

Bear—To be located on a particular bearing, as in "the lighthouse bears 045 degrees"

Bear a hand—Provide assistance, as in "bear a hand with rigging the brow"; expedite

Bearing—The direction of an object measured in degrees clockwise from a reference point (true bearings use true north as the reference, relative bearings use the ship's bow as the reference, and magnetic bearings use magnetic north)

Belay—To secure a line to a fixed point; to disregard a previous order or to stop an action, as in "belay the last order" or "belay the small talk"

Below—Beneath, or beyond something, as in "lay below" (go downstairs); or "below the flight deck"

Berth—Bunk; duty assignment; mooring space assigned to a ship

BIBS—Bibliography for Advancement-in-Rate Exam Study

Bight—A loop in a line

Bilge—Lowest area of the ship where spills and leaks gather; to fail an examination

Billet—Place or duty to which one is assigned

Binnacle—A stand containing a magnetic compass

Binnacle list—List of persons excused from duty because of illness

Bitt—Cylindrical upright fixture (usually found in pairs) to which mooring or towing lines are secured

Bitter end—The free end of a line

Block—Roughly equivalent to a pulley

BMOW—Boatswain's mate of the watch

Board—To go aboard a vessel; a group of persons meeting for a specific purpose, as in "investigation board"

Boat—A small craft capable of being carried aboard a ship

Boat boom—A spar rigged out from the side of an anchored or moored ship to which boats are tied when not in use

Boatswain's (pronounced "BOH-sun") chair—A seat attached to a line for hoisting a person aloft or lowering over the side

Boatswain's (pronounced "BOH-sun") locker—A compartment, usually forward, where line and other equipment used by the deck force are stowed

Bollard—A strong, cylindrical, upright fixture on a pier to which ships' mooring lines are secured

Boom—A spar, usually movable, used for hoisting loads

Boot topping—Black paint applied to a ship's sides along the waterline.

Bow—The forward end of a ship or boat

Bowhook—Member of a boat's crew whose station is forward

Break out—To bring out supplies or equipment from a stowage space

Breast line—Mooring line that leads from ship to pier (or another ship, if moored alongside) at right angles to the ship and is used to keep the vessel from moving laterally away from the pier (another ship)

Bridge—Area in the superstructure from which a ship is operated

Brig—Jail

Brightwork—Bare (unpainted) metal that is kept polished

Broach to—To get crosswise to the direction of the waves (puts the vessel in danger of being rolled over by the waves)

Broad—Wide, as in "broad in the beam"

Broad on the bow or quarter—Halfway between dead ahead and abeam, and halfway between abeam and astern, respectively

Broadside—Simultaneously firing main battery guns; also sidewise, as in "the current carried the ship broadside to the beach"

Brow—"Gangplank" used for crossing from one ship to another, and from a ship to a pier. (Note:"Gangplank" is not a naval term)

Bulkhead—A vertical partition in a ship (never called a wall)

Buoy—An anchored float used as an aid to navigation or to mark the location of an object

BUPERS—Bureau of Naval Personnel

Cabin—Living compartment of a ship's commanding officer

Camel—Floating buffer between a ship and a pier (or another ship) to prevent damage by rubbing or banging (similar to a fender except that a camel is in the water whereas a fender is suspended above the water)

Carry away—To break loose, as in "the rough seas carried away the lifelines"

Carry on—An order to resume previous activity after an interruption

CBR—Chemical, biological, and radiological

CCOL—Compartment Checkoff List

CENTCOM—Central Command

Centerline—An imaginary line down the middle of a ship from bow to stern

Chafing gear—Material used to protect lines from excessive wear

Chain locker—Space where anchor chain is stowed

Chart—Nautical counterpart of a road map, showing land configuration, water depths, and aids to navigation

Chart house—The navigator's work compartment

Chip—To remove paint or rust from metallic surfaces with sharp-pointed hammers before applying paint

Chock—Deck fitting through which mooring lines are led

Chow—Food

CIC—Combat information center

CINCPACFLT—Commander in Chief Pacific Fleet

CIWS—Close-in weapons systems

CJCS—Chairman of the Joint Chiefs of Staff

CMAA—Chief master-at-arms

CNET—Chief of Naval Education and Training

CNO—Chief of Naval Operations

CO—Commanding officer

COB—Chief of the boat

COD—Carrier on-board delivery

Colors—The national ensign; the ceremony of raising and lowering the ensign

Combatant ship—A ship whose primary mission is combat

Commission pennant—A long, narrow, starred and striped pennant flown only on board a commissioned ship

Companionway—Deck opening giving access to a ladder (includes the ladder)

Compartment—Interior space of a ship (similar to a "room" ashore)

Conn—The act of controlling a ship (similar to "driving" ashore); also the station, usually on the bridge, from which a ship is controlled

CONUS—Continental United States

Course—A ship's desired direction of travel, not to be confused with heading

Cover—To protect; a shelter; headgear; to don headgear

Coxswain—(pronounced "COX-uhn") Enlisted person in charge of a boat

CPO—Chief petty officer

Crow's nest—Lookout station aloft

Cumshaw—A gift; something procured without payment

Darken ship—To turn off all external lights and close all openings through which lights can be seen from outside the ship

Davits—Strong arms by means of which a boat is hoisted in or out

Davy Jones' locker—The bottom of the sea

DC—Damage Control

DCA—Damage-control assistant

DCC—Damage Control Central

DCNO—Deputy Chief of Naval Operations

DD—Dishonorable discharge; also destroyer

Dead ahead—Directly ahead; a relative bearing of 000 degrees

Dead astern—180 degrees relative

Deck—Horizontal planking or plating that divides a ship into layers (floors)

Deck seamanship—The upkeep and operation of all deck equipment

Deep six—To throw something overboard (see also Jettison)

DEERS—Defense Enrollment Eligibility Reporting System

DJMS—Defense Joint Military Pay System

Dinghy—A small boat, sometimes equipped with a sail, but more commonly propelled by outboard motor or oars

Dip—To lower a flag partway down the staff as a salute to, or in reply to a salute from, another ship

Division—A main subdivision of a ship's crew (1st, E, G, etc.); an organization composed of two or more ships of the same type

Dock—The water-space alongside a pier

DOD—Department of Defense

Dog—A lever, or bolt and thumb screws, used for securing a watertight door; to divide a four-hour watch into two two-hour watches

Dog down—To set the dogs on a watertight door

Dog watch—The 1600–1800 or 1800–2000 watch

DON—Department of the Navy

Double up—To double mooring lines for extra strength

Draft—The vertical distance from the keel to the waterline

Dress ship—To display flags in honor of a person or event

Drift—The speed at which a ship is pushed off course by wind and current

EAOS—End of active obligated service

Ebb—A falling tide

EMCON—Emission control

Ensign—The national flag; also an O-1 paygrade officer

EW—Electronic warfare

Executive officer—Second officer in command (also called "XO")

Eyes—The forward most part of the forecastle

Fake—The act of making a line, wire, or chain ready for running by laying it out in long, flat bights, one alongside and partially overlapping the other

Fantail—The after end of the main deck

Fathom—Unit of length or depth equal to six feet

Fender—A cushioning device hung over the side of a ship to prevent contact between the ship and a pier or another ship

Field day—A day devoted to general cleaning, usually in preparation for an inspection

Firemain—Shipboard piping system to which fire hydrants are connected

First watch—The 2000–2400 watch (also called evening watch)

Flag officer—Any officer of the rank of rear admiral (lower and upper half), vice admiral, or admiral

Flagstaff—Vertical staff at the stern to which the ensign is hoisted when moored or at anchor

Fleet—An organization of ships, aircraft, marine forces, and shore-based fleet activities, all under one commander, for conducting major operations

Flood—To fill a space with water; a rising tide

Fore and aft—The entire length of a ship, as in "sweep down fore and aft"

Forecastle—Forward section of the main deck (pronounced "FOHK-sul")

Foremast—First mast aft from the bow

Forenoon watch—The 0800–1200 watch

Forward—Toward the bow

Foul—Entangled, as in "the lines are foul of each other"; stormy

FOUO—For official use only

Gaff—A light spar set at an angle from the upper part of a mast (the national ensign is usually flown from the gaff under way)

Galley—Space where food is prepared (never called a kitchen)

Gangway—The opening in a bulwark or lifeline that provides access to a brow or accommodation ladder; an order meaning to clear the way

General quarters—The condition of full readiness for battle

Gig—Boat assigned for the commanding officer's personal use

GMT—General Military Training

GMT—Greenwich Mean Time

GQ—General quarters

Ground tackle—Equipment used in anchoring or mooring with anchors

Gunwale—Where the sides join the main deck of a ship

Halyard—A light line used to hoist a flag or pennant

Hard over—Condition of a rudder that has been turned to the maximum possible rudder angle

Hashmark—A red, blue, or gold diagonal stripe across the left sleeve of an enlisted person's jumper, indicating four years of service

Hatch—An opening in a deck used for access

Hawser—Any heavy line used for towing or mooring

Head—The upper end of a lower mast boom; compartment containing toilet facilities; ship's bow

Heading—The direction toward which the ship's bow is pointing at any instant

Heave—To throw, as in "heave a line to the pier"

Heave around—To haul in a line, usually by means of a capstan or winch

Heaving line—A line with a weight at one end, heaved across an intervening space for passing over a heavier line

Helm—Steering wheel of a ship

Highline—The line stretched between ships under way on which a trolley block travels back and forth to transfer material and personnel

Hitch—To bend a line to or around a ring or cylindrical object; also an enlistment

Hull—The shell, or plating, of a ship from keel to gunwale

IFF—Identification friend or foe

IFR—Instrument flight rules

Inboard—Toward the centerline

Island—Superstructure of an aircraft carrier

Jackstaff—Vertical spar at the stem to which the jack is hoisted

Jacob's ladder—A portable rope or wire ladder

Jettison—To throw overboard

Jetty—A structure built out from shore to influence water currents or protect a harbor or pier

JOOD—Junior officer of the deck

Jump ship—To desert a ship

Jury rig—Any makeshift device or apparatus; to fashion such a device

Knock off—Quit, cease, or stop, as in "knock off ship's work"

Knot—One nautical mile per hour

Ladder—A flight of steps aboard ship

Lanyard—Any short line used as a handle or as a means for operating some piece of equipment; a line used to attach an article to the person, as a pistol lanyard

Launch—To float a vessel off the ways in a building yard; also a type of powerboat, usually over 30 feet long

Lay—Movement of a person, as in "lay aloft"; also the direction of twist in the strands of a line or wire

LCAC—Landing craft, air cushion

Lee—An area sheltered from the wind; downwind

Leeward—Direction toward which the wind is blowing (pronounced "LOO-urd")

Liberty—Sanctioned absence from a ship or station for a short time for pleasure rather than business

Lifelines—In general, the lines erected around the edge of a weather deck to prevent personnel from falling or being washed overboard; more precisely (though not often used), the topmost line (from top to bottom, these lines are named lifeline, housing line, and foot-rope)

Line—Any rope that is not wire rope

List—Transverse inclination of a vessel (when a ship leans to one side)

Log—A ship's speedometer; also book or ledger in which data or events that occurred during a watch are recorded; also to make a certain speed, as in "the ship logged 20 knots"

Lookout—Person stationed topside on a formal watch who reports objects sighted and sounds heard to the officer of the deck

LPO—Leading petty officer

Lucky bag—Locker under the charge of the master-at-arms; used to collect and stow deserters' effects and gear found adrift

Magazine—Compartment used for the stowage of ammunition

Main deck—The uppermost complete deck. (An exception is the aircraft carrier, where the main deck is defined as the hangar bay rather than the flight deck, which arguably fits the criterion of the definition.)

Mainmast—Second mast aft from the bow on a vessel with more than one mast. (On a ship with only one mast, it is usually referred to simply as "the mast.") The tallest mast on a vessel.

Main truck—The top of the tallest mast on a vessel

Make fast—To secure

Man-o'-war—A ship designed for combat

Marlinespike—Tapered steel tool used to open the strands of line or wire rope for splicing

Marlinespike seamanship—The art of caring for and handling all types of line and wire

Master-at-arms—A member of a ship's police force

Mate—A shipmate; another Sailor

MCPON—Master Chief Petty Officer of the Navy

Mess—Meal; place where meals are eaten; a group that takes meals together, as in officers' mess

Messenger—A line used to haul a heavier line across an intervening space; one who delivers messages

Midwatch—The watch that begins at 0000 and ends at 0400

Moor—To make fast to a pier, another ship, or a mooring buoy; also, to anchor

Morning watch—The 0400–0800 watch

MSC—Military Sealift Command

MSTS—Military Sea Transportation Service

Muster—A roll call; to assemble for a roll call

MWR—Morale, Welfare, and Recreation

NAVAIR—Naval Air Systems Command

NAVCENT—United States Naval Forces Central Command

NAVEUR—United States Naval Forces Europe

NAVFAC—Naval Facilities Engineering Command

NAVSEA—Naval Sea Systems Command

NAVSHIPSTECHMAN—Naval Ships' Technical Manual

NAVSUP—Naval Supply Systems Command

NCIS—Naval Criminal Investigative Service

NEC—Naval Enlisted Classification (occupational)

Nest—Two or more boats stowed one within the other; two or more ships moored alongside each other

NETC—Naval Education and Training Command

NEX—Navy Exchange

NJP—Nonjudicial punishment

NKO—Navy Knowledge Online

NSTC—Naval Service Training Command

OCS—Officer Candidate School

OJT—On-the-job training

On the beach—Ashore; also a Sailor assigned to shore duty, unemployed, retired, or otherwise detached from sea duty

OOD—Officer of the deck

OPNAV—Office of the Chief of Naval Operations (the Navy Staff)

Outboard—Away from the centerline

Overhaul—To repair or recondition; to overtake another vessel

Overhead—The underside of a deck that forms the overhead of the compartment next below (never called a ceiling)

PACFLT—United States Pacific Fleet

Passageway—A corridor used for interior horizontal movement aboard ship (similar to a hallway ashore)

Pay out—To feed out or lengthen a line

PCS—Permanent change of station

Pier—Structure extending from land into water to provide a mooring for vessels

Pigstick—Small staff from which a commission pennant is flown

Pilot house—Enclosure on the bridge housing the main steering controls

Pitch—Vertical rise and fall of a ship's bow and stern caused by head or following seas

Plane guard—Destroyer or helicopter responsible for rescuing air crews during launch or recovery operations

Plank owner—A person who was assigned to the ship's company when he or she was commissioned

Plan of the Day (POD)—Schedule of a day's routine and events ordered by the executive officer and published daily aboard ship or at a shore activity

PO—Petty officer

Pollywog—A person who has never crossed the equator

Port—To the left of the centerline when facing forward

QMOW—Quartermaster of the watch

Quarterdeck—Deck area designated by the commanding officer as the place to carry out official functions; station of the officer of the deck in port

Quarters—Stations for shipboard evolutions, as in "general quarters," "fire quarters"; living spaces

Quay—A solid structure along a bank used for loading and offloading vessels (pronounced "*key*")

Rat guard—A hinged metal disk secured to a mooring line to prevent rats from traveling over the line into the ship

RCPO—Recruit chief petty officer

RDC—Recruit division commander

Relief—A person assigned to take over the duties of another

Riding lights—Navigational lights shown at night by a moored vessel

Rig—To set up a device or equipment, as in "to rig a stage over the side"

Rigging—Line that has been set up to be used for some specific purpose (e.g., lines that support a ship's masts are called standing rigging, and lines that hoist or otherwise move equipment are called running rigging)

Rope—Fiber or wire line (fiber rope is usually referred to as line, while wire rope is called rope, wire rope, or wire)

Ropeyarn Sunday—A workday or part of a workday that has been granted as a holiday for taking care of personal business

RT—Radiotelephone (voice radio)

RTC—Recruit Training Command

Rudder—A flat, vertical surface mounted at the stern of a vessel, below the waterline, used in steering; *also*, a part of an aircraft tail section that performs a similar function

Running lights—Navigational lights shown at night by a vessel under way

Scuttlebutt—A drinking fountain (originally, a ship's water barrel [called a butt] that was tapped [scuttled] by the insertion of a spigot from which the crew drew drinking water); also a rumor (the scuttlebutt was once a place for personnel to exchange news when the crew gathered to draw water)

Sea anchor—A device streamed from the bow of a vessel for holding it end-on to the sea

SECDEF—Secretary of Defense

SECNAV—Secretary of the Navy

Second deck—First complete deck below the main deck

Secure—To make fast, as in "secure a line to a cleat"; to cease, as in "secure from fire drill"

SGLI—Servicemembers group life insurance

Shake down—The training of a new crew in operating a ship

Shellback—A person who has crossed the equator

Shift colors—To change the arrangement of colors upon getting under way or coming to moorings

Ship—Any large seagoing vessel capable of extended independent operation

Ship over—To reenlist in the Navy

Ship's company—All hands permanently attached to a ship or station; the crew

Sick bay—Shipboard space that serves as a hospital or medical clinic

Side boy—One of a group of seamen who form two ranks at the gangway as part of the ceremonies conducted for visiting officials

Side light—One of a series of running lights (the starboard side light is green and the port side light is red)

SIQ—Sick-in-quarters

Skylark—To engage in irresponsible horseplay

Slack—To allow a line to run out; also undisciplined, as in a "slack ship"

SOCOM—U.S. Special Operations Command

SOF—Special Operations Forces

SOPA—Senior officer present afloat

Sound—To determine the depth of water; to dive deep (of marine animals); also a body of water between the mainland and a large coastal island

SOUTHCOM—Southern Command

Spar—The nautical equivalent of a pole

Special sea detail—Crew members assigned special duties when leaving and entering port

Splice—To join lines or wires together by intertwining strands; the joint so made

SSBN—Nuclear-powered ballistic missile submarine

SSGN—Guided-missile nuclear submarine

Stack—Shipboard chimney

Stanchion—Vertical post for supporting decks; smaller, similar posts for supporting lifelines, awnings, and so on

Starboard—Direction to the right of the centerline as one faces forward

State room—A living compartment for an officer or officers

Stay—Any piece of standing rigging providing support only

Stem—Extreme forward line of bow

Stern—The aftermost part of a vessel

Stern light—White navigation light that can be seen only from astern

Stow—To store or pack articles or cargo in a space

STRATCOM—Strategic Command

Structural bulkhead—Transverse strength bulkhead that forms a watertight boundary

SUBLANT—Naval Submarine Force, U.S. Atlantic Fleet

SUBPAC—Naval Submarine Force, U.S. Pacific Fleet

Superstructure—The structure above a ship's main deck

SURFLANT—Naval Surface Force, U.S. Atlantic Fleet

SURFPAC—Naval Surface Force, U.S. Pacific Fleet

Swab—A mop; also to mop

TAD—Temporary additional duty

Taut—Under tension; also highly disciplined and efficient, as in "a taut ship"

TDY—Temporary duty

Topside—Weather decks; above (referring to the deck or decks above)

Truck—The uppermost tip of a mast

Turn to—To start working

UA—Unauthorized absence

UCMJ—Uniform Code of Military Justice

UDT—Underwater Demolition Team

UNREP—Underway replenishment

USHBP—Uniformed Services Health Benefit Program

VERTREP—Vertical Replenishment

VFR—Visual instrument flight rules

VLS—Vertical launch system

Void—An empty tank aboard ship

Waist—The amidships section of the main deck

Wake—Trail left by a vessel or other object moving through the water

Wardroom—Officers' messing compartment; collective term used to signify the officers assigned to a ship

Watch—One of the periods, usually four hours, into which a day is divided; a particular duty, as in "life buoy watch"

Watertight integrity—The degree or quality of watertightness

Weather deck—Any deck exposed to the elements

Weigh anchor—To hoist the anchor clear of the bottom

Wharf—Structure similar to a quay but constructed like a pier

Whipping—Binding on the end of a line or wire to prevent unraveling

XO—Executive officer; second in command

Yardarm—The port or starboard half of a spar set athwartships across the upper mast

Yaw—(Of a vessel) to have its heading thrown wide of its course as the result of a force, such as a heavy following sea

APPENDIX B
SAILOR ATTRIBUTES FROM
HOW WE FIGHT

In 2015, the Chief of Naval Operations published *How We Fight: Handbook for the Naval Warfighter*, explaining:

Over the years, Sailors have benefited from a number of handbooks such as the *Watch Officer's Guide* and *The Bluejacket's Manual* to learn the basics of our profession. In addition to rate and warfare specialty training, these references served as a foundation of knowledge on which generations of naval personnel built their professional careers. These books of seamanship, administration, and leadership are terrific guides for excelling in our profession.

How We Fight is a concise, single volume that explains the basic, unique, and enduring attributes associated with being a Sailor, going to sea, and conducting war at sea. It highlights the fundamentals of the environment in which the Navy operates, our uniquely maritime characteristics, our history in this domain, and the way of Navy warfighting. This book should serve as a companion piece to other sources of literature enabling Sailors to understand the essence of being "a Sailor" as they develop their skills as sea going professionals.

Chapter two of *How We Fight* discusses the attributes deemed necessary to be a successful Sailor in today's Navy, and portions of that chapter are quoted here.

ATTRIBUTES OF THE INDIVIDUAL SAILOR: CORE VALUES AND INITIATIVE

. . . no Sailor acts alone. That remains even more so when we have to fight. Yet, to be an effective member of a crew, the Sailor must possess personal characteristics—we can call them virtues or values—that spark the individual actions necessary for the success of the entire organization. It is the responsibility of all navy leaders to inspire and direct such actions if we are to effectively achieve our missions. It is upon these action-causing individual characteristics that successful navy war fighting is founded. First are our core values of honor, courage and commitment. These innate characteristics are the keel upon which all the attributes of individual navy ships and units—indeed, those of the entire Naval Service—are built. These core values are embodied in the Sailor's Creed and United States Navy Ethos. They are ultimately the source of our power as the world's foremost navy.

A value complementary to the three core values is trust. Sailors must trust that others in the crew will perform their tasks and stand their watches to the best of their ability. The captain must trust the crew and the crew must have trust in the captain's skill and decision making. Trust is the operational face of the value of honor, and is an essential requirement for survival in the maritime environment, especially in combat. Like our organization and operational focus, these core values have roots in the environment. To have effect, they must be applied to real life situations within that environment. They must—and have throughout history—be brought into action. In action, the Sailors of the U.S. Navy have always embodied a combination of faithful execution of lawful orders with *great personal initiative* in the absence of orders or when direction is unclear, fragmented, or unavailable. It has often been remarked that it is this sense of personal initiative that has always distinguished U.S. Sailors. Some of this personal attribute is a result of living in a democratic nation in which all citizens are free to make their own choices on how to live and how to be governed. A productive life in such a society requires initiative. This natural tendency is reinforced by a navy culture in which initiative is encouraged, prized and rewarded. Our Navy must always be structured to support individual initiative and each leader must help foster it in his or her Sailors. It is only by fostering this individual characteristic that it can be effectively instilled in the commanding officers and crews of warships and other navy units so that they are ready to take the initiative when it matters most, and in the absence of direction by higher command.

Earlier we discussed how the key personal values and attributes are required by the very fact of being at sea. These are the prerequisite attributes that we expect of each Sailor upon entry into the U.S. Navy, and we make great efforts during basic training and beyond to reinforce these values. But—like the basic designs of our warships—these personal characteristics are shaped by the maritime environment, shaped by the sea. One cannot master the sea without full commitment.

Psychologists advise that to learn to have courage, one must consciously endeavor to act courageous even when the initial instinct is to show fear. This view suggests that one learns to routinely act courageously by conscious and thoughtful repetition.

Through such conditioning one can acquire the habit of courage. In the face of the challenges of the maritime environment—such dangers as violent storms, the transfer of fuel or handling of ordnance in pitching seas, or other inherently dangerous activities routinely carried out—courage is always needed. It is this habit of courage, developed in facing the hazards of the maritime environment that helps to instill the individual courage needed for battle. In the same way, the habits of honor—symbolically demonstrated by navy customs and traditions; and commitment—a requirement of all successful crew efforts—are reinforced through repetitive experience.

ATTRIBUTES OF THE INDIVIDUAL SAILOR: RESILIENCE AND SELF-RELIANCE

Going hand-in-hand, or shall we say hand-over-hand, is resilience. Resilience is defined as the ability to recover rapidly from change or misfortune. In routine activities at sea with their inherent dangers, simple resilience is reflected in the ability to respond to accidents or damage, effectively correct the situation, and continue the task. All Sailors must have a sense of resilience if the crew and warship they are a part of is also to be resilient. Ships are designed for damage control, which is a means of maintaining structural resilience. But the actions necessary to carry out damage control come from resilient Sailors. We train to be resilient, but, as we have noted, the resilience must initially come from within each individual.

In combat, this sense of resilience, particularly when under the fire of a hostile force, means the difference between victory and defeat. As a historical example, the U.S. Fleet suffered a crushing blow at Pearl Harbor, but it was resilient enough to rebound back and win the war. The resilience of the Fleet started with the resilience of the individual Sailor, supported by contingency plans and doctrine, ship repair capacity of both navy and commercial shipyards, and afloat tenders and repair ships, and a supremely effective logistics network.

A more recent example of crew resilience is survival of the USS *Samuel B. Roberts* (FFG-58) after it struck a mine on 14 April 1988. *Samuel B. Roberts* had deployed to the Persian Gulf as part of Operation Earnest Will, the escort of reflagged Kuwaiti tankers during the Iran–Iraq War. Heading to a refueling rendezvous in waters it had previously transited, the ship spotted three Iranian mines which it avoided.

It subsequently struck a fourth unseen mine that blew a 15-foot (5 m) hole in her hull. In addition to flooding the engine room and displacing the ship's two main engines from their mounts, the blast broke the keel—structural damage that almost always sinks the ship. The crew fought fires and flooding for five hours. They saved the ship by taking exceptional damage control actions such as wrapping cables around the cracked superstructure. Throughout, *Samuel B. Roberts* never lost combat capability; her radars and missile launcher remained on line, and she suffered no fatalities.

Yet another characteristic the Navy endeavors to develop in each Sailor is a personal sense of self-reliance that makes his or her individual contribution as a member of the crew even more effective. Self-reliance is not about operating independently; it is about having the capability as well as the initiative to take action without having to wait for support or assistance from somewhere else. In order to be self-reliant—within the confines of a hull and superstructure design shaped in part by the characteristics of the maritime environment—warships carry with them as many provisions, repair parts, ordnance, and other logistical material as can be efficiently stored. This is necessitated by the fact that ships and other units continuously deploy to far regions where there are no opportunities for extensive re-provision or outside help. Just as with the ship itself, self-reliance is necessary at the individual, work center, and watch team levels. Teams must operate in mutual support, each Sailor providing specialized skills. But a team cannot wait for its reliefs to solve a developing problem. An evolving situation needs to be solved before the situation becomes hazardous. This calls for a degree of foresight that is a fundamental aspect of self-reliance.

Developing robust self-reliance requires making the most of every opportunity for training, experience, and self-improvement. Earlier we wrote of the need to constantly replenish one's knowledge of navy operations and functional expertise. This too requires a degree of self-reliance. You must take the personal initiative to teach yourself using the available references and information. Self-reliance requires personal initiative to expand professional knowledge. That is why the Navy maintains a Chief of Naval Operations Professional Reading list, in addition to numerous training manuals, tactical publications and other professional references such as *The Bluejacket's Manual*, *The Chief Petty Officer's Guide*, *Watch Officer's Guide*, and *Division Officer's Guide*. There is also a wealth of on-line courses and electronic learning opportunities.

FROM INDIVIDUAL ATTRIBUTES TO THE FUNCTIONING OF THE CREW

While the necessary attributes of individual Sailors are the framework, the proper functioning of a crew must begin with collective adherence to core values. This is where the mutual trust necessary for maximum performance in danger and combat begins. Reinforcing this trust are extensive exercises to which every navy unit is subjected. Along with internal training and evaluations, such exercises require the team to practice and demonstrate its highest peacetime performance. In combat, this trust must be absolute. Commonly accepted and practiced core values are the keel of absolute trust.

Like individual initiative, the crew must demonstrate collective initiative. No command can achieve operational success without a crew with initiative. In fact, our war fighting doctrine is predicated on it. Perhaps the most dramatic illustration of that is the operation of a ship's Combat Information Center (CIC) or Combat Direction Center (CDC). While sitting in "Combat" during General Quarters, the Commanding Officer cannot and does not direct the myriad of simultaneous activities involving weapons engagements in multiple dimensions. It is the Tactical Action Officer (TAO)—with weapons release authority from the CO who directs the overall war fighting activity. Under the TAO, actual engagements in specific dimensions—air, surface, undersea, the electronic spectrum, or even space—are directed by officers, chief petty officers, or petty officers assigned to specialized tasks: the (missile) fire control officer, anti-submarine warfare evaluator, and electronic warfare supervisor are but three examples. All personnel take action in accordance with their training, standardized procedures and rules of engagement, and appropriate preplanned responses. The TAO prioritizes the activities and gives the action order to fire. Meanwhile—in accordance with our doctrine—the CO's role is to maintain command of the overall situation and command by negation, that is, to stop the release of weapons or otherwise correct and redirect the TAO if the CO concludes that another solution should be used. In this fashion, the CO has the opportunity to concentrate on the integration of all the ship's actions, whether in Combat, on the Bridge, in the Engineering Central Station, Damage Control Central, or at weapons stations—in other words, to see the "bigger picture" and role of the ship as a unit of the task group or fleet. Without such a doctrine, the speed of events in modern day warfare demands a span of attention to detail too great for any one human, even the CO.

This requirement to delegate activities and responsibilities cannot succeed without initiative on the part of each watch stander and participant. No member of the crew can simply wait for "orders from above." All must take decisive action.

A crew member who spots danger—a fire or flooding, as examples— cannot simply report its existence to Damage Control Central, he or she must also take whatever immediate actions are possible to stop it. This requires initiative throughout the crew, and as a crew.

Just as with initiative, individual resilience also sums to a resilient crew, one that will not give up its efforts when faced with difficulty or danger. A resilient crew rebounds from setbacks and uses its collective initiative to find (whether in hours or seconds) new methods for accomplishing the mission. Self-reliance for the crew is the sum of the individual self-reliance of every crewmember. U.S. warships operate forward for long periods of time; they are expected to be able to operate independently, away from sources of supply or repair, and in a hostile physical environment. Ultimately, the ship can rely only on itself and the other ships in its operational task group. There will always be limits to the logistics it can carry. But the crew and warship must be self-reliant to its utmost in order to survive, let alone complete the mission. In a very real sense, there is no choice except to be self-reliant. There is nowhere to escape from everyday dangers, such as fire or flooding or from hostile actions. The crew must continue to "fight the ship" as well as control the damage from enemy action, and have the self-reliance to perform and succeed. As Professor Wayne Hughes of the Naval Postgraduate School describes battle at sea: "No place to hide in ships: where the captain fights, you fight."

FROM THE ATTRIBUTES OF THE CREW TO THE ATTRIBUTES OF THE WARSHIP

Warships are designed to accomplish specified missions and survive in the maritime environment. They are also designed with the attributes that we have discussed in mind. A good warship design both facilitates and requires the crew to be self-reliant, resilient and show initiative.

The systems within the hull are complex. As hard as we try to include automatic and time and labor-saving devices into these systems, they still must be operated by the crew. Decision-making in naval combat is too complex to be performed entirely by machines, even the most advanced computers with artificial intelligence. The crew and the command structure—with command by negation—are the decision-making intelligence of a warship.

As a counterpart to the crew's ability to take initiative, a warship must be designed to ensure flexibility accomplishing its missions. Over its 30 to 50-year lifespan, a warship will be called upon to complete tasks and missions its designers may have never envisioned. Each ship, based on its original planned use, has specific mission-related requirements that affect its design capabilities. Most warships are designed with some degree of multi-mission capabilities. They are capable of conducting simultaneous multi-dimensional combat and a wide variety of peacetime missions.

Warships have and will be used in unanticipated and improvisational ways.

Operating airplanes from cruisers at the advent of taking aviation to sea, or operating U.S. Army helicopters and stability teams from aircraft carriers, as was done during Operation Uphold Democracy, the U.S. military intervention in Haiti in 1994, are but two examples. There are many more, with increasing numbers after the end of the Cold War.

Navy warships are designed to accommodate both changes in mission and changes in configuration. As navy technology advances, new weapons and other systems will emerge to improve navy war fighting capabilities. Warships must be designed with the engineering margins and design flexibility to maintain mission capabilities over a long service life.

Recently, the Navy took innovative steps in the use of modularity in warship design to give certain ship classes the capability to completely replace mission packages. However, whether referred to as being modular, or not, all warships are designed with the attribute of flexibility.

Resilience is another attribute of U.S. Navy warship design. American warships are designed to take battle damage that would incapacitate commercial ships, and, indeed, many of the naval combatants of other nations. Compartmentation, redundancy and separation of mission essential systems, damage control systems, and shock-hardening are but some of the unique features that contribute to operational resilience. In the area of logistics, resiliency is maintained by the world's most extensive fleet of navy at-sea replenishment and resupply vessels.

The U.S. Navy does not maintain "one shot and done" combatants. American naval operational doctrine is based on the assumption of a high degree of resilience in all forces; it is a design attribute of our warships which we rely upon.

TACTICAL ATTRIBUTES OF NAVAL FORCES

The mutually supporting and cumulative attributes of the individual Sailor, crew and warship generate tactical attributes that enhance the flexibility, combat power, and operational effectiveness of U.S. naval forces. The combat capabilities of U.S. Navy forces are extensive and to fully describe them would require extensive volumes. Here we will briefly discuss a few of the key tactical attributes common to U.S. warships when operated together as task groups, forces or fleets.

One tactical attribute, derived directly from our philosophy of warship design and tactical networking, is the ability to operate as a concentrated force or to operate equally effectively when dispersed. Sensors, communications and information processing capabilities, strike and self-protection by means of missiles, guns, decoys, and electronic warfare systems, and logistical self-reliance allow individual warships and other navy units to operate independently and complete tasks that do not require the efforts of a combined force. At the same time, these individual task units can remain networked together to maintain a common operating picture or to quickly revert to combined operational control. Networking has been an attribute of navies since the first use of simple visual communications such as signal flags.

The evolving sophistication of navy communications has continuously increased this networking capability, often with considerable spillover effects to the civilian world. It was the U.S. Navy's experimentation with ship-to-ship and ship-to-shore radio communications during the early 1900s that directly led to the development of the commercial radio broadcast industry.

Networking allows navy forces to be operated in an aggregated or disaggregated manner, greatly enhancing the options available for an operational commander, as well as allowing for the coordinated, perhaps simultaneous application of navy power over long distances and in multiple regions. Task groups and forces can be reconfigured by the inclusion of new units or the release of existing units in order to ensure optimal configurations for assigned tasks and missions. A recent term used to describe this feature is "scalability." A naval group can be scaled to the particular task assigned; the ship types and numbers necessary for counter-piracy operations will be different from those for an amphibious operation. Scalability has been an attribute of our naval forces for years. It stems from individual ship designs and the necessities of the environment.

Another tactical attribute is the ability for dispersed platforms to operate a wide-ranging network and concentrate naval fires (kinetic strikes). Concentrated fire from multiple axes and domains is an attribute that is difficult to replicate by the use of other types of military forces. Naval fires are also unique in that they can be concentrated in any domain from outside that domain. For example, sustained attacks can be made on undersea targets from multiple units, concentrating fire from undersea (submarines), surface (surface ships), and air (ASW aircraft). A strike against shore targets from the sea can also be conducted simultaneously from all these dimensions, supported and enhanced by the use of electro-magnetic spectrum capabilities, cyber warfare, and information from space-based sensors and systems. This ability to concentrate fires from multiple domains is an attribute of navy forces that is critical to joint operations.

In joint doctrine, operational maneuver has often been portrayed as a counterpole to concentrated fires. For a number of years, "maneuver warfare" was a term used to describe a "new" tenet of military operations that sought to avoid "attrition warfare." However, wide-ranging maneuver has always been a natural attribute of navy forces. The sea both enables maneuver and requires us to employ it to prevail in combat. Naval fires and naval maneuver are complementary attributes.

In naval warfare, maneuver is an attribute that can enable the concentration of fires, if necessary, or the detachment and dispersal of forces as determined by the operational commander. The use of the sea as a maneuver space provides navy forces with tremendous tactical and strategic advantages. The mobility and reach of modern naval forces, equipped with advanced strike/naval fires and amphibious capabilities, translate into an ability to attack (and defend positions) anywhere in the littorals. The enemy is left to wonder where our navy forces will strike, forced to both defend the length of his coastline and spread his forces too thin, or concentrate his force in what it considers critical areas, leaving other areas lightly defended. Employing conditions of the maritime environment to create "confusion of the enemy" and "over-commitment of enemy resources" are not in themselves unique to navy operations; but they are representative results of our navy attributes. These attributes in turn contribute to the strategic attribute of assured access.

Another operational attribute of naval forces might be called "cooperative protection." This is not a doctrinal term, but appropriately describes the longstanding defense-in-depth approach that the U.S. Navy has employed for combat operations. The maneuverability inherent at sea facilitates this approach.

Historically, navy defense-in-depth in task group, force, or fleet operations has centered on the protection of a "high value unit," usually the most powerful offensive strike platform such as an aircraft carrier. This concept originated before World War II, but became the standard at-sea formations typifying that conflict.

Other—generally smaller and more numerous—classes of warships would be assigned in operating zones or concentric rings around the high value units to provide the defense-in-depth. Such formations also facilitated the mutual self protection of all the ship in formation. With the great advances in navy technology since that war—particularly in the range and destructiveness of modern weapons and the high level of networking—cooperative protection is less dependent on concentration of forces. However, it remains a routine attribute of operations, facilitated by ship design, operational doctrine, training and experience, and ultimately, the abilities of the crews.

At the tactical level, the term sustainment is an appropriate combination of the attributes of resilience and self-reliance. Sustainment has been defined as "the delivery of tailored support and logistics across the spectrum of conflict from the sea." In light of the need to support the attributes previously discussed, such as the ability to operate forces dispersed over far distances, sustainment could also be described as an operational attribute. As noted, the attributes of navy forces are always mutually supportive, integrated, and cumulative in effect.

Another critical navy tactical attribute is persistent operational stealth. In recent years, stealth has been most often associated with the characteristics of the radar evading properties of fourth- and fifth-generation combat aircraft. This type of stealth was initially demonstrated in combat in Operation Desert Storm in 1991. But our Navy's submarine force has long been the primary practitioners of operational stealth in the U.S. armed forces. This was true even in the era before nuclear propulsion, although nuclear propulsion increased the stealth characteristic of submarines multifold. These stealth characteristics are derived directly from the undersea environment, whose physical properties frustrate most forms of observation. As the ultimate stealth force, ballistic-missile submarines are considered the most survivable leg of the U.S. nuclear triad, while attack submarines armed with cruise-missiles or carrying special operations forces can approach hostile shores submerged and minimal chance of detection, and operate there for months on end. This persistent stealth is a natural attribute of the U.S. Navy's ability to operate in the maritime environment.

APPENDIX C
VISITING YOUR SAILOR'S SHIP: CROSSING THE QUARTERDECK

You might have the opportunity to visit your Sailor's ship. You may be able to simply visit your son or daughter during a port visit or, if you are truly fortunate, there will be an opportunity for you to participate in what is known as a *tiger cruise*. This is a special event that allows families and friends to actually go to sea with their Sailors. Tiger cruises can be a one-day event—under way and back to port in one day—or, in some special cases, can include overnight times. The Navy tries hard to schedule these events when possible because of the obvious morale boost they can provide, but cost factors, such as the price of fuel, and operational needs must take priority.

If you are able to visit your Sailor's ship there are some things to know that will prepare you to maximize the experience. We have learned some of the basic "geography" and language of ships in previous sections; now we will learn some of the customs, cautions, and practices that you will need to understand to have a safe, enjoyable, and worthwhile experience while embarked in a Navy ship.

ARRIVAL

First, some clarification. You have probably encountered the terms "aboard" and "on board" and wondered what the difference is. There isn't much. Both are acceptable. Although "aboard" is usually preferred, you can also use "on board" and be safe. Do not use "onboard" (as one word) when writing, however; that is incorrect in naval usage. You will see it hyphenated as an adjective, however, as in, "We will be using the on-board computers for our calculations." One convention (but not a rule) is that *aboard* deals with people and *on board* deals with equipment, as in, "Be sure to take the laptops on board next week when we go aboard the ship."

You will also encounter the word "embark" (as in the above text), but it is generally used to indicate people (usually not equipment) who are not part of the regular crew, as in, "The reporter will embark next week to interview those Sailors still aboard who took part in the operation," or, "The Marines will embark at dawn for transport to the assault area." Units that contain people can also embark, as in, "The battalion has been embarked for most of the deployment."

The opposite of aboard is *ashore*. The opposite of embark is *debark* or *disembark*. Webster's prefers the latter; the Navy tends to prefer the former.

When you go aboard a ship, you will probably cross from a pier to the ship and you will use the *brow* (not the "gangplank") to cross over. If you are going aboard a ship that is anchored out, you will come aboard from a boat using an *accommodation ladder* rather than a brow. In either case, you will first encounter the equivalent to an entrance hall or foyer in a building; this is called the *quarterdeck*. This may be an open deck area or it may be covered by an awning or actually located just inside the skin of the ship. The quarterdeck is considered a formal, sometimes even ceremonial area. It is not a place for loud talking or laughing. You might note that Sailors coming aboard or going ashore via the quarterdeck go through a ritual of saluting both the national ensign (American flag), which is always located at the ship's stern when not under way, and the quarterdeck watch officer; they will also report their intentions to the latter very formally. You also should report to the quarterdeck watch officer (often called the "officer of the deck" or "OOD"), albeit a bit less formally. You will be required to show proper identification.

Keep in mind that boarding any Navy ship is similar to entering a Navy installation ashore, which means that you are giving full consent to a search of your bags and/or luggage just by being there. Although baggage inspection is not always done, you should be prepared to submit your baggage if requested to do so.

WHAT TO BRING

Although help may be available, you may have to carry whatever you bring up and down rather steep staircases—ladders—and through narrow passageways. Distances on a large ship, such as an aircraft carrier, can be quite long and passages can be particularly cramped. Also bear in mind that stowage space for your belongings will not be spacious. So don't bring more than you will need.

Though the Navy prides itself on keeping its ships as clean as possible, it is also a place where lubricating oils and other substances not friendly to nice clothing abound, so durable, washable clothing is a better choice over your favorite special-care clothing. If you will be embarked for a longer period and must subject your clothing to the ship's laundry, remember that your clothes will be in rather rough company and delicate treatment is not the order of the day—though only legendary, the "button crusher" that is supposedly standard equipment in every ship's laundry did not spring entirely from fertile imaginations!

Odds are you will have to travel some distance through a passageway or two to reach the nearest head, so be sure to bring a robe of some kind for the trek to the shower. Also bring some sort of shower shoes, flip-flops or the like, to prevent stubbed toes and a possible case of athlete's foot.

You never know when you might be rousted from your bunk in the middle of the night in case of a drill or emergency, so it is better to sleep in something you wouldn't mind being seen in as you stumble half-asleep to an assigned mustering station.

Many ships have some form of exercise equipment, so athletic gear is not a bad idea if you are going to be aboard long enough to make it worthwhile. There is nothing quite like a jog on an aircraft carrier's flight deck if you are fortunate enough to be aboard during one of those times when flight operations are not taking place.

Cameras are usually acceptable and are recommended if going aboard is a new experience for you, but follow instructions and use discretion in shooting photographs. If in doubt, ask or don't shoot.

If you bring a compact disk player or the like, keep it small, bring extra batteries—they may or may not be available in the ship's store—and don't count on a lot of available electrical outlets. Be careful about "tuning out" the ship entirely through the use of headphones and loud music—important announcements can be made at any time.

A small flashlight is a good idea. But make sure it has a red lens, or be very careful of shining it near nighttime watchstanders because you can temporarily remove their night vision with white light.

"NAVIGATING" ABOARD SHIP

Finding your way around a patrol craft will not prove too challenging, but people have been known to get lost on aircraft carriers for years—slight exaggeration, but the point is made! Fortunately, crew members are usually more than happy to show off their knowledge and help you find what you are looking for. But there is also a system by which you can find your own way around—and it is logical, the same for all Navy ships, and not terribly hard to learn.

Just as a town or city has a system using street signs and addresses to help you find your way around, so does a Navy ship. Each compartment on a ship has an identifier—which is actually posted on the bulkhead or partition in each compartment—that is roughly equivalent to a street address in a city. Once you understand this system, you will know where you are at any given time on a ship, and you will be able to find any space on a ship even if you haven't been there before.

Each and every space in a ship has a unique identifier that is a yellow rectangle with black letters and numbers, known as the *bullseye*. It will have several lines of information but the top line in this rectangle is made up of numbers and letters, such as:

$$4–95–3–M$$

For each compartment, the numbers and letters will change, but the format will not. That format tells you the following:

- First number = deck or level number
- Second number = frame number
- Third number = compartment's position relative to the centerline
- Letter(s) = code telling you the purpose of the compartment

To understand what those numbers and letters are telling you, a review of some basic ship construction is useful.

You will recall that in chapter 3 we established that ships have a main deck. That main deck is one of the references used in the compartment numbering system, and all "floors" above the main deck are called *levels* and all below are called *decks*. These are indicated by the *first number* of the compartment identifier. Some important clues to deciphering this number system are in knowing that:

the main deck is always numbered "1"
all decks below the main deck are numbers higher than "1" (2, 3, etc.)
all levels above the main deck are preceded with a zero (01, 02, etc.).

These numbers increase as you go away from the main deck. The first deck below the main deck is numbered "2," the next one down is "3" and so forth. One level above the main deck is the "01" level (conventionally pronounced "oh-one level," not "zero-one level." The next one up is the "02 level," and so on. If a compartment extends through more than one deck (such as an engineering space that must be large enough to hold a boiler or huge turbines), the deck number of that compartment refers to the bottommost deck.

It also helps to know that shipbuilders start with a virtual backbone, called a *keel*, that is essentially a very large I-beam running from bow to stern. Other beams, called *frames*, are attached at regular intervals to that backbone—roughly perpendicular (*athwartships*) to it—like ribs to the human spine. Plating is attached to these ribs to form the ship's hull. These frames are numbered, starting at the bow and increasing toward the stern—the farther aft you are, the higher the number of the frame nearest you. This is another clue to navigating your way around

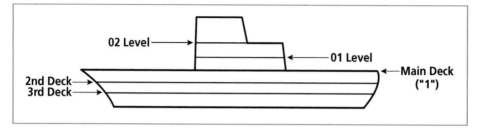

Figure 23. Deck Numbering System

the ship, because the second number of the compartment identifier tells you the *frame number*. It's even more useful to you if you know how many frames the ship has in total; that way, if the ship has three hundred frames, for example, and you are at frame one hundred, you know you are about one-third of the way aft on the ship (or two-thirds of the way forward!). Frame 150 in this case would be exactly amidships.

The third number on that first line of the bullseye is referenced to that imaginary line we described in Chapter 2—the *centerline*—which runs from bow to stern, bisecting the ship into two long halves. This third number in the compartment identifier tells you where you are in relation to that centerline. The bigger the number, the farther away from the centerline (*outboard*). Compartments with even numbers are on the port (left, looking forward) side of the centerline; odd numbers are on the starboard (right, looking forward) side of the centerline. This means that a compartment with the number "3" in this position on the bullseye would be the second compartment outboard from the centerline ("1" being the first) on the starboard side. If you understand this system, you will know that the second compartment on the port side would have the number "4," the third compartment on the port side would be "6," the third on the starboard side would be "5," and so on. If a space straddles the centerline, it has a zero as its third number.

The *last part* of the compartment identifier does not tell you much, if anything, about the location. This letter, or pair of letters, is a code that tells you what the space is used for. Though you don't really need to know these codes to be able to get around on the ship, they can be useful for other purposes and are provided here:

A   supply and stowage spaces

AA   cargo holds

C   control centers (such as CIC)

E   engineering (machinery)

F   fuel stowage (for use by the ship itself; that is, not as cargo)

FF   fuel stowage compartments (when cargo)

J   jet (aviation) fuel for use by embarked aircraft

JJ   jet (aviation) fuel as cargo

K   chemicals and dangerous materials (other than oil and gasoline)

L   living spaces (berthing and messing spaces, heads, passage-ways, etc.)

M   ammunition spaces (magazines, ready service lockers, etc.)

Q   miscellaneous spaces not covered by other letters

T   vertical access trunks or escape trunks

V   void (spaces that are normally empty)

W   water stowage spaces

In the example above (4–95–3–M), the compartment identified is on the fourth deck, is at the ninety-fifth frame, is the second compartment outboard from the ship's centerline, and is a magazine or some other ammunition-related space.

Let's suppose you are in this space and on the ship's 1MC (pronounced "one-em-see"—the general announcing system) you are asked to report to the ship's "Combat Information Center" (CIC), which has a compartment identifier of 03–47–0–C. To get there from this ammunition space, you would know that you would have to go up six ladders (three to get to the main deck [number 1] and three more to go up to the 03 level). You would also know that you would have to go forward rather than aft, because the frames always go up in number as you go aft and down in number as you go forward. If you did all that and arrived in a space numbered 03–47–5–C, you would know that you were close but that you had to head inboard (away from the starboard side toward the centerline) to find CIC (which you know from the "0" is on the ship's centerline). Using this system, you can find any space on any Navy ship.

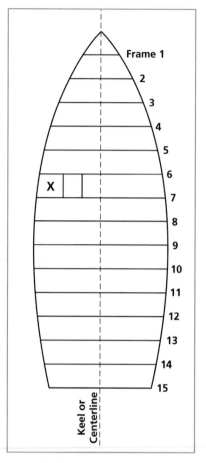

Figure 24. Compartment Numbering System.
In this example, "X" is in compartment
4-6-6-M (fourth deck, sixth frame, third
compartment to port, which is a magazine).

As mentioned earlier, compartment identifiers (bullseyes) are actually posted in each compartment on a ship (sometimes more than once in larger compartments), so you can always have a sense of where you are in a ship. These identifiers are painted on and are easily found. They all adhere to the same format as follows:

4–95–3–M

FR 95–99

GM

The top line is the one we have been discussing, the one that tells you where you are on the ship. The second line tells you what frames the compartment spans, and the bottom line tells you what division on the ship is responsible for maintaining that space (in this case, GM Division, the people who take care of the guided missiles on the ship).

EMERGENCY "NAVIGATION"

Though in many ways you will be safer aboard ship than you are in your own home, bad things do sometimes happen aboard ship. Fire is a more serious hazard aboard ship than even flooding, and you should take precautions to be sure you are ready in the event one breaks out while you are aboard.

Because ports (windows) are rare, ships can be very dark places if power goes out; smoke can also quickly accumulate, making it very difficult to see. As soon as you find out where you will be sleeping, you should plan an emergency escape route—or more than one if possible. Do the same with any other spaces where you will be spending a lot of time. Make several trips to the nearest passageways that will take you to safety, until you become very familiar with the route and can literally travel it with your eyes closed. Practice doing it with your eyes closed so that you will be ready in the event of an emergency. I lived for two years near the engineering spaces in USS *Saratoga* where three men several years before had died during a fire. To preclude that happening to me, I closed my eyes *each and every time* I left my stateroom so that I was more used to doing it that way than with full vision.

You will be told what to do in emergencies. You may be assigned a place to muster (report your presence) in the event of certain emergencies. For example, if someone is thought to have fallen overboard, a quick muster of all hands on board is essential to determine if someone is indeed missing. Be sure that you know where you are supposed to muster and that you know how to get there as expeditiously and safely as possible. Consider alternate routes where possible in the event a fire or something else is in your path.

Remember the term "FUSPAD"! This is an acronym that means:

Forward—Up—Starboard
Port—Aft—Down

This tells you the flow of traffic on a ship during an emergency. If the ship goes to General Quarters (GQ), everyone will be moving at once to get to his or her emergency station. You will know when that happens when you hear a loud "bonging" alarm, the thunder of many footsteps, and the words, "General Quarters, General Quarters. All hands man your battle stations" over the ship's 1MC. If there were not a "traffic pattern," Sailors would collide in narrow passageways and block ladders. (I have known some Sailors you would *not* want to collide with!) So all aboard ship know that in emergencies they must use passageways on the starboard side of the ship if they need to go forward, and they must use ladders on the starboard side if they need to go up to a higher deck or level. Conversely, those who need to move aft or to lower decks must use passageways and ladders on the port side of the ship.

VISITING SPECIAL AREAS

One of the most popular places to visit a ship is her bridge. If you are fortunate enough to be invited to the ship's bridge, be sure to do the following:

- Be aware that the watchstanders have priority at all times. Do not get in their way if they are trying to move about, and do not block their view if they are trying to see out or view a computer display.
- Do not speak too loudly. Watchstanders must be able to hear one another, radios, etc.
- Do not use binoculars or any other equipment unless invited to do so.
- If you are invited to the bridge at night, be sure to use only a red-lensed flashlight and be very careful where you shine it (mostly on the deck).

If you are visiting an aircraft carrier, you should never venture onto the flight deck or the surrounding catwalks during flight operations unless specifically invited and escorted. People who work on the flight deck receive hazardous duty pay for a reason! However, you will not want to miss the opportunity to observe flight operations while you are aboard. There is a place on every carrier's island (usually on the 09 or 010 level) called "Vulture's Row," where you can actually go outside and have a "balcony" view of the "ballet" of Sailors and aircraft below. Be sure to wear ear protection and remove your hat and anything else, like objects in your shirt pockets, that might be blown on to the flight deck. Cameras are usually fine but *never* use a flash.

SOME FINAL THOUGHTS ON SHIPBOARD "NAVIGATING"

Before proceeding up or down a ladder, be sure to look. Because ladders are narrow and steep, you might catch a knee in the face if you start up when someone else is coming down. Sailors often move quickly on ladders, sometimes swinging from the handhold above and deliberately missing the last few steps altogether, so *be vigilant*.

Beware of the infamous "knee-knockers." Doorways that pass through bulkheads are designed to prevent the free flow of water for rather obvious reasons, so the opening does not always reach all the way to the deck. The bottom may be elevated such that you have to step over in order to go through. Obviously, if you are not paying attention, you could well stub a toe or bang a knee as you go through this restricted opening. Often the top of the opening is also lower than a regular door ashore, so you will do well to be alert and *duck* when going through.

Hatches also have a raised edge called a "coaming" around the opening so that water cannot readily flow down through to a lower deck. Be careful to step over this when going up or down a ladder.

If you encounter tape down the middle of a passageway, it is probably because someone is swabbing (mopping) or waxing the deck. Work is done on one half at a time, so that half the passageway is still available for passage. Be sure to stay on the correct (dry) side when proceeding.

TELLING TIME

You have already encountered twenty-four-hour time in Chapter 3. You will do yourself no favors by going aboard without understanding how to tell time this way.

There is another form of timekeeping you may encounter aboard ship, particularly larger ones, that bears some explanation. You may hear bells ringing in a routine but strange pattern. This is more a matter of tradition than of practicality, but it is one of those things that make shipboard life interesting, even a bit exotic.

For many centuries, Sailors did not have the luxury of a personal timepiece. If watches were to be relieved on time, some means of telling the time had to be devised. A system that used a half-hour sandglass and the ship's bell was created and used for hundreds of years.

At the beginning of a watch, the sandglass was turned over to start it running. As soon as it ran out, the watchstanders knew the first half hour had passed, so they rang the ship's bell once and immediately turned the sandglass over to start the second half hour. Everyone on board the ship could hear the bell, so they could keep track of the time. When the sand ran out the second time, the watchstanders rang the ship's bell twice. They continued this until eight bells had been rung, representing the passage of four hours, or one complete watch. The watch was then relieved, and the new watch team started the whole cycle over by ringing one bell when the first half hour had passed, and so on. This bell-ringing tradition has been continued on board many Navy ships even though clocks and watches are now very common.

Even though this system is archaic, you can actually tell time by it (within a half hour). Remember that watches are four hours long and that noon and midnight are among the starting points for watches; the rest is a matter of extrapolation. If a watch begins at noon, then you will hear one bell at 1230, two bells at 1300 (1:00 p.m.), three at 1330 (1:30 p.m.), and so on. The cycle will end at the four-hour point (1600 or 4:00 p.m.) with eight bells and begin again with one bell a half hour later (1630 or 4:30 p.m.).

Today, because bells are rung more out of tradition than for real function, they are not normally rung between taps and reveille (normal sleeping hours for Sailors not on watch), nor are they rung during divine services or in fog, when the ship's bell may be used as a fog signal. Another tradition, still observed in many Navy ships, is the custom of the youngest member of the crew striking eight bells at midnight on New Year's Eve to ring in the New Year.

DOs AND *DON'Ts* ABOARD SHIP

Do read the Plan of the Day (POD). The ship's Plan of the Day comes out the night before the day it covers and lists information pertaining to the coming day's routine, such as what special evolutions or drills are scheduled. It is a good source of information and reading it will reduce the number of questions you will have to ask. It may contain information you might not want to miss, such as a movie schedule.

Don't take long showers. Because the evaporators can make only so much water at a time, care must be exercised not to waste freshwater while a ship is under way or at anchor. Therefore, you should never take what Sailors call a "Hollywood shower" while at sea. This is the kind of shower you probably take at home, where you let the water run for as long as you are in the shower. While at sea, it is important to get in the habit of wetting down (quickly), turning the water off and leaving it off while you soap and scrub, and then turning the water on again just long enough to rinse off. When moored to a pier where the appropriate connections are available, the ship's potable water system can be hooked up to receive freshwater. At these times, abundant freshwater is available so that the strict water conservation practices you use at sea are not necessary. The ship's potable water tanks will all be topped off (filled to capacity) before the ship gets under way.

Do secure doors after passing through. If you have to spin a wheel, work a large lever, or turn a series of small levers in order to go through a door, then you should turn that wheel or work those levers in the opposite direction after you have passed through. Those wheels and levers are the methods you might encounter for securing (tightly closing) a water-tight door (to *keep* it watertight).

Don't open any doors without permission if the ship is at GQ. The ship is "buttoned up" during GQ to prevent fire, smoke, fumes, or water from passing from space to space. To breach that seal without permission is a sin of high order.

Don't move about during a Security Alert. If you hear a Security Alert called away while you are aboard, you should stand fast. The only moving about you should do is to get out of the middle of a passageway or off of a ladder. Armed Sailors and/or Marines will be moving about the ship rapidly and will be in a no-nonsense mode. Do what they tell you—they will not stand on ceremony!

Don't go beyond a RADHAZ sign. You may encounter special signs with the term "RADHAZ" on it, particularly up high in the ship. This indicates a radiation hazard (usually from a radio or radar antenna) and you will do well to heed it. To ignore it can bring you serious injury and even death.

Do stay clear of emergency sites. In the event of an emergency, such as a fire, the word will be passed over the ship's 1MC, "Fire, Fire, Fire," along with the location (another reason to know how to decipher the compartment identification system). You should stay well clear of this area and out of the way of crew members who are proceeding to the area.

Do remove headgear (hat, cap, helmet) when entering or traveling through a shipboard eating area (mess deck, chief's mess, wardroom, etc.). A Sailor on watch (such as a messenger) will keep his or her head-gear on when entering these spaces, but all others do not.

Do be careful of wet paint. Although modern ships are less vulnerable to rust and other forms of corrosion, the sea is a hostile environment to metal. Consequently fresh paint is a fairly common occurrence, so be careful what you touch or lean up against.

Do enjoy the experience. Few people ever venture onto the high seas, and many fewer still in a warship. Make the most of the experience. Ask questions, observe. You will likely speak of your shipboard visit for many years to come.

APPENDIX D
FURTHER READING

While there are many books you could read to learn even more about the Navy, the following are particularly appropriate.

Basic Training for Dummies by Rod Powers (John Wiley & Sons)
Written to cover basic training for all the armed forces, this guide provides detailed information on what to expect in basic training, such as physical training, discipline, classroom instruction, drill and ceremony, obstacle courses, simulated war games, self-defense, marksmanship, and other ways to "survive and thrive in boot camp."

The Bluejacket's Manual by Thomas J. Cutler (Naval Institute Press)
From the days of oars and coal-fired engines to the computerized era of the twenty-first century, *The Bluejacket's Manual* has been an essential part of the American Sailor's sea bag for more than one hundred years, serving as an introduction to the Navy for new Recruits and as a reference book for Sailors of all ranks.

The Naval Academy Candidate Book by Sue Ross (Silver Horn Books)
A how-to book based on hundreds of interviews with Naval Academy professors, administrators, admissions officials, midshipmen, graduates, congressional staffers and panelists, and parents from across the

United States. It explains how your daughter or son can prepare for the Navy, gain admission to the Academy, and survive after she or he get there.

Newly Commissioned Naval Officers Guide by Fred Kacher
(Naval Institute Press)
This desktop guide is a user-friendly first stop for officer candidates and midshipmen seeking information as they transition to naval officers. It offers practical advice in the basic tenets of leadership, naval policy, etiquette, and personal and professional management. In a conversational style, Commander Kacher demystifies the new roles and responsibilities of young officers as they grapple with concepts very different from their experiences as enlisted Sailors or college students. Useful insights from officers who have recently made the transition and advice from successful commanding officers are included. This manual also provides a concise overview of the U.S. Navy's history, along with a recommended reading list, and serves as a gateway to the many online and print assets available to new officers.

Reef Points (Naval Institute Press)
Published each year by the Naval Institute Press, this pocket-sized guide is issued to every "Plebe" on his or her very first day at the U.S. Naval Academy. It contains a lot of useful and traditional information that these "freshmen" will need to know as they transition from civilian life to that of the Naval Academy and the Navy in general.

A Sailor's History of the U.S. Navy by Thomas J. Cutler
(Naval Institute Press)
This compact history is unique in two important ways. First, it is written thematically rather than chronologically. This allows recent history to be blended with more distant (but important) events in ways that will reinforce the timelessness as well as the timeliness of the U.S. Navy, thereby having a greater appeal to today's Sailor. The other unique characteristic of this history is that it focuses wherever possible on the roles of ALL Sailors rather than just the officers. Some emphasis upon what it was like to be a Sailor (working and living conditions) at different times is included as well.

APPENDIX E
NAVY RATINGS

In the Navy rating system, a rating is an occupational specialty. You might call it a "job" or an "occupation" in the civilian world. Before Sailors can qualify for a rating, they first work their way through the "general apprenticeship levels" (E-1 to E-3), which help prepare them for a rating. In order to advance beyond the E-3 paygrade, Sailors must have a rating. Once promoted to E-4, they have a rating and, except in special circumstances, will likely keep that rating for the rest of their careers.

Each of the Navy's ratings is identified by a two- or three-letter abbreviation such as ET (for Electronics Technician) or GSM (for Gas Turbine Systems Technician—Mechanical). Each rating is further identified by a unique symbol called a specialty mark included on a rating badge worn on the left sleeve of dress uniforms.

There are two categories of ratings: general and service. Occupations for paygrades E-4 through E-9 are called general ratings. Each general rating has a distinctive badge. Examples of general ratings include Operations Specialist, Gunner's Mate, and Logistics Specialist.

Some general ratings are further subdivided into service ratings, which indicate some additional specialization. For example, the general rating of Gas Turbine Systems Technician (GS) is subdivided into two service ratings: GSE (electrical) and GSM (mechanical). There can be service ratings at any petty officer level; however, they are most common with E-4s through E-6s. In the higher paygrades (E-8 and E-9), service ratings sometimes merge into a general rating. For example, those Gas Turbine Systems Technicians who specialize in electrical and mechanical systems (GSE and GSM) would become simply GSs once promoted to senior chief petty officer (E-8), because a Senior Chief Gas Turbine Systems Technician needs to know about both the electrical and mechanical systems.

General ratings are sometimes combined at the E-9 level when the work is similar. For example, the work done by a Senior Chief Utilitiesman and by a Senior Chief Construction Electrician are very similar, so when these individuals are promoted to master chief, both become Master Chief Utilitiesmen. These are referred to as compression ratings.

Specialty marks were added to enlisted uniforms in 1866 and were often designed to represent an instrument originally used to perform a particular task. For example, the mark for a Quartermaster (QM), who worked mainly in navigation, was a ship's helm, while the Boatswain's Mate (BM) mark used two crossed anchors. The custom of representing the type of work with a specialty mark for each rating continues, often using traditional (sometimes obsolete) instruments, such as crossed quills for Yeoman (YN), who performed administrative work in the Navy, even though quills are no longer used as writing instruments.

Each rating—with its specialty mark—is briefly described below. When a general rating also has service ratings, these are included in the description. Compression ratings are also included. Those ratings that merge into compression ratings are also noted.

AB

Cross anchors,
winged

Aviation Boatswain's Mate

ABs operate, maintain, and repair aircraft catapults, arresting gear, and barricades. They operate and maintain fuel- and lube-oil transfer systems. ABs direct aircraft on the flight deck and in hangar bays before launch and after recovery. They use tow tractors to position planes and operate support equipment used to start aircraft. (**Service ratings**: ABE [launching and recovery equipment]; ABF [fuels]; ABH [aircraft handling].)

AC

Microphone, winged

Air Traffic Controller

ACs assist in the essential safe, orderly, and speedy flow of air traffic by directing and controlling aircraft under visual (VFR) and instrument (IFR) flight rules. They operate field lighting systems, communicate with aircraft, and furnish pilots with information regarding traffic, navigation, and weather conditions. They operate and adjust GCA (ground-controlled approach) systems. They interpret targets on radar screens and plot aircraft positions.

AD

Two-bladed
propeller, winged

Aviation Machinist's Mate

ADs maintain jet aircraft engines and associated equipment or engage in any one of several types of aircraft maintenance activities. ADs maintain, service, adjust, and replace aircraft engines and accessories, as well as perform the duties of flight engineers. (**Compression rating**: AF [Aviation Maintenanceman].)

AE

Globe, winged

Aviation Electrician's Mate

AEs maintain, adjust, and repair electrical-power generating, converting, and distributing systems, as well as lighting, control, and indicating systems in aircraft. They also install and maintain wiring and flight and engine instrument systems, which include automatic flight control, stabilization, aircraft compass, attitude reference, and inertial navigation systems. (**Compression rating:** AV [Avionics Technician].)

AG

Circle on vertical arrow, winged

Aerographer's Mate

The Navy has its own weather forecasters, AGs, who are trained in meteorology and the use of aerological instruments that monitor such weather characteristics as air pressure, temperature, humidity, wind speed, and wind direction. They prepare weather maps and forecasts, analyze atmospheric conditions to determine the best flight levels for aircraft, and measure wind and air density to increase the accuracy of antiaircraft firing, shore bombardment, and delivery of weapons by aircraft.

AM

Crossed mauls, winged

Aviation Structural Mechanic

The maintenance and repair of aircraft parts (wings, fuselage, tail, control surfaces, landing gear, and attending mechanisms) are performed by AMs working with metals, alloys, and plastics. AMs maintain and repair safety equipment and hydraulic systems. (**Service rating:** AME [safety equipment].) (**Compression rating:** AF [Aviation Maintenanceman].)

AO

Flaming spherical shell, winged

Aviation Ordnanceman

Navy planes carry guns, bombs, torpedoes, rockets, and missiles to attack the enemy on the sea, under the sea, in the air, and on land. AOs are responsible for maintaining, repairing, installing, operating, and handling aviation ordnance equipment; their duties also include the handling, stowing, issuing, and loading of munitions and small arms.

AS

Crossed maul and spark, winged

Aviation Support Equipment Technician
ASs perform intermediate maintenance on "yellow" (aviation accessory) equipment at naval air stations and aboard carriers. They maintain gasoline and diesel engines, hydraulic and pneumatic systems, liquid and gaseous oxygen and nitrogen systems, gas-turbine compressor units, and electrical systems.

AT

Helium atom, winged

Aviation Electronics Technician
ATs perform preventive and corrective maintenance on aviation electronic components supported by conventional and automatic test equipment. They repair the electronic components of weapons, communications, radar, navigation, antisubmarine warfare sensors, electronic warfare, data link, fire control, and tactical displays. (**Compression rating**: AV [Avionics Technician].)

AW

Spark-pierced electron orbits over wave, winged

Naval Air Crewman
AWs perform a wide variety of functions in many of the Navy's aircraft, such as operating electronic equipment (radars, radios, etc.), performing search and rescue techniques, etc. (**Service Ratings**: AWF [mechanical]; AWO [operator]; AWR [tactical helicopter]; AWS [helicopter]; AWV [avionics].)

AZ

Two-bladed propeller on open book, winged

Aviation Maintenance Administrationman
AZs perform clerical, administrative, and managerial duties necessary to keep aircraft-maintenance activities running smoothly. They plan, schedule, and coordinate maintenance, including inspections and modifications to aircraft and equipment.

BM

Crossed anchors

Boatswain's Mate

BMs train, direct, and supervise others in marline-spike, deck, and boat seamanship; ensure proper upkeep of the ship's external structure, rigging, deck equipment, and boats; lead working parties; perform seamanship tasks; are in charge of picketboats, self-propelled barges, tugs, and other yard and district craft; serve in or in charge of gun crews and damage-control parties; and use and maintain equipment for loading and unloading cargo, ammunition, fuel, and general stores.

BU

Carpenter's square
on plumb bob

Builder

Navy BUs are similar to civilian construction workers. They may be skilled carpenters, plasterers, roofers, cement finishers, asphalt workers, masons, painters, bricklayers, sawmill operators, or cabinetmakers. BUs build and repair all types of structures, including piers, bridges, towers, underwater installations, schools, offices, houses, and other buildings. (**Compression rating:** CU [Constructionman].)

CE

Spark on telephone
pole

Construction Electrician

CEs are responsible for the power production and electrical work required to build and operate airfields, roads, barracks, hospitals, shops, and warehouses. The work of Navy CEs is like that of civilian construction electricians, powerhouse electricians, telephone and electrical repairmen, substation operators, linemen, and others. (**Compression rating:** UC [Utilities Constructionman].)

CM

Double-headed
wrench on nut

Construction Mechanic

CMs maintain heavy construction and automotive equipment (buses, dump trucks, bulldozers, rollers, cranes, backhoes, and pile drivers) as well as other construction equipment. They service vehicles and work on gasoline and diesel engines, ignition and fuel systems, transmissions, electrical systems, and hydraulic, pneumatic, and steering systems. (**Compression rating**: EQ [Equipmentman].)

CS

Open book with linked old-fashioned keys and a quill

Culinary Specialist

CSs operate and manage Navy dining facilities and bachelor enlisted quarters. They are cooks and bakers in Navy dining facilities ashore and afloat, ordering, inspecting, and stowing food. They maintain food service and preparation spaces and equipment and keep records of transactions and budgets for the food service in living quarters ashore.

CT

Crossed quill and spark

Cryptologic Technician

Depending on their special career area, CTs control access to classified material, translate foreign-language transmissions, operate radio direction-finding equipment, employ electronic countermeasures, and install, service, and repair special electronic and electromechanical equipment. CTs require special security clearances. (**Service ratings**: CTI [interpretive]; CTM [maintenance]; CTN [network]; CTR [collection]; CTT [technical].)

DC

Crossed fire axe and maul

Damage Controlman

DCs perform the work necessary for damage control, ship stability, firefighting, and chemical, biological, and radiological (CBR) warfare defense. They instruct personnel in damage control and CBR defense and repair damage-control equipment and systems.

EA

Measuring scale
fronting level rod

Engineering Aide

EAs provide construction engineers with the information needed to develop final construction plans. EAs conduct surveys for roads, airfields, buildings, waterfront structures, pipelines, ditches, and drainage systems. They perform soil tests, prepare topographic and hydrographic maps, and survey for sewers, water lines, drainage systems, and underwater excavations. (**Compression rating:** CU [Constructionman].)

EM

Globe with longitude,
latitude lines

Electrician's Mate

The operation and repair of a ship's or station's electrical powerplant and electrical equipment are the responsibilities of EMs. They also maintain and repair power and lighting circuits, distribution switchboards, generators, motors, and other electrical equipment.

EN

Gear

Engineman

Internal-combustion engines, either diesel or gasoline, must be kept in good order; this is the responsibility of ENs. They are also responsible for the maintenance of refrigeration, air-conditioning, and distilling-plant motors and compressors.

EO

Bulldozer

Equipment Operator

EOs work with heavy machinery such as bulldozers, power shovels, pile drivers, rollers, and graders. EOs use this machinery to dig ditches and excavate for building foundations, to break up old concrete or asphalt paving and pour new paving, to loosen soil and grade it, to dig out tree trunks and rocks, to remove debris from construction sites, to raise girders, and to move and set in place other pieces of equipment or materials needed for a job. (**Compression rating:** EQ [Equipmentman].)

EOD

Mine on crossed torpedo and aircraft bomb

Explosive Ordnance Disposal Technician

EODs render safe all types of ordnance, both conventional and unconventional, improvised, chemical, biological, and nuclear. They perform a wide variety of ordnance-related tasks, including underwater location, identification, render-safe, demolition, recovery, and disposal of foreign and domestic ordnance. They also support military and civilian law enforcement agencies.

ET

Helium atom

Electronics Technician

ETs are responsible for electronic equipment used to send and receive messages, detect enemy planes and ships, and determine target distance. They must maintain, repair, calibrate, tune, and adjust electronic equipment used for communications, detection and tracking, recognition and identification, navigation, and electronic countermeasures.

FC

Rangerfinder with inward spark on each side

Fire Controlman

FCs maintain the control mechanism used in weapons systems on combat ships. Complex electronic, electrical, and hydraulic equipment is required to ensure the accuracy of guided-missile and surface gunfire-control systems. FCs are responsible for the operation, routine care, and repair of this equipment, which includes radars, computers, weapons-direction equipment, target-designation systems, gyroscopes, and rangefinders.

FT

Rangefinder

Fire Control Technician

FTs maintain advanced electronic equipment used in submarine weapons systems. Complex electronic, electrical, and mechanical equipment is required to ensure the accuracy of guided-missile systems and underwater weapons. FTs are responsible for the operation, routine care, and repair of this equipment.

GM

Crossed cannons

Gunner's Mate

Navy GMs operate, maintain, and repair all gunnery equipment, guided-missile launching systems, rocket launchers, guns, gun mounts, turrets, projectors, and associated equipment. They also make detailed casualty analyses and repairs of electrical, electronic, hydraulic, and mechanical systems. They test and inspect ammunition and missiles and their ordnance components and train and supervise personnel in the handling and stowage of ammunition, missiles, and assigned ordnance equipment.

GS

Turbine with ducting

Gas Turbine Systems Technician

GSs operate, repair, and maintain gas-turbine engines, main propulsion machinery (including gears, shafting, and controllable-pitch propellers), assigned auxiliary equipment, propulsion-control systems, electrical and electronic circuitry up to printed circuit modules, and alarm and warning circuitry. They perform administrative tasks related to gas-turbine propulsion-system operation and maintenance. (**Service ratings:** GSE [electrical]; GSM [mechanical].)

HM

Caduceus

Hospital Corpsman

HMs assist medical professionals in providing health care to service people and their families. They act as pharmacists, medical technicians, food-service personnel, nurses' aides, physicians' or dentists' assistants, battlefield medics, X-ray technicians, and more. Their work falls into several categories: first aid and minor surgery, patient transportation, patient care, prescriptions and laboratory work, food-service inspections, and clerical duties.

HT

Crossed fire axe and maul with carpenter's square

Hull Maintenance Technician

HTs are responsible for maintaining ships' hulls, fittings, piping systems, and machinery. They install and maintain shipboard and shore-based plumbing and piping systems. They also look after a vessel's safety and survival equipment and perform many tasks related to damage control.

IC

Telephone receiver over globe

Interior Communications Electrician

ICs operate and repair electronic devices used in a ship's interior communications systems—SITE TV systems, public-address systems, electronic megaphones, and other announcing equipment—as well as gyrocompass systems.

IS

Magnifying glass and quill

Intelligence Specialist

Military information, particularly classified information about enemies or potential enemies, is called "intelligence." Intelligence specialists analyze intelligence data. They break down information to determine its usefulness in military planning. From this intelligence data, they prepare materials that describe in detail the features of strategic and tactical areas all over the world.

IT

Four sparks

Information Systems Technician

ITs are responsible for the Navy's vital command, control, communications, computer and intelligence systems, and equipment. They use state-of-the-art multimedia technology such as fiber optics, digital microwave, and satellites on a global basis and work with telecommunications equipment, computers, and associated peripheral devices. (**Service Rating:** ITS [submarines].)

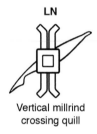

LN

Vertical millrind crossing quill

Legalman

Navy LNs are aides trained in the field of law. They work in Navy legal offices performing administrative and clerical tasks necessary to process claims, to conduct court and administrative hearings, and to maintain records, documents, and legal-reference libraries. They give advice on tax returns, voter-registration regulations, procedures, and immigration and customs regulations governing Social Security and veterans' benefits and perform many duties related to courts-martial and nonjudicial hearings.

LS

Crossed keys

Logistics Specialists

LSs are the Navy's supply clerks. They see that needed supplies are available, including everything from clothing and machine parts to forms and food. They serve as civilian warehousemen, purchasing agents, stock clerks and supervisors, retail sales clerks, store managers, inventory clerks, buyers, parts clerks, bookkeepers, and even forklift operators. They also provide postal system services for the Navy to ensure an efficient interface between the U.S. Postal Service and the Fleet.

MA

Star embossed in
circle within shield

Master-at-Arms

MAs help keep law and order aboard ship and at shore stations. They report to the executive officer, help maintain discipline, and assist in security matters. They enforce regulations, conduct investigations, take part in correctional and rehabilitative programs, and organize and train Sailors assigned to police duty. In civilian life, they would be detectives and policemen.

MC

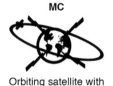

Orbiting satellite with
lightning bolts

Mass Communications Specialist

MCs are public affairs and visual information experts. They present the Navy story to audiences in the Navy and to the rest of the world through a variety of media. MCs write and produce print and broadcast journalism news and feature stories for military and civilian newspapers, magazines, television, and radio. They use photography, web design, graphic design, and other related skills in the performance of their duties.

MM

Three-bladed propeller

Machinist's Mate

Continuous operation of the many engines, compressors and gears, refrigeration, air-conditioning, gas-operated equipment, and other types of machinery afloat and ashore is the job of the MM. In particular, MMs are responsible for a ship's steam propulsion and auxiliary equipment and the outside (deck) machinery. MMs may also perform duties in the manufacture, storage, and transfer of some industrial gases. (**Service Ratings:** MME (auxiliary); MMN [nuclear]; MMW [weapons].)

MN

Floating mine

Mineman

MNs test, maintain, repair, and overhaul mines and their components. They are responsible for assembling, handling, issuing, and delivering mines to the planting agent and for maintaining mine-handling and mine-laying equipment.

MR

Micrometer and gear

Machinery Repairman

MRs are skilled machine-tool operators. They make replacement parts and repair or overhaul a ship engine's auxiliary equipment, such as evaporators, air compressors, and pumps. They repair deck equipment, including winches and hoists, condensers, and heat-exchange devices. Shipboard MRs frequently operate main propulsion machinery in addition to performing machine-shop and repair duties.

MT

Guided missile and electronic wave

Missile Technician

MTs perform organizational and intermediate-level maintenance on ballistic missile weapons systems; they also operate and maintain their fire-control systems, guidance subsystems, and associated test equipment, as well as missile and launcher/tuber groups and all ancillary equipment. They operate and maintain strategic weapons systems, associated ship/weapon subsystems, and test and handling equipment.

MU

Lyre

Musician

MUs play in official Navy bands and in special groups such as jazz bands, dance bands, and small ensembles. They give concerts and provide music for military ceremonies, religious services, parades, receptions, and dances. Official unit bands usually do not include stringed instruments, but each MU must be able to play at least one brass, woodwind, or percussion instrument. Persons are selected for this rating through auditions.

Navy Counselor

NC

Anchor crossed with quill

NCs offer vocational guidance on an individual and group basis to Navy personnel aboard ships and at shore facilities and to civilian personnel considering enlistment in the Navy. They assess the interests, aptitudes, abilities, and personalities of individuals. An NCR (Navy Counselor Recruiter) focuses on bringing people into the Navy and helps new recruits make early career decisions. NCCs (Navy Career Counselors) primarily work with personnel further along in their careers, assisting them with such things as advancing their education, converting their ratings, and improving their chances for retention and promotion.

Navy Diver

ND

U.S. Navy Mark-V diving helmet and breastplate

NDs perform underwater construction, salvage, repair, maintenance, demolition, reconnaissance, and search-and-rescue tasks using a variety of diving equipment. They also support Special Warfare and Explosive Ordnance Disposal personnel (see SO and EOD ratings).

Operations Specialist

OS

Arrow through oscilloscope

OSs operate radar, navigation, and communications equipment in a ship's combat information center (CIC) or on the bridge. They detect and track ships, planes, and missiles. They operate and maintain IFF (identification friend or foe) systems, ECM (electronic countermeasures) equipment, and radiotelephones. OSs also work with search-and-rescue teams.

PR

Parachute, winged

Aircrew Survival Equipmentman

Parachutes are the lifesaving equipment of aviators when they have to bail out. In times of disaster, a parachute may also be the only means of delivering badly needed medicines, goods, and other supplies to isolated victims. PRs pack and care for parachutes as well as service, maintain, and repair flight clothing, rubber life rafts, life jackets, oxygen-breathing equipment, protective clothing, and air-sea rescue equipment. An Aircrew Survival Equipmentman was originally called a "Parachute Rigger," which explains the rating abbreviation "PR."

PS

Book with quill

Personnel Specialist

Those Sailors in the PS rating provide enlisted personnel with information and counseling related to Navy occupations, opportunities for general education and job training, requirements for promotion, and rights and benefits. PSs maintain and audit pay and personnel records and determine military pay and travel entitlements. They prepare financial and accounting reports related to individual pay and travel transactions and operate associated accounting systems.

QM

Ship's helm

Quartermaster

QMs are responsible for ship safety, skillful navigation, and reliable communications with other vessels and shore stations. In addition, they maintain charts, navigational aids, and records for the ship's log. They steer the ship, take radar bearings and ranges, make depth soundings and celestial observations, plot courses, command small craft, conduct honors and ceremonies with passing ships, maintain signaling equipment, and send and receive visual signals by flashing light, semaphore, and flaghoist. QMs stand watch and assist the navigator and officer of the deck (OOD).

Religious Program Specialist

RP

Globe on anchor within compass

RPs assist Navy chaplains with administrative and budgetary tasks. They serve as custodians of chapel funds, keep religious documents, and maintain contact with religious and community agencies. They also prepare devotional and religious educational materials, set up volunteer programs, operate shipboard libraries, supervise chaplains' offices, and perform administrative, clerical, and secretarial duties. They train personnel in religious programs and publicize religious activities.

Special Warfare Boat Operator

SB

Cutlass and cocked flintlock pistol on an anchor

SBs drive a variety of special warfare craft. They support SEALs and other Special Operations Command forces during their maritime and riverine missions and conduct unconventional small boat operations such as coastal/riverine patrols. They collect intelligence on enemy military installations in coastal areas, perform parachute/helicopter insertion operations, and support military and civilian law enforcement operations.

Ship's Serviceman

SH

Crossed key and quill

Both ashore and afloat, SHs manage barbershops, tailor shops, ships' uniform stores, laundries, drycleaning plants, and cobbler shops. They serve as clerks in exchanges, soda fountains, gas stations, warehouses, and commissary stores. Some SHs function as Navy club managers.

SO

Flintlock pistol on an
anchor and trident

Special Warfare Operator

SOs are better known as SEALs—an acronym from one of their primary missions: conducting insertions/extractions from the sea, air, or land. SOs also conduct covert, special operations missions in virtually any environment throughout the world, capture high-value enemy personnel and terrorists, collect information and intelligence through special reconnaissance missions, carry out small-unit, direct-action missions against military targets, and conduct underwater reconnaissance and demolition of natural or man-made obstacles prior to amphibious landings.

ST

Earphones pierced
by arrow

Sonar Technician

STs operate sonar and other oceanographic systems. They manipulate, control, evaluate, and interpret data for surface and submarine operations. STs coordinate submarine and auxiliary sonar and underwater fire-control interface, operate surface-ship underwater fire-control systems and associated equipment for the solution of antisubmarine warfare problems, and perform organizational and intermediate maintenance on their respective sonar and allied equipment. (**Service ratings:** STG [surface]; STS [submarine].)

SW

I-beam suspended
from hook

Steelworker

SWs rig and operate all special equipment used to move or hoist structural steel, structural shapes, and similar material. They erect or dismantle steel bridges, piers, buildings, tanks, towers, and other structures. They place, fit, weld, cut, bolt, and rivet steel shapes, plates, and built-up sections used in the construction of overseas facilities. (**Compression rating:** CU [Constructionman].)

UT

Valve

Utilitiesman

UTs plan, supervise, and perform tasks involved in the installation, operation, maintenance, and repair of plumbing, heating, steam, compressed-air systems, fuel-storage and -distribution systems, water-treatment and -distribution systems, air-conditioning and refrigeration equipment, and sewage-collecting and disposal facilities. (**Compression rating:** UC [Utilities Constructionman].)

YN

Crossed quills

Yeoman

YNs perform secretarial and clerical work. They greet visitors, answer telephone calls, and receive incoming mail. YNs organize files and operate duplicating equipment, and they order and distribute supplies. They write and type business and social letters, notices, directives, forms, and reports. They maintain files and service records.

INDEX

ABOUT THE AUTHOR

Thomas J. Cutler has been serving the U.S. Navy in various capacities for more than fifty years. The author of many articles and books, including several editions of *The Bluejacket's Manual* and *A Sailor's History of the U.S. Navy,* he is the Gordon England Chair of Professional Naval Literature at the U.S. Naval Institute and Fleet Professor of Strategy and Policy with the Naval War College. He has received the William P. Clements Award for Excellence in Education as military teacher of the year at the U.S. Naval Academy, the Alfred Thayer Mahan Award for Naval Literature, the U.S. Maritime Literature Award, the Naval Institute Press Author of the Year Award, and the Commodore Dudley Knox Lifetime Achievement Award in Naval History.

Would you like to learn more about the Navy your son or daughter joined?
Become a member of the U.S. Naval Institute and support the advancement
of the naval profession and the men and women who serve in our Navy,
Marine Corps, and Coast Guard.

Being a parent is challenging, and even more so for those proud mothers and fathers who send their sons and daughters off to defend our great nation. We are often contacted by concerned American parents—just like you—who have many good questions about the military culture their child has joined. It is normal to feel both extremely proud and a bit nervous about this major step in your child's life? Do you often wonder about the details of your Sailor's new profession? Where your son or daughter could be stationed? How you can stay current on news impacting their lives? What will happen if hostilities break and America goes to war?

The U.S. Naval Institute can help answer your questions.

For more than 140 years, the Naval Institute has served as an important bridge between the Navy, Marine Corps, and Coast Guard and the American public. We are a private, independent, 501(c)(3) nonprofit, member-based organization dedicated to the professional advancement of the naval profession and the men and women who serve in our Navy, Marine Corps, and Coast Guard.

The U.S. Naval Institute can help you better understand today's Navy and the challenges its Sailors face in several important ways:

1. **Learn more about the organization and operations of today's Navy, Marine Corps, and Coast Guard.** The Institute helps Americans better understand their Sea Services by publishing *Proceedings* magazine every month. *Proceedings* serves as the peer-reviewed journal of our nation's naval professionals. Each issue is packed with the latest cutting-edge thoughts on strategy, policy, and tactics.
2. **Learn more about the history and heritage of the naval services.** The Institute also publishes *Naval History* magazine six times per year to preserve and share the stories of the men and women who shaped our nation's legacy of valor. Each action-packed edition puts you at the center of the battles that were fought to keep our nation free.
3. **Stay up-to-date on the latest breaking news.** *USNI News*, founded in 2012, has rapidly become the world's go-to source for all naval news. The *USNI News* team of reporters scours the globe for the very latest information affecting the Sea Services to provide the public a better understanding of our Sailors', Marines', and Coast Guardsmen's contributions to our common defense.
4. **Take a deep dive into knowledge—read a book.** The Naval Institute Press has been a leader in maritime publishing since 1898 and now publishes about 80 new titles a year, including histories, biographies, strategy, ship and aircraft

guides, textbooks, and novels. The Naval Institute Press helped launch the careers of Tom Clancy with *The Hunt for Red October* and Stephen Coonts with *Flight of the Intruder*. Institute members receive generous discounts on the Press' more than 800 books in print.

If you wish to understand the Navy, Marine Corps, or Coast Guard; learn more about critical issues facing our nation; and advance the professionalism of the men and women who serve in uniform, please consider joining us, more than 50,000 strong, and become a U.S. Naval Institute member today.

United States Naval Institute
Member Services
291 Wood Road, Annapolis, MD 21402–5034
(800) 233–8764
www.usni.org